Migration and Development

Migration and Development

Dependence on South Africa:
A Study of Lesotho

Gabriele Winai Ström

Scandinavian Institute of African Studies, Uppsala

This book was first published in 1978 under the title

Development and Dependence in Lesotho
the Enclave of South Africa

as a doctoral thesis at the Department of Political Science,
University of Uppsala.

The printing of this new updated edition has been made
possible by financial support from
the Swedish Council for Research in the Humanities and
Social Sciences and the Swedish International Development
Authority (SIDA).

ISBN 91-7106-252-1
(1978 91-7106-123-1)

Printed in Sweden by
Motala Grafiska, Motala 1986

Contents

Preface and acknowledgements

During the 1980s Lesotho has joined with other countries in a common effort for the liberation of South Africa. A century ago Moshoeshoe I created the tradition of independence from South Africa by developing international links with other countries. The present king, Moshoeshoe II, with the support of his former Prime Minister, Chief Leabua Jonathan, has continued this royal tradition.

The increasing awareness of the political history of Lesotho can partly be explained by an interest in the types of influences that small dependent states possess. Lesotho is also of interest in examining the future conditions of a liberated South Africa.

When this book was first published, although censored in Lesotho, it was quickly sold out. Interest in a new edition has increased as the government of Lesotho has sought to broaden its foreign relations while giving more open support to the anti-apartheid struggle.

I was already preparing a new edition when, in January 1986, there was a coup d'etat by the constitutional monarch of Lesotho. By that time support for the Jonathan government had already declined. Political change became necessary with the additional pressure of South African sanctions against Lesotho. The coup met with almost no internal opposition, as had been the case after the earlier coup of 1970. Whether this is a sign of a move to a more popular government remains to be seen.

This book analyses the political conditions in a migrant labour state and its internal and international linkages. Through a deeper knowledge of these conditions we can more accurately foresee the future development of this part of southern Africa.

I would like to thank all those who have assisted with the updating of this book. I particularly wish to thank Anna Norrman of the Department of Peace and Conflict Research at the University of Uppsala, who typed this offset edition, and Karl Eric Ericson of the Scandinavian Institute of African Studies, Uppsala, who have the responsibility for its distribution. The Swedish Council for Research in the Humanities and Social Sciences and the Swedish International Development Authority (SIDA) financed this book.

Bromma October 1, 1986

Gabriele Winai Ström

Preface

It is unusual that a dissertation gets such strong political
reactions as this book received, when first published. It was
not only censored in South Africa and Lesotho, but it resulted
in extra-ordinary cabinet meetings and discussions in the
parliament of Lesotho.

Today it is, however, accepted in Lesotho as one of the best
analyses of recent political events. Since the book is also
still high in demand by both academic and politically interested
readers elsewhere I am happy to see this second edition published.

Leif Lewin

Johan Skytte Professor of Eloquence and Government
Chairman of the Department of Government,
Uppsala University

List of tables and diagrams

Abbreviations

AAPC	All-African Peoples' Conference
ANC	African National Congress (of South Africa)
BAC	Basutoland African Congress (called BCP after 1960)
BCP	Basutoland Congress Party
BFL	Basutoland Federation of Labour
BNP	Basotho National Party
CPDO	Central Planning and Development Office, Maseru
CPL	Communist Party of Lesotho
EDESA	Economic Development for Equatorial and Southern Africa (Investment Bank)
FAO	Food and Agricultural Organization of the United Nations
FP	Freedom Party
H.M.S.O.	Her Majesty's Stationary Office (London)
IBRD	International Bank for Reconstruction and Development (also called World Bank)
IDEP	Institute for Economic Development and Planning, Dakar
IDR	Institute for Development Research, Copenhagen
IDS	Institute for Development Studies, Sussex
ILO	International Labour Organization
IMF	International Monetary Fund
LCW	Lesotho General Council of Workers
LNDC	Lesotho National Development Corporation
MFP	Marema-Tlou Freedom Party (emerged from MTP and FP, 1962)
MTP	Marema-Tlou Party
ODA	Overseas Development Agency
OAU	Organization for African Unity
OMI	Oblates of Mary Immaculate (Catholic Order)
PAC	Pan-African Congress (of South Africa)
SIDA	Swedish International Development Agency
UBLS	University of Botswana, Lesotho and Swaziland (after Nov. 1975 split into NUL, National University of Lesotho, and UBS, University of Botswana and Swaziland)
UDP	United Democratic Party
UNDP	United Nations Development Programme

1 Introduction

This case study deals with some political conditions of development in Lesotho. The focus is on political parties, state institutions and development policies during the period 1960 to 1975. Lesotho* is an enclave state surrounded by the Republic of South Africa and sovereign since 1966.

In this introduction I first discuss my focus, method and theoretical framework, and finally comment on source material on political conditions in South Africa.

My main focus of attention is on the state level, where I have related the state on the one hand to the international level, particularly Southern Africa, and on the other hand to the socio-economic and political conditions within the country.

Chapter 2 concerns the socio-economic structure in Lesotho as a background to the rest of the study. It has a longer historical perspective than the other chapters. The aim is to investigate in what way Lesotho became part of the international capitalist system, thus indicating where we should look for causes of present socio-economic relations.

In chapter 3 I analyse the ideas and the support of the two political parties in Lesotho which dominate the country's political life. In Lesotho there is a deeply rooted tradition of popular participation in politics. The conflict between dependence mechanisms and development goals is thus partly revealed in economic and political events.

In chapter 4 the changes in organization of and control by state institutions are characterized. Changes in the state institutions regarding organization and popular participation may reflect changes in the forms of dependence.

Chapter 5 is devoted to the development policies resulting mainly from features discussed in previous chapters. The development policies themselves, however, are also important in determining future political conditions for development. I also give two examples of how development policies in two areas, mineral and financial policies, are implemented. These were the two policy areas in which the government claimed to be most successful.

* Lesotho was named Basutoland by the British during the colonial period 1868-1966.

The purpose of case studies is to draw attention to generalizations that have been established otherwise, or to illustrate such generalizations. My aim is to draw attention to mechanisms of dependence and my method is to relate a number of questions on general tendencies, treated in the literature as typical signs of dependence, to the situation in Lesotho.

The extremeness of dependence in Lesotho makes it a test case for generalizations about tendencies treated in the theoretical literature on underdevelopment as signs of dependence. Thus when I study political conditions in Lesotho I raise the following questions:

1. Is production becoming less diversified and more disintegrated?
2. Are inequalities in welfare, wealth and income increasing?
3. Is the power base of the government decreasing?
4. Are state institutions growing in size and state activities growing in scope?
5. Is foreign control of human and material resources in society increasing?
6. Is economic growth increasingly emphasized as a goal of government policies, at the same time as the regime repeatedly fails to reach this goal?

The tendencies indicated in these six questions are sometimes treated as automatic indicators of dependence, although not always grouped together in the same study.[1] It is time to systematically compare different signs of dependence with detailed empirical studies. Although it is not possible to reliably prove or disprove generalizations on the basis of one case study, and although the above signs of dependence are only some of those given in the theoretical literature on development and underdevelopment, a comparative discussion should be of general interest.

The six general questions raised are derived from the study of other societies than Lesotho, during the same period but also in the Third World. It is often argued that they are general signs of dependence, although other tendencies are also mentioned as typical of different kinds of dependence. Looking at these signs as caused by dependence does not exclude that they can also have other causes in other societal situations.

The first two questions are raised in chapter 2. The third and fourth questions are dealt with in chapters 3 and 4, and finally, in chapter 5, we shall meet the fifth and sixth questions.

Comment on question 1. Production tends to become less diversified and more disintegrated in dependent societies. What is meant is that specialization on a few economic activities tied to foreign companies is commonly believed to be a general sign of dependence. This is connected with a tendency for the specialized sectors to become integrated with the centre of the international system at the same time as these sectors become increasingly isolated both from each other and the rest of productive activities in the dependent country. This has implications for production, for employment and for the development of socio-economic and political groupings.

Comment on question 2. Dependent societies are believed to tend towards more pronounced inequality than both capitalist centre societies and less dependent Third World societies. This tendency is
sometimes called "marginalization" in the theoretical literature on
development and underdevelopment, meaning that more and more people
tend to be deprived of possibilities to participate in employment
and other aspects of society.

Comment on question 3. Minority governments thus tend to rule in
dependent countries, since the majority tends to be left outside
political participation. The demands of potential political majori-
ties tend to be in conflict with the demands of centre capitalist
interests. The socio-economic structure evolving from earlier dependence relations makes small elites powerful and tied to the
centre.

Comment on question 4. The growth of state institutions empirically
found in Third World dependent societies cannot be explained by the
same factors as those explaining the expansion of state institutions
in socialist countries or centre capitalist countries. State institutions in dependent societies tend to be large in relation to the
low level of economic and welfare activities. The growth of state
institutions in dependent societies is instead seen as an effect of
the centre economies' need for administrative and political control
in dependent countries.

Comment on question 5. Foreign economic control from abroad is
sometimes considered the crucial sign of dependence. The dependence
approach as summarized below in its Latin American version is, however, careful to stress that this is neither the only nor always
the most important sign of dependence. This all depends on the historical duration of dependence and the way in which socio-economic
and political structures have been transformed through dependence.
Thus it is clear that Southern Africa and most of Latin America
belong to a part of the Third World where dependence was established
early by the most industrialized part of the world. Internal conditions might today be just as important signs of dependence as foreign control. I will came back to this aspect.

Comment on question 6. The last sign of dependence referred to a-
bove is the most vague and least systematically studied. It is
mainly in Latin America that we find some discussion of the effects
of external dependence on the formulation of government policies.
Remembering the specific conditions of different Latin American
countries, there are many examples of attempts to industrialize on
a national basis which have failed to result in growth except for
in small modern enclaves. Economic growth through foreign capital
involvement but with little actual development in the countries
concerned is also common. This latter aspect is often referred to
as "growth without development".

In the following I define development, very crudely, in the same way as the United Nations: improvement in living conditions for the poor people in the Third World. This is a much narrower definition than is generally found in the literature on underdevelopment and development. The more narrow definition applied by the United Nations is, however, sufficient here, since I treat it as a value that is universally agreed upon and against which changes in political conditions are measured. I do not elaborate in this study on how improvement in living conditions can be measured.[2]

Dependence is defined as a subordinate relation to the outside world. The internal signs and effects of external dependence are particularly stressed in this study. Dependence originated historically through foreign intervention from what is now the most industrialized part of the world. Today it works, however, both through the internal socio-economic structure established in the peripheral societies and through unequal foreign relations. It is treated as a crucial cause of underdevelopment, as is commonly done by the dependence school in studies of underdevelopment and development.

In my opinion T. T. Ewers and Peter von Wogau (1973) have made the best summary of this school and the theoretical implications for subsequent research.[3] According to them, the following elements are common to scholars who use dependence as an explanatory category:

a. The situation of the countries in the Third World can only be explained if the role of external factors is accounted for. The political and socio-economic structure of a country in the Third World is not the result of an autonomous historical process. The internal and the external factors of dependence are today intertwined into an almost indistinguishable whole.

b. The present conditions in Third World countries were originally caused by external factors but the effects are typical characteristics of the socio-economic structures of these countries today. Underdevelopment therefore means change, not lack of change.

c. To overcome underdevelopment, external dependence has to be reduced. This can be done through transformation within the peripheral society.

d. Earlier static descriptions of conditions in Third World countries should be replaced by an analysis which accounts for the dynamics of change as well as the necessarily inter-disciplinary character of studies of underdevelopment.

Ewers and Wogau point out that the inclusion of external factors explaining underdevelopment was considered new by the theorists of social change predominating during the 1960s. But it was new in different ways to different scholars. Marxist scholars earlier stressed that a change in the total international system was necessary to change peripheral conditions. Imperialism as defined by Lenin and Luxemburg had, according to Ewers and Wogau, been seen as relevant mainly in relation to its effects on the class struggle in the centre. The perspective introduced by the dependence approach was that internal conditions of the peripheral countries could both be analyzed and changed from the periphery. Non-marxist scholars on

the other hand rediscovered imperialism as an important dimension.[4]
This re-discovery was largely a result of a crisis in the analysis
applied by development planners who had earlier neglected negative
internal effects of international relations but heavily stressed
the possibilities to develop society from within.

Thus, the essence of the dependence approach is that relations
with the surrounding world determine development in countries which
are subordinately linked to the international capitalist system.
This relation, thus, is not only a background variable.

The dependence approach grew out of a dialogue between marxists
and non-marxists involving Latin American political scientists,
sociologists and economists centred in Santiago de Chile. It influenced neo-marxist scholars, mainly in France, but soon extended
to non-marxist scholars, mainly in North America. In the Latin
American version of the dependence approach, the focus is put on
the way dependence mechanisms are expressed internally. This focus
is applied also in this case study. In Europe and North America,
however, scholars focussed more often on the external part of the
dependence relation.[5] The dependence approach of course is not
applicable only to peripheral societies. Not only do dependence
relations affects the dominating party in an often neglected way,
but such relations, although less extreme, exist also between developed countries. The mechanisms of dependence differ according to
socio-economic and political conditions within the country under
study.

A. G. Frank's book "Capitalism and Underdevelopment in Latin
America"[6] was one of many contributing to the theoretical dialogue,
mentioned above. Since this book was one of the first to be published in English (1967), it was singled out and got wide publicity
in Europe and North America. It should, however, be seen as a part
of a broader discussion at the time, summarizing the work of other
scholars of Latin America. What Frank had in common with most other
scholars with whom he discussed was the descriptive generalization
of the international system as a capitalist-dominated system consisting of central and peripheral parts. His specific interest was
in tracing the historical roots of underdevelopment. He was criticized for mistaking today's society for the final stage of history.[7]
This bias in Frank's work is, however, not inherent in his method
of analysis, but rather a result of his focus. This focus is not
shared by many other scholars applying a dependence approach.

The dependence approach has been applied on African societies
only later. Samir Amin, choosing analytical categories applicable
to counter-dependence-strategies, bases his theory on the Latin
American theoretical discussion and applies a dependence approach
to conditions in African societies. After a thorough analysis of
change in the system of international capital accumulation,[8] he has
devoted some efforts to defining both the effects of this system on
the periphery and to defining a relevant counter strategy.[9] Amin
has a more relativistic view of history than Frank. He stresses the
fact that centres have become peripheries and peripheries have
become centres over time. But strategies for countries to change
their peripheral positions which were relevant earlier in history

are, according to Amin, no longer efficient, mainly because of the
new situation of world wide and tighter integration of the different
parts of the international capitalist system.

The following "characteristics of underdevelopment" are elements
of Amin's core theory:[10]

1. Unevenness of productivity between sectors of production.
2. Disarticulation, meaning that the various sectors of the economy are disconnected from each other and that the economy is
   not self-centred, but directed towards external markets,
   lacking some of the sectors of production generally found in
   centre countries.
3. Domination from outside, meaning unequal foreign exchange
   relations.

Amin uses a broader development concept than the one applied here.
To Amin, development is a complex process of social transformation,
involving changes in capital accumulation and production. His argument is that development, i.e. social transformation, will result
if these characteristics of underdevelopment are overcome. He calls
this strategy "self-centred development". This is primarily based
on a self-centred production. He does not recommend isolationism
or autocracy, but stresses efforts to increase production also in
the lacking sectors, i.e. production of means of production, and
production to meet internal demand. Amin is thus primarily focussing
on alternative strategies of raising production for internal needs.
Although Amin often refers to the prime importance of political
action and socialist transformation of society if the increase in
production is to be distributed to improve living conditions in the
Third World countries concerned, his own focus is on capitalist
accumulation, production and the creation of an internal market.[11]

An analysis of internal political conditions under dependence
is given by the Latin American scholar F. H. Cardoso, who elaborates
the political implications of changes in social groupings in Brazil
as a result of the increasingly tight linkage of the Brazilian economy to the United States and Europe via multinational corporations.
Cardoso's writings are theoretically ambitious and recently he has
been concerned with specifying hypotheses in order to operationa-
lize the concept of dependece. By testing each hypothesis he has
found that changes in external relations are expressed in new
forms and mechanisms of dependence internally.[12]

It is not clear from the dependence approach how external and
internal conditions interact in the given case. When the colonial
system was established, it was easy to discriminate between external and internal conditions. But the closer we come to the reality
of today and the more detailed the study becomes, the more difficult is it to define the difference. In early formulations of the
dependence approach this problem was solved in a simple manner by
classifying the social structure into three: foreign, middlehand
and internal.

Empirical case studies are needed to improve our knowledge and
to develop research methods which give the concept of dependence a
better basis. This can, according to Ewers and Wogau, be done by

way of <u>middle range questions</u>, through which the concept of dependence can be specified into several hypotheses, which are then related to the case under investigation.

The following two points have frequently been made in the post second world war discussion on development among political scientists concerned with Third World studies. Both points have been made in the theoretical writings on societies in the Third World, but we should not forget that they are also of consequence for our understanding of societies in general.

a. *The dependence approach* Many political scientists with widely different theoretical backgrounds agree, mainly after the dialogue in Latin America from 1960 to the mid-1970s, that the way societies are linked to the international system affects their internal socio-economic and political conditions. To understand the conditions of development we thus have to take international factors into account.

b. *The criticism of the dependence approach.* This has likewise come from scholars of different theoretical schools. The dependence approach is criticized for neglecting the specific situation of each country. The specificity of each country is seen as important both for explaining the different forms that society takes in different countries and for stipulating a relevant development strategy.

The criticism of the dependence approach has resulted in studies of specific conditions in peripheral areas. Such documentation is crucial for all further discussion. It is necessary to seek knowledge both at the general and the specific level. But if there was earlier a tendency to neglect the specific conditions of each country, there is now a risk that the generalizations of the dependence approach is neglected. Seeking detailed information on specific countries it is of course not contradictory to an interest in the general mechanisms of dependence.

The international system of which Lesotho is a peripheral part is dominated by multinational banks and firms through an hierarchically structured pattern of wealth and control. Viewing this international, mainly capitalist, system as a system of nation states does not disclose the essence of relations between the dominating and dependent parts of the system. These relations often transcend borders, but are also found within the same country. Thus, when I attempt to evaluate the inter-state relations between Lesotho and South Africa, I do this against the background of political and socio-economic conditions prevailing in the respective countries. Only when the character of these internal conditions are taken into account is it possible to understand the type of relations between the states. This is a conclusion of my study, but it probably holds true also for other subsystems than the Southern African subsystem.

Earlier studies of the Republic of South Africa usually concluded that there were sections of subsistence production in that country. Lesotho was then considered to be a subsistence section similiar to the peripheral parts of the Republic. Recent well-documented studies

of the character of production in South Africa argue instead that
such sections of subsistence production no longer exist, not even in
the peripheral parts of this country.[13] Some documentation on the
character of production in Lesotho is taken up for discussion in the
chapter 2, since the conclusion has relevance for comparison with
the Lesotho government's own view and its development policies.

The Republic of South Africa contains the most industrialized
part of Africa. The government of South Africa intervenes frequently
to secure the interests of national and international capital. The
two legs on which this government bases its growth plans are black
labour and foreign capital. Foreign contract workers have for a
century been a major part of mine labour. Lesotho has during this
century been one of the most important recruitment areas for South
African mines, farms and industries.

The South African Chamber of Mines has controlled labour recruitment for the mines since the end of the 19th century. It is a powerful institution in the Republic and employs nearly 40 per cent of
the male labour force of Lesotho at any given time.[14] Although
industry is the fastest growing sector of the economy, the mines
still provide half of the export value of South Africa. Multinational firms, both those controlling the mines and others, invest in
South African industrial growth.[15] South Africa provides capital
owners in Europe and the United States with higher profits than
they get in most other parts of the world. Hard-working black employees are a basic condition of these profits.[16]

The fact that Lesotho is a labour reserve for the growth of the
South African economy has important implications for political and
living conditions.

Sources on Lesotho

Christian Potholm has rightly stressed in his introduction to the
book "Southern Africa in Perspective", 1972,[17] that the literature
on political conditions in Southern Africa is value-loaded and divided into either ultra-conservative or radical. According to Potholm,
the former kind is produced by those close to the fascist National
Party of South Africa and the latter kind by those sympathetic with
the liberation movements. This extreme polarization of the literature on Southern Africa reflects of course the deep conflicts in
this part of the world. There is a censorship at universities and
in the press, emergency regulations prevail in most of the black-
declared areas of South Africa, including the Transkei.[18] This has
resulted in a lack of research critical to basic features of the
apartheid system in studies published in this region. Those who have
left Southern Africa are on the other hand often highly critical but
lack data. Literature including both facts and criticism is scarce.

The literature on Basutoland/Lesotho is scarce and varies in
quality and bias.[19] On the one hand there are propagandistic pamphlets without empirical connections, on the other hand there are
careful fact-collections without attempt to analyse these facts.
Examples of the former are many publications from the South African

Institute of International Affairs in Johannesburg and pamphlets of
the liberation movements. Examples of the latter are many publications from the Institute of Race Relations and the Christian Institute in Johannesburg and the Africa Bureau in London. The latter
have summarized data on social and economic conditions among black
people in Southern Africa including Basutoland.

But there are also fact-collections made in a biased way, full
of paternalistic conclusions. The African Institute in Pretoria has
published several studies on Lesotho of this kind. These publications contain the first tables on economic conditions in Lesotho
around the time of independence, and they have been used as a basis
for decision-making and long term planning by the Lesotho government. The conclusions in these Africa Institute of Pretoria studies
often point to the backwardness of people in Lesotho and their lack
of knowledge of their own interest.

In Lesotho, collecting data has met with less practical difficulties than in the Republic of South Africa, at least during the
period I study. Still, there is very little research done. A problem, when relating Lesotho to South Africa is also that facts are
often available for only one of the countries. This tends to result
in studies which often do not refer to Lesotho's integration into
South Africa. Among others, Archie Mafeje, social anthropologist
from South Africa, has made the crucial comment that it is almost
impossible to make a realistic study of Lesotho isolated from South
Africa.[20]

The position of the colonial enclave Basutoland has been discussed in diplomatic correspondence between South Africa and the
British colonial power. Basutoland played a strategic military and
economic role in relations between London and its crown colony South
Africa. This correspondence is spread over the entire period of
colonial rule from 1870 to 1960, when Great Britain agreed to future
independence for Lesotho.[21]

Only lately, British and American social scientists have started
to publish works on political conditions in Lesotho. Sandra Wallman,
Allan Macartney, Richard Weisfelder and Jack Spence have made most
thorough studies of politics in Lesotho.[22] Wallman's focus is on
village politics, Macartney's and Spence's on government decision
making, and Weisfelder's on party debate.

An example of an empirical study of industrial development in
Lesotho applying a centre-periphery analysis is Percy Selwyn's
"Industries in the Southern African periphery".[23] But his analysis
is limited to a cost-benefit approach and takes the political and
social conditions as given. He gives economic data on an area
otherwise lacking in documentation. His conclusions are, however,
restricted by the partial and static way he applies a centre-
periphery analysis. He does not discuss changes over time in economic centre-periphery relations between Lesotho and South Africa.

I have made use of the kind of literature mentioned above, but
my main sources for this study have been documents produced by
government, local and international organizations, (particularly
the World Bank and the International Monetary Fund, who record some
of the most crucial data for macro-political and macro-economical

conclusions) political parties, trade unions, parliamentary minutes, statements by politicians, government statistics and other surveys. I have choosen to make public some earlier restricted data, since they are a few years old now and should be of wider general interest.

My interviews with people in differing social backgrounds have been important to check and counter-check written documentation. Listening actively to the points put forward by people with different perspectives on social change in Lesotho has been important for my general background information in a foreign country. I have only referred to the names of people in public positions. Interviews with government and opposition leaders were written down immediately and sent to the interviewees who have approved them.

2 Socio-Economic Change

The Republic of South Africa is often looked upon as a nation dominating its neighbours in trade and investment relations. By examining aggregate figures of these relations it is possible to show
extreme and growing dominance.[1] To look upon Southern Africa as a
system of hierarchically ordinated nations may be useful for some
purposes,[2] but it explains little of the actual exploitative mechanisms involved. Nor does it indicate the possibilities for change
in these mechanisms. For that purpose we have to investigate the
directions of change and the character of socio-economic relations.

In this chapter I will first focus on the present socio-economic
relations of Lesotho*. Secondly, I will compare with the situation
as it was about one hundred years ago. Thirdly, I will comment upon
what is known about the Sotho society before 1830. Finally, I will
briefly discuss the changes in the roles of chiefs. The aim is to
find out what caused the present socio-economic relations and in
what way Lesotho became a part of the international capitalist
system. I have no ambition to cover the history of Lesotho, but
rather to indicate in what direction we might look for causes of
present socio-economic relations to localize mechanisms of dependence.

The Labour Reserve Society of Today

Lesotho is a labour reserve society. The majority of the population
have long been in contact with wage employment in South Africa.
Prevailing habits are shaped to a large extent by industrial work
and consumption values there. In spite of this participation in an
industrialized society the poverty and underdevelopment of Lesotho
resembles that of other Third World countries.

* Lesotho is the name of the country (Basutoland during the colonial period) of the people, Basotho, who speak the language
  Sesotho. Sotho is the ethnographic term for all those who speak
  the Sesotho language.

Agricultural Population?

In an underdeveloped country a large proportion of the population
are normally occupied in agricultural production. This is often
thought to be the case also in the so-called labour reserve societies. The South African Chamber of Mines argues that the low wages
paid to the mine workers are supplemented with subsistence food production in labour reserves, including Lesotho.[3] The First Five-Year
Plan of Lesotho, 1970, also describes "agricultural production..."
as "the major local source of income for approximately 85 per cent
of the population".[4] A "low degree of monetization of agricultural
production (less than 30 per cent of the estimated value in 1966/67)
was thought to be the reason why agricultural produce was recorded
to be so low, and "indicative of the large size of the subsistence
sector". The Five-Year Plan of 1970 also states that "subsistence
activities in general accounted for more than half of the gross
domestic product".[5] In the 1970 agricultural census, 90,7 per cent
of the total population are described as "agricultural population",
1 per cent lower than in 1960. This "agricultural population" grew
from 888,258 individuals to 908,979 from 1960 to 1970 (see table
2.1.).

Table 2.1. *Number of Holdings and Population of Holdings 1950-1970*[6]

		Holdings			Agricultural Population (1)		
Year	Total	Subsis-tence hold.	Inst. hold. (2)	Ave.size of hold-ing (3) (hectare)	Number	% of to-tal popu-lation	Average per hold-ing (per-sons)
1950	149 861	149 800	61	2.33	660 600	–	5.4
1960	161 250	161 250	–	2.18	888 258	91.1	5.1
1970	187 515	187 421	94	1.98	908 979	90.7	4.9

(1) Only on individual subsistence holdings
(2) Missions, business etc.
(3) Arable land

Source: For 1950 "Basutoland Agricultural Survey 1949-50"; for 1960
"1960 Agricultural Census Basutoland" Part 3; for 1970 "1970
Census of Agriculture Report". Bureau of Statistics, Maseru
1973.

But if we scrutinize the actual "agricultural population" on the so
called "subsistence holdings" in tables 2.1. and 2.2. we find that
neither agriculture nor subsistence agriculture is a characteristic
occupation of the population of the country. The figures in table 2.1.

indicate only the number of people living in the countryside and
the number of holdings they have the legal right to farm on. People
are rarely seen in the fields.

Even during the ploughing periods people are seldom seen in
the fields. In the evenings, and even then only rarely, tractors
plough and women and children weed their plots. In response to
questions they say their fields would yield only about one bag
of maize in those years they decide to make use of their fields.
They would themselves have to pay the cost of ploughing and mil-
ling. Fifteen bags of mealie meal was the yearly consumption for
a family of five. Thus 14 of these bags would have to be
bought.[7]

Since commercial thinking and monetarized economy characterizes
the Lesotho society commercial agricultural has been easy to introduce. Where development assistance projects or wealthy chiefs have invested in food production such production has increased. In 1985
one third of food requirements was produced inside Lesotho compared
to in 1975.

A direct effect of increased real wages in the mines during
1973-1977 was a decrease in actual land use, 100,000 Hectares were
taken out of production. In 1976 70 per cent of the official incomes of an average rural household was remittance from migrants
to South Africa, compared to 40 per cent in 1970. In spite of an
increasing unemployed labour force it was neither seen as economically viable nor worth the dependence on land distributing authorities.

Agricultural experts from the United Nations Food and Agriculture Organization (FAO) have documented how easily new techniques
have been introduced in Lesotho. Tractors were already used in
88 per cent of the Leribe Pilot Project area in 1971, when the
project started. Three years later 98 per cent of the area was
tractor ploughed. Fertilizer, the use of which is normally resisted
by a population for two or three years, was immediately taken into
use in Lesotho as long as the price was low.[8] However, to begin
with it resulted in less time being devoted to agriculture rather
than an increase of total production.

Untouched by Modern Economic Development?

According to the World Bank, Lesotho at independence "was virtually
untouched by modern economic development. It was, and still is,
basically a traditional subsistence peasant society".[10] This conclusion about Lesotho as an "untouched" agriculture society with
subsistence production contrasts with other observations. The same
World Bank report as quoted above mentions that "60 per cent of
the male labour force were absent as migrant workers in South
Africa".[11] The high figures of the agricultural propulation hardly
make sense when compared with the large number of wage earners
absent in South Africa. More than 200,000 citizens of Lesotho worked in South Africa at any given time.[12] This figure did not fluctuate over the year. Lower figures are usually given in official

Table 2.2. *Lesotho: Estimated Employment of the Labour Force, 1967, 1970,1973 and 1984. (Thousands of workers)* [9]

	1967	1970	1973	1984
Population (1) (including workers temporarily abroad)	990	1,059	1,131	—
Active labour force	400	430	460	500
Male	250	270	290	—
Female	150	160	170	—
Persons in cash employment	142	150	197	194
In South Africa	125	130	175	159
Employed in mines (2)	80	87	110	114
Employed in other activities	45	43	65	45
In Lesotho	17	20	22	35
Employed in public sector	6	7	7	20
Employed in private sector	11	13	15	15
Residual (mainly persons engaged in subsistence agriculture)	258	280	263	306

(1) Based on projections of the *de jure* population since the April 1966 census.
(2) These estimates could be subject to considerable error, especially given the uncertainty of the nationality status of many of these individuals.
Source: IMF Staff estimates and IMF report Nov 1985.

Table 2.3. *Employment in the "modern" sector in Lesotho 1980*

Mining (diamonds) - closed 1982	800
Quarry	200
Building industry	4,000 - 9,000
Manufacture	3,500 - 7,500
Government (electricity)	500 - 850
Trade and tourism	7,500
Transport	750 - 3,000
"Modern" agriculture	200
Government administration	10,000
Government work	2,000
Insurance, service etc.	1,500
Education	6,500

Source: Lesotho Government and World Bank, both 1980.

tables. The high figure of 200,000 includes also those who seek employment of their own. Even higher figures are given unofficially. If short-time employment, which is frequent among women, is included, the figure rises to about 300,000 out of a total population of 1,4 million in 1985.[13]

The number of mine workers from Lesotho has increased by about 5,000 per year in absolute terms from 1963 to 1974. In 1975 12,000 workers went on strike. In 1976 the increase was 50,000. This means that South Africa's recruitment of miners in Lesotho has increased steadily after independence until 1978. At the same time the proportion of Basotho in the mines had increased from 9 per cent in 1963 to 25 per cent in 1976.[14] (See Diagram 2.A. below.) In 1966, the South African government decided to forbid all new employment of Basotho citizens outside mines and farms. (Those who already held employment in industries and public administration were allowed to continue working.) Whether or not the restriction actually had the effect of preventing Basotho from getting jobs outside mines and farms is, however, doubtful. According to some estimates the employment in other sectors has increased. The large number employed earlier in seasonal agricultural jobs in the Orange Free State has, however, decreased with mechanization.[15]

In conclusion there has been an increase in the recruitment of mineworkers and probably also an increase in the recruitment of workers for industries in spite of the South African government restrictions on the employment of foreign labour for work outside farms and mines. The percentage relation between mine workers and others might therefore be the same as before independence. The main change is that less people work on farms. After 1974, when Malawi withdrew its migrant labour force the recruitment of Basotho increased. After 1980 the recruitment of South African labour increased and took over mining jobs leaving almost no room for new recruitments from Lesotho.

A recent study of agricultural households in the Thaba Bosiu region shows that 80 per cent of all the income of the households with some farming land came from off-farm production. Although the landless households in the region were not included and in spite of the fact that all costs connected with off-farm production had been deducted, 59 per cent of the total income of the households was received through wage employment in South Africa and 21 per cent from off-farm production in Lesotho. Only 6 per cent came from crop production and 13 per cent from commercial production of wool, mohair and cattle for export. The Thaba Bosiu is not an extreme region. The same proportions are true for 1980.

Similar studies made in the agriculture projcets of Thaba Tseka and Leribe indicate that an even greater proportion of the income usually comes from off-farm production. Thaba Tseka is situated in the middle of Lesotho in a mountainous part, whereas Leribe is situated on the lowlands on the border to the Orange Free State.[16]

Diagram 2.A. *Basotho Men Employed in South African Mines, 1963-1980*

(average end-of-month employment each year in thousands)

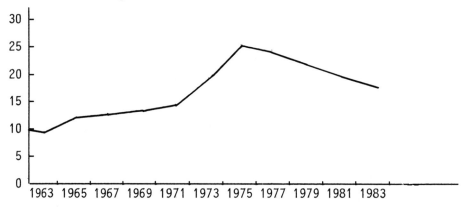

Basotho as a proportion of South African Black Mine Workforce, 1963-1983 (per cent)

Table 2.4. *Sources of Net Income in the Area of Thaba Bosiu Rural Development Project*

Weighted averages for all land-owning households	Crops	Livestock	Misc.	Migrant Labour	Other Off-farm	Total
%	6	13	1	59	21	100
		19			80	

Source: Thaba Bosiu Rural Development Project, Evaluation Study
No 1, Maseru April 1975.

The table below summarizes the results of a survey of land-holders in the area selected by government for a pilot scheme for its agricultural policy. The survey was undertaken by an adviser to the Ministry of Agriculture, C. Hellman. Hellman commented that the category off-farm included work in mines, South African farms, business and trade (café, tractor, beer, etc.). He also considered the values of crop production as biased upwards because of high mortality of livestock those years and because farmers had a tendency to underestimate their incomes from off-farm activites.[17]

Table 2.5. *Sources of Net Income in the Area of the Leribe Agriculture Scheme*

Weighted averages for all land-owning households	Crops	Livestock	Misc.	Migrant Labour	Other Off-farm	Total
%	19.3	1.4	-		79.3	100

Source: Leribe Agricultural Scheme. Economic Surveys of a Random
Sample of Farmers 1970/71-1972/73 by C. Hellman, Maseru
Aug 1974.

Only about 3-5 per cent of the households in Lesotho could in 1973 earn an adequate living from agriculture and/or livestock production, according to inofficial estimates by the Planning Office in 1974. All the mentioned figures have been confidential for a long period of time. They were not discussed publicly. I can only speculate about the reasons for this. One reason might be that the government did not believe them to be correct. Another reason might be that experts of agricultural technology have tended to restrict the publication of their surveys, since these might give the donor-

organization an impression that aid in these field is useless. A
third possibility is the already mentioned fact that the Chamber of
Mines, the largest single employer of migrant labour, is interested
in keeping up the illusion that backward agriculture provides food
for the families of low-paid workers in the mines. The image of a
subsistence agricultural sector in the black areas - including
Lesotho - also gives backing to the idea that there are two separate societies in South Africa based on different modes of production. This is an important foundation of apartheid ideology.

Thus caution should be applied when looking at the estimates
of subsistence agriculture which should be seen as an estimate of
mainly home economics, care for children, old and sick. The population of Lesotho is "industrialized" in the sense that it is participating in the building up of an industrialized economy outside
the borders of their own country. The low wages paid for their
work in combination with equal distribution of land holdings to all
households has given the result that they do not have the means for
farming. Although many have the knowledge and the skill necessary
for farming they have neither time nor money to invest.

Export-Oriented Production?

The Gross Domestic Income is estimated to be three times as large
as the Gross Domestic Product because of migrant labour earnings.
Otherwise the typical patterns of many underdeveloped countries is
visible. Manufacturing and other secondary production is extremely
small, whereas primary production and the service sector domiante
total production. The widening gap between export of raw material
and import of goods is largely due to an increase in the value of
imports of food and manufactured goods,whereas exports of unprocessed wool, mohair, livestock and diamonds remain at about the same
value. The gap in the balance of payments was filled by migrant
labour earnings in spite of the increase in the number of foreign
experts. The table below describes the national income over the
period 1972/73 to 1979/80.

Most of Lesotho's small production is export-oriented. A few
products dominate the exports: wool, mohair and cattle make up
about 70 per cent of the total export. This concentration on a few
unprocessed products vulnerable to international market conditions, adds to the insecurity of the living conditions in Lesotho
in the same way as labour market conditions of South Africa.
This concentration is documented also for other dependent societies.[19]

Lesotho's cattle is sold to South Africa to be slaughtered and
processed there. Wool and mohair are sold unprocessed to Europe via
Port Elizabeth in South Africa, where purchasers, from France and
England mainly, bargain about the price of the wool and mohair from
Lesotho. The export from Lesotho has always been sold separately
from the produce of South Africa. A highly fluctuating price was
paid to the producers until 1972/73, when producers organizations

Table 2.6. *Relation between National Product and National Income 1972/73 - 1979/80*

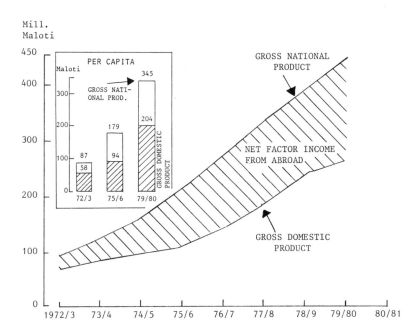

Year	Gross domestic product at market prices	Net factor income from abroad	Gross national product at market prices	PER CAPITA	
				Gross domestic product	Gross national product
	Current prices; Mill. Maloti			Maloti	
1972/73	64,3	31,5	95,8	58	87
1973/74	87,8	44,5	132,3	78	117
1974/75	98,0	60,1	158,1	85	137
1975/76	111,0	101,0	212,0	94	179
1976/77	143,3	125,8	269,1	118	221
1977/78	186,4	145,0	331,4	151	268
1978/79	240,6	156,1	396,7	191	314
1979/80*	263,2	181,8	445,0	204	345

* = indicates preliminary estimates

Source: Economic Indicators 1972/73 - 1979/80
        World Bank (UNDP) Team
        Maseru, Lesotho, June 1981

for these two products were set up in London by South Africa,
Australia and New Zealand, the top three producers in this field.
Lesotho, the fourth biggest producer of mohair, is still not represented in the mohair producers' organization. After this was formed
the country has, however, benefitted from a more stable export
revenue.[20]

The production of wool and mohair employs mainly boys at the age
of 6 to 12, who look after the sheep and the goats, when they do
not go to school. The export of wool and mohair has increased
slightly, but has existed for about a century in Lesotho, as well
as in the Transkei, the Orange Free State and the Cape Province.
Whereas in Lesotho and the Transkei this export remains the only
major production, other produce has become more important in the Cape
Province and in the Orange Free State. Lesotho is today specialized
in two sectors: export of labour and export of wool and mohair.
These two sectors are both outward oriented and have little economic
exchange between them. This situation is characteristic of a disintegrated society. The main expanding sector after independence
has been tourism. So far it has resulted in little net increase in
employment opportunities and little increase in national income.

The lack of production internally is an important condition for
the migrant labour system to continue. People are in practice forced
to supply their labour to the employers of South Africa even at low
wages. The result of low wages is a lack of means to keep any kind
of production alive leaving no possibility to invest for the future.

In South Africa, apartheid is virtually a state-authorized system to justify that the wages paid to the large majority of black
employees are kept at a low level and to administer this wage system. This affects the employees from Lesotho. They are automati-
cally classified as "black" and their status as "foreign black"
gives them even fewer rights and lower wages than the already
underprivileged South African blacks. Present economic tendencies
and legal structure therefore do not favour people in Lesotho.

Unequal Income Distribution?

The distribution of income was during 1940 to 1970 extremely
equal in Lesotho, although at a low level. Estimates in the Second
Five Year Plan for example are, however, based on the distribution
of land holdings and cattle ownership. Since the importance for
income of the holding of land is generally low and decreasing, the
table below underestimates the actual differences in income.

The official per capita income in 1973/74 was 100 rand and in
1979/80 345 rand. Many people live near starvation, but it is also
true that this would look different if we know more about the amount
saved and earned by Lesotho's citizens in South Africa.[22] Also the
actual distribution of wealth might then change. Since there are
hardly any government sponsored insurance schemes, workers try to
save privately for this purpose. This is done in banks, building
societies and insurance companies mainly in South Africa. Information about these savings is not systematically collected. People

Table 2.7. *Income Distribution in Lesotho, 1972*

Population Group	% of Total Income Received	% of Total Income Received Excluding Expatriates
Lowest 5%	3	4
Lowest 20%	15	16
Lowest 40%	30	32
Highest 40%	52	50
Highest 20%	33	30
Highest 5%	16	11

Source: CPDO estimates based on the 1970 Agricultural Census and the 1972/73 Urban Household Budget Survey (The Urban population is about 5 per cent of the total) 21

also save in Lesotho with South African branches. Cattle and housing is still a medium of investment but banks etc. have long been important. [23]

There is no documentation on the size of different occupational groups. Table 2.8. does, however, indicate the differentiation of incomes in selected occupations in Lesotho and South Africa. This gives us reason to believe that there is today an unequal distribution of incomes among the wage employees. Education and skill constitute the most important basis for differentiation within the group of black employees in South Africa.[25]

Table 2.8. *Lesotho: Average Annual Cash Earnings in Selected Occupational Groups, 1970/71-1974/75* [24] *(In Rand)*

	1970/71	1971/72	1972/73	1973/74	1974/75
A. Employment within *Lesotho*					
1. Government					
Including:	564	656	684	...	...
Minimum wage for					
unskilled	228	228	228	228	228
Minimum clerical salary	342	342	342	342	342
Maximum professional					
base salary	4,800	4,800	4,800	4,800	4,800
2. Catering	651	812	1,405	...	...
3. Commerce	386	395	525	...	...
Including, for banking:					
Minimum wage for					
unskilled	...	...	...	...	670
Minimum clerical salary	...	...	...	...	1,320
Minimum teller's salary	...	...	...	...	1,920
Maximum teller's salary	...	...	...	...	3,800
4. Manufacturing	402	473	768	...	...
5. Other identified services	703	890	899	...	...
B. Employment in *R.S.A. mines*(1)	216	229	264	350	528
Including:					
Minimum unskilled above-					
ground wage	...	...	...	...	325
Minimum unskilled below-					
ground wage	...	...	...	...	576
Minimum clerical wage	...	...	...	...	720
Maximum skilled below-					
ground wage	...	...	...	...	1,500

(1) These data relate to calendar years ending three months before the fiscal year shown. In addition to cash earnings, mine workers receive payments in kind (in the form of food, accomodation, medical attention, et), which were generally valued at R 360 per annum in 1974.

Sources: International Monetary Fund, Economic Development in Lesotho 1975. Data on average cash earnings in Lesotho were provided on a preliminary basis by the Statistican's Office. Average cash wages of Bantu employed in South African mines were derived from *Bulletin of Statistics*, Department of Statistics, Pretoria, March 1974. Other data were provided by cabinet personnel and the Salaries Commission.

A Grain Exporting Society - 1830 to 1930

The picture of a society almost totally dependent on off-farm production - 80 per cent of the total income of all "farm households"
- differs entirely from the descriptions of the former colony of
Basutoland a hundred years ago. What is now Lesotho used to be a
rich and very efficient agricultural economy. It was both self-
reliant for food and certain handicraft products and well-integra-
ted into the cash economy of South Africa through large exports
of wheat, maize and sorghum, as well as through the consumption of
manufactured goods.

Diagram 2.B. *Some Important Historic Data Mentioned in this Chapter*

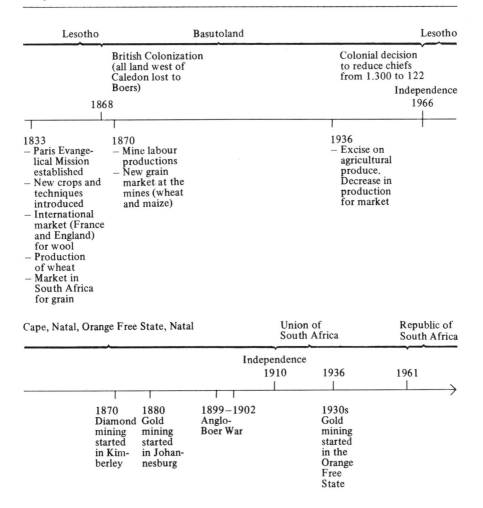

In 1837, the inhabitants of Lesotho, which then stretched west
of the present border marked by the Caledon river, "had grain sto-
red for four to eight years" and "in 1844 white farmers 'flocked'
to them to buy grain".[26] The country seems to have accumulated
wealth throughout the nineteenth century, despite periods of wars.
Moshoeshoe's "Lesotho" lost what is today half of the Orange Free
State to the Boer Republic. Thereafter Great Britain annexed the
remaining eastern part as a colony. This was in 1868 at the same
time as the Boer Republic lost the diamond rich areas of Kimberley
to Britain. Basutoland recovered quickly and in 1872 "exported
100,000 bags of grain - wheat, mealies and sorghum - 2,000 bags
of wool and a considerable number of cattle and horses".[27]

The Basotho farmers benefitted from their long experience of
agricultural production in an area - the Orange and Caledon valleys - which is the best naturally irrigated region of South
Africa's interior. They managed, during the whole of the nineteenth century, to compete successfully in the drier areas with
Boer cattle farmers, who were inexperienced but attempted to
establixh themselves in grain production.[28]

The Basotho responded quickly to new techniques and to new
crops like wheat and maize. Before the colonial annexation, a
newspaper in the Orange Free State described the country in the
following terms:

> Nowhere else in South Africa is there a more naturally indus-
> trious nation, as honest and as peaceable as the Basuto.
> Before the wa the quantity of wheat, maize and millet which
> this tribe produced was truly incredible.[29]

In 1871, after the colonization, a missionary described the
occupations of the inhabitants in the following way:

> Hitherto our Basuto have quietly remained at home, and the move-
> ment which is taken place beyond their frontiers has produced
> no other effect than to increase the export of wheat and other
> cereals to a most remarkable degree. While the district in
> which the diamonds are found is of desperate aridity, the val-
> leys of Basutoland, composed as they are of a deep layer of
> vegetable mould, watered by numerous streams and favoured with
> regular rains in the good season, require little more than a
> modicum of work to cover themselves with the richest crops.[30]

In spite of the loss in 1868 of a large lowland area west of the
present Lesotho borders, the Basotho were self-sufficient in food
and exported the surplus to the diamond mines which were opened
up in Kimberley in 1870 and to the gold mines which were opened
up in the Johannesburg area in the mid-1880s. They do not seem to
have had economic reasons to go to the mines for work. (We should,
however, keep in mind that the missionaries' records seldom distinguish between poor and rich people in Basutoland.) Yet the grain
exporting country experienced competition. In 1887 a missionary
mentioned new problems:

> The establishment of the railway... (from the coast to Kimber-
> ley and Johannesburg) ... has profoundly modified the economic

situation of Basutoland. It produces less and finds no outlet
for its products. Its normal markets, Kimberley and the Free
State, purchase Australian and colonial wheat. Money is scarce,
so scarce that the Government has had to receive tax in kind.
... Basutoland, we must admit, is a poor country. Money is
rare, more especially these days. The price of wool has fallen
by half. Last year's abundant harvest has found no outlet for,
since the building of the railway, colonial and foreign wheat
have competed disastrously with the local produce. [31]

This quotation indicates that money was already widely in use
in Basutoland in 1887, and wool export to Europe as well as wheat
export to the mines were important parts of the production. There
are varying data on the number of men and women who took jobs outside Basutoland. A high proportion of the men worked in the mines
already in the 1880s.[32]

In the opening stages of migrant labour, before 1911 the employees had short term contracts and they were paid at a relatively much higher rate than they are today.[33] The short contracts
still gave the workers time for farming, and the high wages allowed them to save money for investments. People thus had the means
to produce and invest in agriculture.

Table 2.9. *Annual Cash Earnings in Gold Mines, 1911-69.*

Date	Current rands		Index of Real Earnings 1936 = 100		Earnings gap Ratio W:B
	White	Black	White	Black	
1911	666	57	102	100	11.7 : 1
1916	709	59	94	90	12.0 : 1
1921	992	66	90	69	15.0 : 1
1926	753	67	85	88	11.2 : 1
1931	753	66	90	92	11.3 : 1
1936	786	68	100	100	11.5 : 1
1941	848	70	94	89	12.1 : 1
1946	1 106	87	99	92	12.7 : 1
1951	1 607	109	113	89	14.7 : 1
1956	2 046	132	119	89	15.5 : 1
1961	2 478	146	129	89	17.0 : 1
1966	3 216	183	149	99	17.6 : 1
1969	4 006	199	172	99	20.1 : 1

Source: Francis Wilson *Labour in the South African Gold Mines,
1911-1969* [34]

Table 2.10. *Migrant Labour from Basutoland - Lesotho, 1911-1976*

Populations Census	Men	Women	Total	Per cent of de jure population
1911	21 658	2 972	24 630	5,8
1921	37 827	9 314	47 141	8,7
1936	78 604	22 669	101 273	15,3
1946	95 697	32 331	128 028	18,6
1956	112 790	41 992	154 782	19,5
1966	97 529	19 744*)	117 273	12,0
1976	129 103	23 551	152 654	12,5

*) In 1966 South Africa enforced restrictions on migrant labour
which mainly affected women.

Source: Bureau of Statistics, Lesotho
Department of Labour, Lesotho
van der Wiel, A.C.A., <u>Migratory Wage Labour</u>, its role in
the economy of Lesotho, Mazenod, Book Centre, Mazenod,
Lesotho, 1977.

Lesotho is not suitable for farming. This is a frequent conclusion in reports on agriculture in Lesotho after independence.
Sandra Wallman, for example, wrote in 1976 that "natural factors
combine with traditional farming practices and with increasing
pressure of population and land to make Lesotho unsuitable for
farming".[35]
What changed the "natural factors" so completely and what impe-
ded a continuation of the development of farming practices and
successful production described above? Until the 1930s, agricultural production was large enough to make Basutoland self-sufficient
and able to export. Production was larger than ever before in history and there was enough to feed the population. The rain factor
has not changed. Soil erosion has been mentioned as one explanation. But geographical surveys indicate that shortage of farm
labour is an important cause to soil erosion.[36]
In the 1930s agricultural produce started to decrease in absolute terms. Not until then was the socio-economic structure of the
farming community in Basutoland broken down and left with migrant
wage labour as the dominant source of income, although there were
migrant men and women going to South Africa as contract labour
long before that, see table 2.10. It is from then on that the present methods in agriculture have come into use. Women instead of
men worked over-time in the fields, often without the equipment
used earlier.[37]
Migration was the result of poor agriculture. This is another
proposition often heard in Lesotho after independence. The causal
relationship might just as well be the opposite. There are important changes in political conditions which might be part of the
explanation. Agriculture was actively broken down through, for
example, the following decisions:

1. In 1932, the South African Prime Minister, General Hertzog wrote to the British Secretary of State, J. H. Thomas, to ask for restrictions on wheat farming in Basutoland. White farmers in South Africa had long complained that the black farmers were more successful. When there was economic recession in South Africa - as part of the general international recession - these complaints were articulated in political terms.

> We find it increasingly difficult to resist the daily pressure on the part of the people of the Union for measures restricting competition in our local markets from territories outside the Union. The depression, as you might well imagine, has much accentuated this demand.[38]

This claim was repeated in 1933, in a memorandum from the Minister of Justice, Jan Smuts. The argument used in order to make Britain decide in favour of the South Africans was to threaten with a) restrictions on recruitment of labour to the British-owned mines b) incorporation of the High Commission territories.[39] In 1935, Britain answered by handing over an "Aide-mémoire" to the South African Ministry of Native Affairs, which suggested "improved co-operation between the Union and the High Commission Territories". Restrictions on agricultural produce were introduced by the colonial government in Basutoland. South African subsidies to the white farmers in the Orange Free State had already been given. Capital-intensive agricultural methods and boreholes were spread as a result of state subsidies.[40]

2. Before the British colonial restrictions were enforced in Basutoland, an investigation of the economic conditions in the colony was made. This investigation resulted in an ambitious mission report, "The Pim Report" in 1935. The whole system of rule needed to be changed, concluded the report. The chiefs were too rich, and there were far too many of them. Recommendation was made to dismiss most of the existing 2,000 chiefs, appointed by the colonial government. The chiefs were at this time still in charge of land allocation, they led the farming practices.[41] These practices broke down gradually. The drainage and irrigation system for example, depended largely upon the organizational work carried out by the chiefs and their advisors. The changing role of the chiefs will be described and analyzed in greater detail further on in this chapter.

The Iron Workers and Peasants before 1830

Why was the Lesotho society able to absorb innovations and accumulate wealth so successfully during the 19th century? What kind of society existed before the 1830s, when techniques introduced by the missionaries and traders were rapidly absorbed by the Basotho? It is easy to get the impression that human history started in Southern Africa when the missionaries arrived. These have been the history writers of Lesotho, just as they have been in other parts of Africa. The written history of Lesotho is still that of its

colonizers. The views of the government of South Africa today dominate the interpretation of the history, including Lesotho. Until the late 1970s the interior of Southern Africa was usually
described as an empty land before the settlement of the Portuguese, the Boers and the British.[42]

According to the South African official history, spread also
in Lesotho, the so-called Bantu people came from the North at the
same time as the Europeans invaded the interior from the Cape and
Natal in the 18th and 19th centuries. French missionaries settled
in the country of the famous king Moshoeshoe in 1833. One of these
French missionaries was a young man, Eugene Casalis, from the
Paris Evangelical Church, who became not only the Foreign Secretary of King Moshoeshoe but also a prominent historian of Lesotho.
Moshoeshoe had already started to gather scattered Sotho, Nguni
and Xhosa groups under his government's control. During the early
19th century, there was a long period of several wars, the *Lifa-
qane*, involving Nguni and Sotho. Moshoeshoe named the new nation
Lesotho after the dominating language group Sotho.[43] Anthropolo-
gical and archeological sources give us some information about
the economy and social structure of the Sotho society. Language
determined who belonged to the Sotho people.[44]

Iron was worked in what is today Southern Transvaal from at
least A.D. 1,000 and in what is now the Orange Free State from
between A.D. 700 and 800. In the region of today's Lesotho there
is only vague evidence of iron ore mining, but in the now lost
region, which until colonial annexation in 1868 belonged to Lesotho, there is clear evidence that mining, smelting and crafts were
practiced. The production of leather and metal work covered not
only internal consumption but these goods were also exported.
Grain production and cattle-keeping were also prominent.[45]

The Sotho were distinguished from their neighbours by their
skill as craftsmen and by the fact that most of them lived in
stone houses in relatively permanent settlements rather than in
scattered homesteads. The following examples taken from different
travellers' records, show that Sotho towns were fairly large and
much larger than any of the white settler towns at that time:

Dithakong 10,000-15,000 inhabitants (1801)
Kaditshwene 13,000-16,000 inhabitants (1820)
Masweu 10,000-12,000 inhabitants (1820)
Taung 1,300-1,400 (1824) and 20,000 (1836)
Kgwakgwe (1824) covered a large area and had more inhabitants
than any South African town, known to the eye-witness, A Euro-
pean missionary
Phitshane, on Molopo river, had a population of "upwards of
20,000" (1824)
Thaba 'Nchu 9,000 (1839).[46]

MAP 1. Distribution of Sotho before 1822 and 1822–40, also the Tsetse zone in the Transvaal. *After C. C. Saunders* (References are filed in the University of Cape Town). Tsetse distribution C. Fuller, *Tsetse in the Transvaal and Surrounding Territories*, Pretoria, 1923.

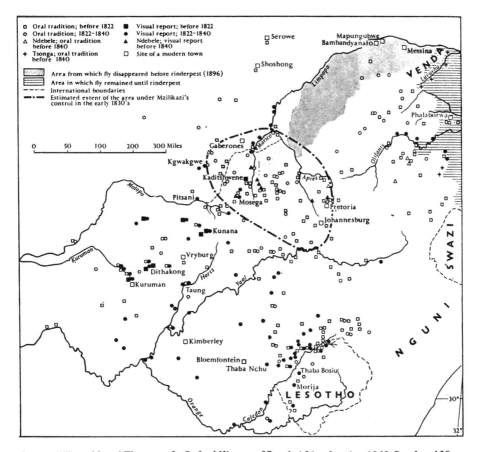

Source: Wilson, M. and Thomson, L. *Oxford History of South Africa,* London 1969, Part I, p. 138.

Each large settlement was a "capital" in which an independent chief lived with most of his followers, and each was surrounded by cattle posts. Small groups of hunters had their customers among the chiefs and leading families and occupied areas distant from the capital and cattle posts. Many of the settlements were situated on hill tops, exactly like the capital of Moshoeshoe at Thaba Bosiu, described in detail by the French missionary Eugene Casalis mentioned above.47

Cultivated fields spread in the valley below the capital, sometimes covering "several hundred acres". These fields were "at least twenty miles in circumference". During the sowing and reaping seasons, families could camp in the fields, but their huts might be

burned if they failed to return to the capital when the work was
done. Packoxen were constantly used for bringing in grain from the
fields (some of which were twenty-five miles distant from the owner's home) and for transporting articles of trade.[48] Sorghum,
sweet reed, kidney beans, pumpkins, sweet melons and gourds were
grown. Maize was probably unknown until 1822 and was introduced
on a larger scale only later.[49] There is documentation of a fairly
extensive trade in metal goods. Hides of wild animals and ostrich
feathers were also exchanged by some of the Sotho speakers who
purchased grain from people living in the neighbouring regions.
Hemp and tobacco were used both for consumption and barter. The
skill of the Sotho craftsmen was reported early by contemporary
travellers from Greece and the Arab countries. The fact that they
refused to buy European knives, as they were inferior to their own,
was reported with astonishment by travelling European traders.[50]

In 1843, David Livingstone reported from the Transvaal: "The
manufacturing of iron seems to have been carried on here uninter-
ruptedly from a very remote period." Travelling eastward through
the Transvaal he came to Banalaka and reported: "They smelt iron,
copper and tin and in the manufacture of ornaments know how to mix
the tin and copper so as to form an amalgam. Their country abounds
in ores." Livingstone also described an extensive trade in hides
and skins. 20,000 to 30,000 hides were tanned and many of these
were sold to China. This trade across the Indian Ocean had been
going on already before the Portuguese appeared on the scene in
the 16th century.[51]

Livingstone's report on the abundance of ores spread quickly
in Europe and led to a rapid inflow of capital. Present official
versions of history which claim that the British "discovered" the
mineral deposits are obviously false. The mining was taken over
directly from the people in the region, who already knew the mining profession well. The Sotho saying: "You should never tell
the existence of a mineral deposit to a European because then you
will lose it" still hinders prospecting in Lesotho, according to
a UNDP report.[52] The saying is based on bitter historic facts.

Diagram 2.C. *Some Dates on the Integration into the International
Capitalist System over Time*

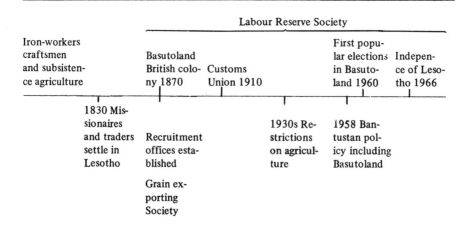

The Changing Role of Chiefs

In the following section a closer look will be taken at the group
called chiefs. Here the term "chief" is used mainly according to
the British way of defining the word. The British definition is
connected rather with a certain group of families inheriting their
colonial jobs. The colonial law regarded the position of chiefs
as hereditary.

In the Sesotho language the title of "chief", "morena", is given to persons who hold superior economic and social positions.
The actual holders of such positions have been changing over time.
This indicates an emphasis on the role and function of a chief
rather than the individual holder of such posts. Missionaries,
traders, and civil servants, both Basotho and foreigners are called "chiefs".

We know little about who ranked high in the socio-economic
structure before the 1830s. Trade was probably monopolized by
people called "chiefs". The surplus appropriated from agriculture
and trade was probably redistributed to soldiers, iron-workers
and others. The Sotho city states were not organized in the form
of military kingdoms as the societies of the Nguni (including the
Swazi), although soldiers probably ranked high as well as cultiva-
tors, craftsmen and herdsmen. Order was assured through compromise
and negotiation as well as by more violent methods. Even when
there were wars a during the reign of Moshoeshoe (1820-1870),
(who at times controlled more than 10,000 soldiers), travellers
recorded that the freedom to criticize authority in public assembly was greater than was then permitted in England and France.[53]

Cleavages were expressed in terms of opposing lineages. But
much of this oral history was written down by missionaries and
the chiefs themselves only during the 19th century. It aimed at
tracing divisions and showing links between the ruling lineages
of existing chiefs. But there is little known today about the
actual underlying causes of conflict.[54]

In pre-colonial times new chiefs were established through the
procedure of a young leader moving away from his followers
to settle down in a territory which might or might not overlap
with that claimed by the chief who he left. He asserted the independence of his court, *lekhotla*, by refusing to send cases of
appeal to any other authority. Independence did not mean, however,
that the chiefdoms were totally isolated from each other. Emissa-
ries were exchanged, trade relations existed and the chiefs and
their advisors often met.[55]

In Basutoland as in Bechuanaland and Swaziland, the British colonial policy after annexation was to delegate most of the administration and decision making at the local level to the chiefs, the
missions, and the traders.

The chiefs existed before colonization as did missionaries and
traders. But the roles of these three groups changed. The colonizers made the chiefs collect taxes in addition to their traditional roles of judges and distributors of land. The greatest change,
however, was an increase in the number of chiefs, who in practice

became colonial employees installed for life. Their positions were
inherited by their sons. For a long period, the missions held the
supreme right to decide on the organization and content of education, health and other services. White traders had the exclusive
right to buy the produce of Basutoland and to import manufactured
goods into the colony. They were also responsible for the roads
of Basutoland. Many Basotho worked for the traders to keep the
roads in good condition.

In contrast to most of the chiefs in South Africa, those of Basutoland served the colonial power and represented it. In many
areas of South Africa, the chiefs were discriminated against. British magistrates took over their functions as tax collectors and
judges, for example in the Cape Colony. Common land ownership was
abolished except in the small areas called Native Reserves.[56] In
Basutoland, the chiefs were often looked upon as traitors by their
own people, whereas in certain areas of South Africa they sided
with the rest of the people against the colonial power.[57] In the
Transkei and the Ciskei, for example, chiefs joined the liberation
movements.[58] This tendency is, however, vague and there are examples of hereditary chiefs, who are accepted by the South African
government also in these areas.

British colonial policy in Basutoland has often been described
as "laissez-faire". According to some sources, this gave the people
room to manoeuvre. According to my impression, this room was only
for elite groups. Until the second world war a high degree of autonomy was enjoyed by chiefs, traders and missionaries in their relationship with London. A similar autonomy was enjoyed by wheat
producers, gun smiths and the ox wagon owners, among others. British interests were that the colony should cost little and serve
British capital interests in South Africa. The British civil servants who were placed in Basutoland at an early stage played minor
roles. The local groups of colonially appointed chiefs, British
traders and missionaries of European extraction assumed state
functions at political, economic and ideological levels. As long
as the local groups served this interest well, few British administrators were considered necessary. But during the 1930s this
was no longer the case: tax collection did not function and labour
was scarce in the territory for the labour offcies to recruit.
Neither chiefs responsible for the collection of taxes nor the traders responsible for recruitment of labour to build roads had control over where the villagers stayed and worked.

The Pim Report, mentioned earlier, stated that there was a
"complete lack of any kind of government." What Pim might have
meant was that the groups trusted earlier by the colonial government were no longer ruling in the British interest since the main
interest of British companies in Southern Africa during this period was an increase of labour and control of labour. Suggested
reforms aimed at building up a bureaucracy to take over from the
chiefs and the missionaries. The traders still functioned well
according to the report.[59]

New offices for tax collection were now set up in South Africa.
The Basotho were integrated into the pass law system of South

Africa, through which the movement of labour was more strictly
controlled. The interests of the British were thus met. The chiefs
were reduced in number from about 1,300 to 120 over the period
1938 to 1946. Their judical functions were taken over by trained
lawyers who seldom were chiefs.[60]

However, the few chiefs who were still left ranked high in the
socio-economic structure. They were still the largest land holders.
Some of them, the Principal Chiefs, had contacts with the financial decision makers through their advisory roles in the National
Councils. Tax collection was, however, taken over by educated Basotho commoners and British employees. The today common belief
that the many lower chiefs, who have reemerged after independence,
base their power on land distribution has to be reconsidered. The
role of the chiefs will therefore be taken up for discussion a-
gain in chapters 3 and 4.

The policy to dismiss thousands of lower chiefs from their gazetted right to get an income from the villagers at the same time
as introducing excises on agricultural produce hit many of them
hard. The precolonial roles had lost importance. Together with
their advisors and families they emerged as a frustrated social
stratum. Their frustration continued a basis for later anti-colonial mobilization. The party connections of this stratum will be
discussed in the next chapter.

The chiefs who remained as salaried and so-called gazetted
chiefs after the reform were appointed and dismissed by the colonial government. Earlier the chieftainship itself had the power
to recruit new chiefs in addition to those inheriting their positions. Not even the Paramount Chief had the right to dismiss a
chief. These powers of the colonial government were taken over
by the Lesotho government after independence.

Conclusions

During 1884-1966 the area which constitutes the Lesotho of today
was administered as a separate colony, Basutoland, by the British
colonial headquarters through the British representatives in
South Africa. The British interest was to secure food exports
and labour for the mines. From being a diversified society based
on iron-mining, leather work and subsistence agriculture, the
Lesotho society became increasingly specialized after the 1830s.
Missionaries first settled in Lesotho from the 1830s and their
records show that the welfare of the population increased as a
result of growing trade both with the Southern African region and
with Europe. The regional trade involved grain, whereas the international trade concentrated on wool and mohair. Increasing monetization and modernization of technology were important new elements.
Control of the new means of production by citizens of Lesotho
seems to have been kept for a considerable period after colonial
annexation. The grain producers were a new elite of both chiefs
and commoners but through the excises on agricultural produce

enforced during the 1930s this elite was deprived of part of its income. Through the excise many grain-producers could no longer compete.

According to the dependence approach, economic disintegration is to be expected in peripheral societies. In Lesotho, we have found this in the form of separation between the export markets of wool-mohair on the one hand and labour on the other. Until the 1930s there was a third important separate sector — that of commercial grain production, which then started to decline.

One result of the deprivation of the wealthy groups was a more equal distribution of wealth within Basutoland. Yet, eqaul distribution was kept at a very low level. This might be said to contradict the pattern expected in dependent societies. This distribution of holding of land and wealth introduced during the 1930s has remained until the mid-1970s. The wage distribution changed towards a more unequal pattern already during the mid-1960s. A small group of well-paid state employees after independence in Lesotho and another small group of skilled professionals in South Africa earn much more than the average with wages kept at subsistence level.

The decrease in agricultural production had several reasons. One earlier neglected reason is the state intervention from both South Africa and the British colonial power to actively prevent commercial farming in Basutoland in the mid-1930s. This was done at the explicit demand of white farmers in South Africa, who experienced difficulty in meeting competition from the wheat producing farmers in Basutoland. But the actions taken were not against the interests of the British mining companies in South Africa. These had an interest in the destruction of alternative income possibilities in the regions where mine-workers were recruited. Basutoland became such an area with the start of the large-scale exploitation of the diamond and gold mines in South Africa.

The official statistics on the present population of Lesotho do not disclose that commercial production once flourished within agriculture and that there is today little evidence to support a general belief of the existence of a subsistence agriculture. Today's poverty-stricken migrant workers are the descendants of the Sotho-speaking iron workers and craftsmen of a period before colonization. Already from about 1,000 A.D. there were iron-working societies in central South Africa.

Socio-economic relations in Sotho society have changed gradually. During the time when iron was worked, the miners, smelters and craftsmen competed with chiefs for elite positions. For half a century after the colonial annexation, the chiefs experienced little competition from these groups. Instead they gained increasingly central positions through their organizational control of communal work in the villages and through the support given directly to them by the colonial government. They were able thereby to appropriate part of the surplus for themselves through the mechanisms of grain marketing. After the 1930s the role of the chiefs clearly became less important. This was casued by a de-

crease in agricultural production, as a result of the mentioned
restrictions on the production in this field. Almost all the
chiefs (about 9/10) lost their earlier incomes from their administrative and judical roles. The remaining higher chiefs can be
compared to "landlords" since people are still given plots through
the chief, although using them mainly for housing. A new kind of
village chief has emerged after independence, directly dependent
on the post-independence government. These chiefs are mainly occupied with questions of security and information.

The exploitation on a large scale of mines, farms, and industries was initiated by the capital owners of the metropolitan
centres of Western Europe and the United States, and established
through colonial military intervention. The people already settled in the area resisted politically and militarily and were only
gradually annexed. The mine owners controlled state power in
South Africa although not without opposition from both white and
black groups.

During the 1930s political pressure on a mass basis was mobilized by boer farmers and foremen as well as by black workers. But
the groups of whites were only allowed to share the power. Today
Lesotho, with its 200,000 to 300,000 contract workers, is linked
to the centre of the international system in a subordinate manner
via employers in South Africa. This has resulted in only partial
compensation for the work done by these migrant contract workers.

Keeping in mind the separate colonial history of Basutoland,
there are still many similarities between Lesotho and those parts
of South Africa which were declared Native Reserves in 1911, including the Transkei. These have been ecologically destroyed and
now lack employment opportunities. As in Lesotho, half of their
labour force in employed in the white-declared industrialized
parts of the Republic. Like Lesotho they were the last regions
to be colonized and some of them played an important role as grain
producers until the mid 1930s.

3 Political Parties

What are the political conditions for development in a labour reserve like Lesotho today? Is it possible to organize political action for a development strategy and what ideas of development are
expressed in the extreme dependence situation of this enclave state?

During the rule of Moshoeshoe I and the 98 years of colonial rule
that ended in 1966, separate state institutions for Lesotho/Basuto-
land were built up. But what political base did these state institutions have at independence and after? While studying the development policies of the state institutions, I soon found that all
decision-making was connected with either of two strong parties:
the Basutoland Congress Party (BCP) and the Basotho National Party
(BNP). In this chapter I focus on the groups supporting these two
parties and the political ideas they aim at implementing.

Organizational Patterns in Lesotho

Political discussion has long been widespread in Lesotho. In spite
of severe restrictions at times, people not only articulated their
ideas of what the future society should be like but also organized
their implementation.

However, the frequent movement of people between contract work
in industrial areas of South Africa and the countryside of Lesotho
makes it difficult for any kind of permanent organization to develop among the Basotho. There are many who argue that the very reason
for the migrant workers' system is that it is an efficient method
to prevent trade unions and political activities contrary to the
interest of the employers in South Africa. Basotho migrants also
move within South Africa between different places of work. There
is a concentration of Basotho migrants in South African towns like
Soweto, Vereeniging and Welkom. The individual wage earners have
gradually become less and less integrated into the power structure
of the home villages of Lesotho. There are also legal restrictions
on meetings and certain types of organizations both in Lesotho and
South Africa. Frustration is associated both with the actual moving
away and the isolation from family and friends on the part of the
wage earner, and also with the waiting for money and messages on
the part of the dependent family members. These difficulties have,
however, existed almost a century. They have led to the demand for
an organization providing improved communication links between the
people.

The employers provide, with some success, a channel for communicating money and messages of a social character through their recruitment offices and personnel departments.[1] The Evangelical church
and its Catholic competitor have also discussed the need for frustrated workers to find human relations and a feeling of belonging
at their places of work. With little success they have attempted to
organize meetings of a religious and social nature for migrants in
South Africa.[2] But the respective branches of the Catholic church
in Lesotho and in the industrial areas of South Africa have different origins. This is an obstacle to co-operation. The catholic
church in Lesotho has historically been integrated with chieftainship. Most of its priests belong to the "Oblates of Mary Immaculate"
(OMI).   This Order is the politically most conservative in
Southern Africa and particularly active in anti-communism campaigns.

It is much more conservative than the Order dominating among
priests in the Johannesburg area.[3] The Evangelical church faces a
similar problem of schismatic organization. But the difficulties
facing the churches and employers to act as communicators stem not
only from differences in ideas and organization within and between
the churches but also from the fact that the workers and their
families have little trust in their employers and the church officials.

The organizations which have succeded best in forming the linkage
between the migrant wage earners and their dependants have been the
BCP, the trade unions, the African National Congress (ANC) and the
Pan-African Congress (PAC). These movements have not only provided
an organization favouring the interests of the migrant wage earners.
They have representatives spread geographically. They were able to
present an integrated picture of the diverse social forces facing
the migrant families but however, are trusted only as long as they
refuse co-operation with the establishment.

The very breakdown of the earlier existing society in Lesotho
and the increased movement of people had given the political parties
an important role to play in the pattern of communication. Most
other institutions, including the extended family, were gradually
loosing their importance. The average family household had only
4-5 members.[4] The reaction to the exploitation of people through
low wages and racial discrimination can also explain why there
was much political discussion and political organization among
people in Lesotho. Another background explanation is that, during
the last century there have been competing mission churches in
Lesotho. The ordinary citizens of Lesotho had become used to the
possibility of choosing between alternative views and contacts
affecting their lives in different ways. During the first period
of their existence the parties have also been connected with either
of the most important churches: the Catholic church with the BNP
and the other churches with the BCP. Voting seems, however, to
have had little connection with the religious conviction and both
parties have succeeded in involving new members from both churches.
But to what extent is the conflict between the two parties an
expression of a social cleavage? The background of the different
parties and the conflict between them might give us an answer to
this question.

Stability in Political Cleavage over Time

Political cleavages expressed in party conflicts have shown a remarkable stability over time, both ideologically and with regard to the
support given to them. Since 1958, when party politics were first
formally allowed, there have been two major power blocks opposing
each other throughout the country in almost every village: the
radical-oriented BCP and the more conservative BNP. The small
royalist and liberal-oriented Marema-Tlou Freedom Party (MFP),
formed in 1962 and standing ideologically between these blocks,
has never managed to get a countrywide following, but has regional
support around the royal village and Maseru.[5] Two minor parties,
with only a few hundred followers each, are worth mentioning because
of their importance for the relation between the BCP and BNP: the
Communist Party of Lesotho (CPL), operating during 1961-1970 mainly
within the BCP, and the United Democratic Party (UDP) 1967 onwards
which made up the main legally articulated opposition[6] in the
Interim Parliament, appointed by Leabua Jonathan in 1973.

Major changes in Lesotho's political party structure took place
in 1952 and in 1958. In 1952 most of the politically conscious
citizens of Basutoland joined a common independence movement, the
Basutoland African Congress (BAC), under the leadership of Ntsu
Mokhehle. In 1958 a group of lower chiefs, chief's advisors and
Catholic teachers broke away from the BAC and formed the BNP, under
the leadership of Leabua Jonathan. The BNP continued an anti-
colonial policy but stressed co-operation with South Africa when
independence had been attained. The government of South Africa
accepted the BNP as a party working within the framework of its
policy for the Southern Africa region.

In 1959, The BAC changed its name to Basutoland Congress Party
(BCP). The opinion expressed earlier - that real liberation would
mean co-operation with other liberation movements in Southern Africa
and would entail changes in the social structure of Basutoland -
was now stressed. Even the BAC had expressed attitudes which were
not only anti-colonial, but also anti-chiefs, anti-traders and anti-
churches. But after changing its name, the BCP became more explicit
and detailed on how power should be transferred from the established
groups to the majority of the people. The BCP often talked about
the right of the unfavoured and exploited sections of the population to the same opportunities as the chiefs, the traders and the
priests.[7] This line of thought was not only a direct reaction to
British colonial policy in Basutoland and to the actions of the
Nationalist Party government in South Africa. It was inspired by a
general discussion in the colonies expressed, for example, at the
All-African People's Conference (AAPC) under the leadership of
Kwame Nkrumah. The BCP leader, Ntsu Mokhehle, was an active member
of the Steering Committee of the AAPC from 1958 to 1962.[8]

In 1957, that is before the BNP was formed, the Marema-Tlou
Party (MTP) was announced. It supported the status of the Paramount
Chief and the Principal Chiefs. It was formed as a reaction to BAC's
increasing criticism of chiefs. The BAC leadership had repeatedly
criticized the chiefs for being "an arm of a conservative colonial

Diagram 3.A. *Origin of the Political Parties with Reference to Time and Political Bias*

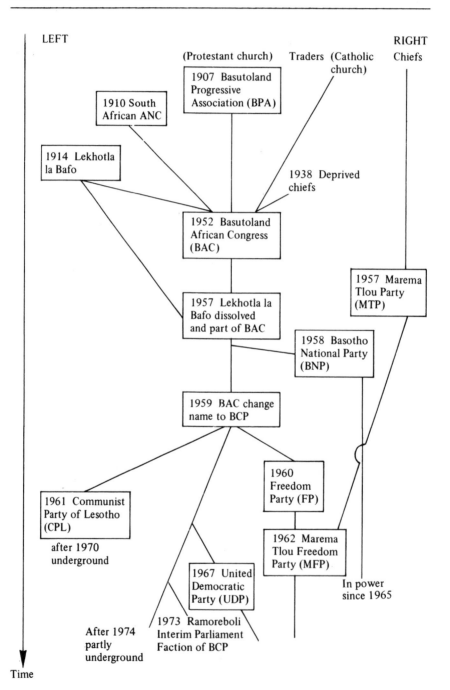

Government". The new pro-chief party, MTP, however, did not manage
to get many supporters.[9] In 1962, it joined the small liberal Freedom Party (FP) under the former deputy leader of the BCP, Bennett
Khaketla. Khaketla had left the BCP in 1960 together with a handful
of other BCP members protesting against what they saw as an authoritarian stand against individual chiefs, traders and priests.

The FP under Khaketla had not managed to get much popular support either.[10] But the new joint party Marema-Tlou Freedom Party
(MFP) rapidly organized support in the area around the royal village
of Matsieng and among traders and intellectuals in Maseru. The MFP
profited from the popularity of the young Paramount Chief, Moshoeshoe II. He had returned from his university studies in Oxford in
1960 to succeed Regent Mantsebo. In the 1965 elections the MFP
gained 4 seats, apart from the fact that the 22 Principal Chiefs
and 11 others, who were appointed to the Senate by Moshoeshoe II,
also favoured the MFP. But in the 1970 election three seats were
lost. The MFP kept only one seat in the House of Commons.[11]

The Communist Party of Lesotho (CPL) was formed in 1961 and
worked within the framework of the BCP. The BNP had already turned
out to be highly anti-communist. It saw communism as an unknown
evil, from which the people in Lesotho must be saved. In this campaign the BNP was assisted by South African mass media and the
Catholic priests in Lesotho. In 1970, when the BNP carried out a
coup d'état to stay in power in spite of its loss in the general
elections, the CPL was banned and "communist books and propaganda"
were seized or burnt by the police.[12]

Exclusion of individual members from both the BCP and the BNP
has led to several attempts to form new parties, but none of them
have managed to get more than a few hundred followers. In 1967,
the United Democratic Party (UDP) was formed by a few members from
the BCP who favoured a more liberally oriented policy. This party
stood for elections in January 1970, but did not win any seat.[13]
The UDP was, however, called in by the coup leader Leabua Jonathan
to be present at the negotiations demanded by the imprisoned leaders
of the BCP and the MFP in March 1970. These negotiations aimed at
the formation of an interim government but never succeeded. In 1973,
the coup government nominated an "Interim Parliament" with 93 seats,
of which the UDP received two. (See table 3.1.D.)

Table 3.1. *Composition of Lesotho's National Assemblies 1960, 1965,
1970 and 1973*

A. *1960 Indirectly Elected National Council:*

80 seats of which
  40 were indirectly elected
  22 principal and ward chiefs
  14 nominees of the High Commissioner after consultations with
     Resident Commissioner and the Paramount Chief
   4 British colonial representatives.

(cont. next p.)

The 40 elected seats were distributed in the following way:
  30 Basutoland Congress Party led by Ntsu Mokhehle
   1 Basuto National Party led by Leabua Jonathan
   5 Marema Tlou Party led by Seephephe Matete
   4 Independents.

Comment: This National Council elected four members to an Executive Council of eight. Only one out of these four was a BCP member (Bennett Khaketla, who left the BCP a few months later). Four members of the National Council were ex-officio British expatriates.

B. *1965 Directly Elected Parliament:*

60 seats, elected through general suffrage in one-man constituencies:
  31 went to the BNP led by Leabua Jonathan
  25 went to the BCP led by Ntsu Mokhehle
   4 went to MFP (Marema Tlou-Freedom Party) led by Dr Seth Makotoko
     and Bennet Khaketla.

33 seats in the Senate composed of:
  22 chiefs, all the principal chiefs in the country
  11 nominees of the Paramount Chief, Moshoeshoe II.

C. *1970 Directly Elected Parliament,* (which never sat because of a coup d'état).

60 seats elected through general suffrage in the same way as in 1965 but with different constituency boundaries (drawn up by an expert on constituency boundaries from the Transkei, Johannes Pretorius, chief electoral officer, provided by the South African government).
  36 seats went to the BCP led by Ntsu Mokhehle
  23 seats went to the BNP led by Leabua Jonathan
   1 seat went to the MFP led by the lawyer Seth Mohaleroe and
     Bennett Khaketla.

33 seats in the Senate were distributed in the same way as in 1965:
  22 principal chiefs of which five supported the BNP and the
     others supported the MFP
  11 nominees of the King.

D. *1973 Interim Parliament, nominated by Leabua Jonathan.*

The seats were distributed in the following way:
  20 representatives of the BCP
  32 representatives of the BNP (12 of these were members of the
     Council of Ministers)
   4 representatives of MFD
   2 representatives of the UDP·
  22 principal chiefs
  11 representatives of other important organizations (womens orga-
     nizations, High Court, traders' organizations etc.).

Leabua Jonathan, officially called Prime Minister, had nominated 20 individuals to represent the BCP in the Interim Parliament.
Only five of these, however, had actually represented the BCP in
earlier elections. Two of these five decided to join the Interim
Parliament. They were then immediately excluded as members of the
BCP. The Deputy President of the BCP, Gerhard Ramoreboli, was one
of the two. Fourteen of the other fifteen who decided to join the
Interim Parliament were ordinary members of the BCP. Only some of
them were known BCP supporters. A policy statement was issued by the
BCP Executive Council to the effect that all sixteen BCP members
who decided to join the Interim Parliament were expelled from the
party.[14]

The reasons given by the BCP for the exclusion were:

1. the political parties had not been given the right to select
the persons who were to represent them in the Interim Parliament

2. the persons selected were not elected by the people through
the ballot box

3. participation in the Interim Parliament without any form of
BCP participation in the Council of Ministers would be a betrayal
of the people who had given their mandate to the BCP.

The so-called BCP and MFP nominees in the 1973 Interim Parliament did not criticize the government.[15] In November 1975, Jonathan
appointed Gerard Ramoreboli Minister of Justice in what he called
a "National Government". Two of the MFP nominees were appointed
Ministers without portfolio.[16] Critical opinions against government
policies came mainly from the two nominees of the small UDP.[17]
But also some nominees representing the BNP launched minor points
of criticism. Among these BNP nominees were prominent members of
the BNP who have since left either the BNP or have been dismissed
from the Council of Ministers. Most of the Ministers in Jonathan's
government were changed during the period of 1970-1976. The only
Minister who was being retained with Jonathan was his close relative, C. D. Molapo. Molapo was also the General Secretary of the
BNP for a considerable time.[18] He left, however, both government
and party in 1983.

After 1974, the BNP existed mainly as a core group around the
Council of Ministers. But it still had somewhat of a dialogue with
the dismissed members staying in their home villages.[19] The BCP works
underground without acknowledging those who claimed to represent
the party in the Interim Parliament. Acting leaders were made
known to the public and stand to begin with in contact with the
exiled leaders of Botswana, Zambia and Mozambique. In 1973 and
1974, many BCP members had left Lesotho to take refuge in these
countries.

In December 1973 the government uncovered a plan allegedly
worked out by BCP leaders and former BNP leaders to form a "United
Front" against the Jonathan regime.[20] Whilst no immediate action
was taken against these leaders, the regime used the alleged con-
spiracy as a pretext for a prolonged campaign of repression against
BCP supporters, which finally forced the BCP to re-organize.

Splits in both the exiled BCP and the BNP resulted in new con-
stellations and changes in ideologies after 1975. Let me, however,
first analyze the constitutions and historical origins of the two
parties.

Comparison between the Constitutions of the BCP and the BNP

Important differences between the BCP and the BNP are expressed in
their party constitutions. Militant struggle is favoured as a means
to reach the aims stated in the introduction to the BCP constitution. The BCP wants to "fight oppression, exploitation, and discrimination in all its manifestations", "fight against incorporation
of any part of Lesotho into South Africa", and "fight colonialism
and imperialism".

But the ways in which this fighting should materialize are only
vaguely indicated: "to encourage the establishment and strengthening of trade unions", "to instill love and patriotic spirit among
the youth", "to strive for a democratically elected government"
and "to cooperate with other parties and organizations having the
same aims and objects as those of the Congress Party."[22]

The BNP starts out on a softer tone:[23] it "believes in freedom
from discrimination, freedom of religion as well as all fundamental human rights as embodied in the United Nations Character".
It says nothing on incorporation into South Africa, nor exploitation, colonialism and imperialism. Instead it is firm in its
opposition to any organizations or any other party "interfering
in the religious affairs of any Church" and "firmly opposed to
the Communist ideology and detests anybody who aligns himself
with it or who propagates that ideology."

The BNP anti-communist stand has resulted in co-operation with
movements and governments which fear communism and seek to form
anti-communist international alliances. The Taiwanese government
has been the most reliable diplomatic relation of the Lesotho
government during the 1970 political crisis. The Christian Democratic *"Adenauer Stiftung"* is another anti-communist international contact sought. In July 1975, however, a BNP caucus meeting
decided to stress the paragraph in the party's constitution which
stated that it was only anti-christian communism that the party
should fight. The meeting stated that the Party should freely
communicate with all but "Anti-Christian Communists". This statement made it easier for the Lesotho government both to take part
in world conferences on Anti-Communism and to welcome trade delegations from socialist countries during the same period.[24]

A value promoted by the BNP is the acceptance "of the supreme
authority of the Almighty God, who takes care of all nations.
Upon this faith the party will endeavour to foster progress,
hapiness and prosperity among all inhabitants of Lesotho in such
a way that the Basotho nation will live in harmony and peace".
... "The Party will strive to promote the development in Lesotho

in all possible ways".[25] The BCP aims in its Constitution, at "unity
between chiefs and commoners and also amongst people of all denominations". The BNP pledges support for the hereditary chieftainship
in Lesotho on the understanding that "chiefs must rule according to
the wishes of the people". Whereas peace and harmony are mentioned
only in the BNP constitution, the fight against exploitation and
the strengthening of trade unions are mentioned only in the BCP
constitution. The BNP mentions the Organization of African Unity
(OAU), but expresses only hope that African governments will co-
operate in the development of Africa as a whole. The BCP states a
condition for the party's co-operation with other organizations:
these should have aims not imcompatible with those of the BCP.

Table 3.2. *Aims of the Basutoland Congress Party (extract from the
BCP Constitution) translated from Sesotho*

a) To fight for the freedom of Africa, including Lesotho.

b) To strive for the unity between chiefs and the commoners and
   also between people of different denominations.

c) To instill love and patriotic spirit amongst the youth of
   Lesotho.

d) To fight oppression, exploitation and discrimination in all its
   manifestations.

e) To encourage the establishment and strengthening of the trade
   unions.

f) To strive for the establishment of a democratically elected
   government and fight against incorporation of any part of Lesotho into South Africa. To fight against colonialism and imperialism.

g) To co-operate with all African movements whose aim is to put
   an end to oppression in all its forms and whose policies are
   not inconsistent with those of the BCP.

h) To establish and to further political co-operation between the
   organizations of Africa and the World at large, whose policy,
   aims and objects shall not be incompatible with those of the
   BCP.

The BNP Aims are not openly in conflict with the interests of
South Africa, not even its belief in the OAU and its objectives
and in the UN charter, as long as it did not aim at actively
materialize these objectives.[26] The BCP Aims are, however, in
direct conflict with the security interests of the South African
government. Instead of only believing and hoping that other
African governments will co-operate for development, as does the
BNP, the BCP itself wants to co-operate with movements which aim
to put an end to oppression. This means explicit support to the
liberation movements in Southern Africa.[27]

There are some *ideals* which the BNP and the BCP hold in common:
a. The importance for economic development of training, education and skills.
b. National self-determination.
c. A critical attitude towards racial discrimination.[28]

Table 3.3. *Aims of the Basotho National Party (extract from the British version of the BNP constitution)*

a) The Party accepts the supreme authority of the Almighty God who takes care of all nations. Upon this faith the party will ende- avour to foster progress, hapiness, and prosperity among all the inhabitants of Lesotho in such a way that the Basotho nation will live in harmony and peace.

b) The Party believes in freedom from discrimination, freedom of religion, as well as in all fundamental human rights as embodied in the United Nations Charter.

c) The Party will oppose anybody, any organization or any other party interfering in the religious affairs of any Church.

d) The Party pledges support for the hereditary chieftainship of Lesotho on the understanding that chiefs must rule according to the wishes of the people.

e) The party is firmly opposed to the Communist ideology and de- tests anybody who aligns himself with it or who propagates that ideology.

f) The Party believes in the OAU and its Objectives and hopes that African Governments will cooperate in the development of Africa as a whole.

g) The Party will strive to promote the development in Lesotho in all possible ways.

But these ideals are interpreted in different ways: a) The BNP stresses the possibilities of buying and hiring services and skilled experts, whereas the BCP stresses the possibilities of the people to gain skills, training, and education by themselves. b) BNP stres- ses the historically superior role of the chieftainship and conti- nued traditional life. The nation is sometimes identified with chieftainship, sometimes with the geographical area of Lesotho. BCP stresses the right of citizens of Lesotho, including those for- ced to earn their living in South Africa, to decide on matters of their own interst. National self-determination is seen by the BCP as majority rule and the right to have a say individually, not through the chief or head of family. c) BNP is emphatically against racial discrimination and discrimination of minorities within the borders of Lesotho. This tends to favour the wealthy white minori- ties in Lesotho. These have been protected by the BNP against the abolishment of their economic privileges and against the claim for equal opportunities.

Both parties speak for the whole nation, but sometimes exclude
certain groups as being opposed to the values of the party. The BCP
sometimes excludes the established groups of today's Lesotho: the
wealthy white foreigners, traders, missionaries, and chiefs. The
BNP excludes the communist-inclined and anti-Christians.

There are interesting differences between the BNP and the BCP
concerning membership qualifications. In order to be a member of
the BNP one has to be a resident of the country. One becomes a member immediately after signing an oath which includes "belief in the
power of the Almighty God to lead the country, and full support of
a democratic life based on Christian principles". One can only be
a party member in one's village of residence except for special
reasons. A member will be expelled if he does not appear before
his village committee after being summoned three times and cannot
present good reasons for his absence. There are therefore few possibilities for a migrant worker to be a member of the BNP. The typical member of the BNP is a Catholic woman. BNP meetings were
often held after Church on Sundays.

According to the estimates of the BNP executive, the party had
about 6,000 members in 1969. Of these only about 1,000 had paid
their membership fee. In the BNP only individual membership exists.
Financial support is given on a voluntary basis. No fixed membership fee is charged. Many traders and missionaries provide large
sums for the party, while the poorer members of the party are not
required to pay anything.[29]

In order to become a member of the BCP a subscription fee of 25
cents had to be paid. All new members then placed on 18 months of
probationary membership before being fully recognized. No oath was
taken and no residental conditions are required by the constitution. This allows non-Christians and migrant workers to become
members of the party. An annual fee of another 25 cents has to be
paid each year before July. Otherwise the membership rights are
lost.

According to the estimates of the BCP, this party had 60,000
paying members in 1969. Organizations are also able to joint on a
collective basis by paying a total fee of R 2 annually. The Lesotho
Federation of Trade Unions (LFTU), (earlier The Basutoland Federation of Labour, BFL), was one such organization. Basutoland Co-
operative Industries (BCI) was another. In 1973 the BFL had 12,000
members and in 1969 BCI had possibly 1,000 members. Some of these
also held individual BCP membership cards.[30] According to estimates
in 1980 the relation between the two central trade union organizations is still the same. After serious attempts in 1976-78 from
trade union representatives of African and Asian trade unions a
formal agreement has been signed between these earlier competing
trade union organizations.

If we compare the constitutions with regard to party organization, we find some similarities. The BNP copied the BCP constitution in some of its organizational aspects. The BCP, in turn, originally copied the constitution of the Convention People's Party (CPP)
in Ghana. As organizations, both the BCP and the BNP are centralized. The consitutions describe a powerful leadership. Both parties

have retained the leaders they had when the parties were formed.
But there are important differences.

The BCP constitution requires secret ballot elections when party
committees elect higher authority. (This is not required by the BNP.)
The Annual Party Conference of the BCP, elected by the lower committees, has the last word on policy matters and elects the BCP executive including the Leader. The Annual Conference draws up policy in
accordance with motions from the lower committees. The power of the
leadership is observed mainly in two respects: a) the Executive has
the right to expel members after giving a written explanation to the
expelled member and to the District Committee under which the member
is organized. b) The Leader has the right to appoint Treasures in
the Party Districts: this gives the Leader the last word on financial matters.[31]

The BNP executive is elected by a separate body called the Supreme Council (SC). This SC, although much smaller, has got rights similar to those of the Annual Conference of the BCP. It consists of
the Leader, five members appointed by the Leader, three representatives nominated by the Party District Committees and six representatives elected by an Annual Conference. The Annual Conference of the
BNP has no decision-making power except that of electing six members of the SC. The SC has, according to the party constitution, the
right to deprive a person of his or her membership without giving
any reason. It can dissolve an elected party committee at village,
constituency or district levels and thereafter re-constitute its
membership without giving any reason. After 1972, this right of the
SC was transferred to the Leader by decision of the SC itself. The
annual elections of BNP Village Committees continued in many villages after the emergency of 1970, but they were stopped in 1972 and
thereafter the Committees have been appointed directly by the Leader. This is in accordance with a decision taken by the SC.[32]

The Leader of the BNP is not elected. The procedure of choosing
a Leader is not mentioned in the Party Constitution. The Leader
should be the Chairman of the Executive. Neither post is therefore
elected. The President of the SC, however, is elected annually by
the SC. In the elections during the 1960s, the Leader of the BNP,
Leabua Jonathan, was elected President. The BNP has not held an
Annual Conference since 1969. The Supreme Council together with BNP
members appointed by its Leader, Leabua Jonathan, have however, met
for discussions of urgent political problems each year after 1972.
Because the Leader has held the constitutionalized power to appoint
all committees since 1972, these committees do not necessarily represent the opinions of the BNP members.

The Leader of the BCP is elected annually by the Annual Conference, if it is possible to hold such a conference. A suggestion by
the BCP leader to change the party constitution in 1959 and introduce elections every five years instead of each year, was turned
down by the Annual Conference.[33] The last Annual Conference publicly held by the BCP took place in 1969. In December 1973, a Conference was planned but stopped by the government without reason on
the very day of convening. Many of the delegates were arrested,
others were able to go underground or into exile. Elections at vil-

lage, constituency and district levels took place in 1972 and in
1973, but have since been stopped by the government.[34]
    The BCP builds its financial strength on membership fees. It re-
ceives some assistance from other African countries and liberation
movements. Initially this assistance came via the All-African People's Conference and later via the Afro-Asian Solidarity organization. There is much speculation but little evidence of who the
actual donors are. The BNP claims that the BCP receives its funds
from the Soviet Union and China. There is however no evidence of
that. According to the general secretary of the MFP (formerly deputy leader of the BCP) Bennett Khaketla, the BCP has never received
any direct financial assistance from any communist government.
Ghana, during the 1950s, and the Liberation Committees of the OAU
during the 1960s did channel funds to the BCP according to the same
source. Even in 1967, when Lesotho was independent, the BCP was
still receiving assistance from the OAU Liberation Committee.
Assistance through this channel stopped thereafter.[35]
    The BNP does not build its financial strength as the BCP on
membership fees. It has always relied mainly on voluntary gifts.
South African trading companies sponsored the party in the election
campaign before the 1970 election. Individual Catholic priests also
provided substantial sums. The largest sponsor in the 1965 election
was the government of South Africa, who donated R 15,000 to the BNP.
A further R 10,000 came from the West German *Adenauer Stiftung*. The
BNP leader lost in his constituency. Three months later he stood in
a by-election for a safe BNP constituency at Mpharane. He was then
given 100,000 bags of grain by the Prime Minister of South Africa,
H. F. Verwoerd, as a personal gift "to help him feed the starving
people of Lesotho". A large proportion of this grain was distributed in the constituency of Mpharane before the by-election was
held.[36]
    The importance of the size of financial assistance for an expla-
nation of the success of different parties should not be overesti-
mated. It is generally believed in Lesotho that large funds spent
on pamphlets and transport facilities have little effect and that
voters consider reliance on membership fees to be better than reliance on outside assistance.
    In 1965 the BCP received funds for transporting its members by
landrover and bus to large meetings in the lowland, whereas the BNP
then had to rely more on horseback for transport to small meetings
all over the country. In 1970, the situation was the opposite. The
BNP had government transport facilities at its disposal, whereas the
BCP campaigned through convincing people by face to face contacts
at many meetings at the homes of people all over the country. The
BCP could print and spread many pamphlets in 1965 just as the BNP
did in 1970. The BNP also used the government radio for its campaigns, and this advantage given to the BNP was successfully criticized by the BCP as immoral.[37]

Political Ideas, Origin and Support of the
Basutoland Congress Party

The organization of the first political mass movement in Basutoland,
the Basutoland African Congress (BAC), started in 1952. Migrant workers in South Africa and villagers in Basutoland formed the ideas
which made up its policy. The origin of the BAC was among groups of
African National Congress (ANC) members in South Africa and members
of the *Lekhotla-la-Bafo* (The Commoners League) in the densely popu-
lated villages of the Western lowlands of Basutoland.

Ideas of Democratic Socialism and Popular Participation

According to its leader, Ntsu Mokhehle, the two important questions
that the BAC won members on, when it was formed in 1952, were:
1) opposition to incorporation of Basutoland into the Republic of
South Africa and 2) self-rule.

During the 1950s, laws for Basutoland were proclaimed from the
British High Commission in Pretoria and Mokhehle argued that fighting colonial domination was the same as to fight white domination
of South Africa. The situation of the opposition in Basutoland differed, however, somewhat from that in South Africa at the time. It
was easier, after 1948, to argue with Great Britain for the independence of Basutoland than it was to argue with South Africa for
equal rights for black and whites. The anti-British Nationalist
Party in South Africa had come into power in 1948. The BAC tried
to convince Britain that a transfer of Basutoland to South Africa
under these circumstances was not only against the interests of
the Basotho, but also contrary to the interests of the British.
The BAC co-operated with other Panafricanist movements during
this time period.38

During the 1950s, Ntsu Mokhehle and the group around him convinced an increasing number of villagers and migrant workers that decisions taken by people themselves were better than decisions by
employers, chiefs, clergymen, traders and colonial officers. The
BAC leaders went around educating their followers in the evenings,
at their homes and places of work. Self-confidence spread and made
possible the continued growth of the BAC movement. A belief in
future self-government with popular participation was one important basis for the opposition to incorporation of Basutoland into
South Africa.

Ntsu Mokhehle has explained this mobilization of people in Basutoland in the following words:

> The questions the BAC won members on during the 1950s were deci-
> ded by the people in the villages. We discussed the problems in
> the way they appeared in the villages, problems in relation to
> the trading stations, problems in land allocation and so on.
> We were of course aware of the fact that we had to fight also
> at the government level and take over the Legislative Council.

The focus was at the village level in our party work. It was
through winning people in the questions that concerned themselves and to make them see their right, that we could become
the strong party we became.[39]

The development of political consciousness that Mokhehle describes was initiated by a well-organized movement based on ideas inherited from the South African ANC and the *Lekhotla-la-Bafo* in Basutoland. Mokhehle himself was a member of both and so were most
people around him. The training of workers and villagers to become
conscious of their own political power was essential since these
would otherwise have little possibility to articulate their aspirations, according to Mokhehle.

Oppressed people have no time to think freely. They are under
pressure of the chiefs, the trading stations and the churches.
The BCP tried to make people conscious of their rights in relation to these. We referred to history, to say that people had
been powerful before even in relation to chiefs. We managed to
slowly take over the decision-making at the village level, to
make people see that they could decide for themselves and that
the result of these decisions were better than the decisions
made by chiefs, traders and others.[40]

The political ideas dominating the BCP after 1958 were those of
democratic socialism. Lesotho was seen as a society of exploited
workers and peasants in conflict with the exploiting traders,
chiefs and colonialists, aided by the churches. The BCP saw the
hierarchical system of chieftainship as a potential basis for continued foreign dominance in Lesotho after independence. Common land
ownership was basic to the BCP policy at village level. Common land
without the chiefs being in control of the allocation was an important political aim. Popular participation in development was considered more important than rapid economic growth and the co-operative movement was seen as one important method to reach this aim.[41]

In the 1960 election the BCP became the largest political party,
but was not allowed to take government power. In those District
Councils and Village Committees in which the BCP was in the majority, the BCP was however able to implement its development ideas.
Ambitious projects of social welfare, agricultural production, and
small-scale co-operative industries were started.[42] Attempts were
made to create jobs through restructuring the village economies.
Co-operatives were established, for example using the skills of
repatriated migrants and craftsmen who had gained their skills in
post second world war programmes for ex-soldiers in Basutoland.
A whole range of co-operative industries and agriculture schemes
was started. No official financial assistance was given by Britain
to these projects, but non-governmental and idealistic work by
British individuals was important. The co-operative ideas had,
however, been introduced by the British co-operative educators
during the 1940s. Some financial assistance came initially from
Ghana or from migrant workers via the District Councils. Some of
these co-operative production units and shops were able to compete
with the trading companies.

These co-operative enterprises established during the early 1960s through the efforts of the District Councils and the BCP later were organized under a common association, the Basutoland Co-operative Industries. After the BNP gained power in 1965 most of these were however closed down by the BNP government. The Lesotho Chamber of Commerce, consisting only of white large-scale traders urged the government to close these with reference to their disorganized book-keeping. According to the BCP the reason was rather that the co-operatives competed with the established traders. The co-operatives concerned the following professions among others:[43]

- cattle service
- wool producers
- building groups (brick-making)
- cabinet-makers
- water engineers
- shoe-makers (still operating)
- carpenters (still operating)
- knitters and cloth-makers.

Before the 1965 election the BCP could refer in its programme (under point 8) to successful existing co-operatives. These had by then become an important part of Basotho life. The BCP programme was summarized in the following way by the journalist Jack Halpern in 1965:[44]

1. Improvement of all social services
2. Free and universal education
3. Unyielding opposition to South African influence in Lesotho
4. Nationalization of the diamond diggings
5. Thorough geological survey of the whole country
6. Improvement of agriculture
7. NRC, the recruitment organization of the South Africa Chamber of Mines, should be replaced by a government agency
8. Introduction of more co-operative movements
9. Minimum wage
10. Vote for all, including women
11. Encouragement of industries with help of the United Nations
12. Freedom of worship, keeping religion out of the political arena

Point number 9 above, about minimum wages, was soon found to be less relevant as a party goal since unemployment was considered a greater problem. The silence on land tenure in connection with agricultural development (point 6 above) was broken. Immediately after the elections common landownership was stressed. Otherwise exactly the same programme was presented for the 1970 election. On the question of how the BCP could believe in any kind of development in the midst of a country ruled by a hostile government and with powerful international companies expanding in the region, one of the BCP ideologists G. M. Kolisang answered in 1972:

If society would function in a way where the only dynamic element was the dominating capitalist part, the South African economy would have finished off Lesotho or would be doing this in the future, because it is impossible to put borders around the country.

But there are other processes going on within South Africa and also outside, which oppose the same process that seek to dominate Lesotho, and these processes together with dynamic processes going on within Lesotho itself resist the encroachement of South African finance.

In other words, if we were dealing with a static situation where the only dynamics lay in the strong South African economy, the logical thing to do would be to leave Lesotho alone and ultimately the force and the power of South Africa would finish Lesotho off.

The workers of Lesotho give their hope to a dialectical relationship which emerges out of conflicting forces. Lesotho has throughout history survived because of trends opposing the dominating capitalist forces ruling in Southern Africa.[45]

Popular confidence in the future possibilites of the BCP strategy has long been a mystery to political observers from Western countries.[46] One important reason for this confidence, I think, is the strong belief in history being dialectical that has been spread by *Lekhotla-la-Bafo* and the BCP. According to this dialectical view of history, the forces opposing the present order will sooner or later be the dominating element in society. Another important reason for the mentioned confidence among BCP supporters is the feeling of not being alone in the struggle for better living conditions. The co-operation with the liberation movement in South Africa is the basis for this feeling.

In 1975 the BCP leader Mokhehle, then in exile, described the alternative policy with which the BCP would replace that of the BNP. He referred to the restructuring of the economy for an increased control and gradual improvement in living conditions:

> We would conquer the process to make houses, to make cloth, to make things that people use in their daily work. We would try to disengage as much as is practically possible *(from the international economic system)*. ... Only South Africa gains of the kind of development policy that Jonathan stands for. Look at Optichem *(the fertilizer factory)*, ... Domolux *(lamp factory)*, ... and the carpet factories. Everything used in production is imported and everything produced goes for export. We would not say no to development aid, maybe not even to factories resting on mechanization. But the policy would be to slowly link together the parts of production we have with the needs we have.[47]
> (Authors note within brackets)

Land, people and education were seen as the main resources. The BCP was more optimistic about the possibility of creating better living conditions through training people and utilizing the resources the country already had. These are just some of the development schemes which were made politically issues in Parliament during the period of 1960 to 1970:

a. The water should be exploited in small-scale electricity plants instead of being exported from the large scale Oxbow-Malimabatso project which meets the needs of the Chamber of Mines in South Africa, as was the plan of the Colonial power and later of the BNP Government.

b. The diamond resources should be exploited in labour intensive surface mining with some mechanization instead of capital intensive mining with technology and capital controlled by the De Beers monopoly.

c. Cloth production from the wool and mohair of Lesotho should be expanded.[48]

Origin in Lekhotla-la-Bafo and African National Congress

When the BAC was formed in 1952, it had support both in the form of finance and personnel from the African National Congress (ANC) in South Africa. Many individuals from Basutoland who were politically active had long been members of the ANC. The BAC co-opted two political organizations in Basutoland: the *Lekhotla-la-Bafo* formed in 1913 by villagers at Mapoteng in Western Lesotho, and the Progressive Association (BPA) formed by a group of commoners as early as in 1907. The *Lekhotla-la-Bafo* had about 1,000 followers and the BPA about 2,000.[49] None of these ever became a party, but they acted as pressure groups now and then. They kept a political discussion alive in the interest of commoners in opposition to the colonial power and high-ranking chiefs. The former followers of the BPA were among those who left the BAC to form the BNP in 1958 under the leadership of Leabua Jonathan.[50]

To understand the policies of the BCP it is important to study the *Lekhotla-la-Bafo*. This organization continuously adopted a dialectical view of social change. Its members were self-educated men, active in reinterpreting the historic knowledge of South Africa and Basutoland and presenting findings together with demands for increased power to the commoners of Basutoland.[51] Chiefs and church representatives were seen as traitors because of their roles as employees and supporters of the colonial exploiters. The commoners had a right to decide for themselves, like they had done before, and they had the chance to succeed since, according to the *Lekhotla-la-Bafo*, relations between people were continuously changing. The preamble of the constitution of *Lekhotla-la-Bafo* reveals a critical opinion towards Moshoeshoe I:

> Whereas the late Chief Moshoeshoe and his successors in office did not satisfy the people in their government by the establishment and sustenance of a national assembly known as a "Pitso" and held at Thuta-Ea-Moli.
> - And whereas the said Pitso was in the year 1903 abolished and the present Basutoland National Council constituted, composed of the chiefs and their advisors.
> - And whereas the present composition of the National Council,

is not in the best interests and good government of the territory by reason of the exclusion from membership of persons and associations other than the chiefs and their advisors: it is resolved:

(a) to form an association to safeguard, promote and protect the best interests and welfare of its members and persons other than the chiefs and their advisors.

(b) to seek recognition and representation of Commoners in the National Council and the Constitution.[52]

According to the *Lekhotla-la-Bafo* the chiefs had become "hirelings of the foreigners", and had "helped the Resident Commissioner to subvert the traditional democratic institutions of the country and had forfeited the trust of the common man". Christian missionaries along with the British Civil Servants were seen as destroyers of the "Basotho personality". The Catholic Church in particular was criticized since it accepted gifts of large areas of land from the Paramount Chief. In the period 1912-1939 when Griffith was Paramount Chief he did everything possible to advance the interests of the Roman Catholic church. He was indifferent and even hostile to other missions and their supporters. Conflicts both within the BAC and the *Lekhotla-la-Bafo* have usually centred around the kind of strategy to use in relation to the chiefs. Common ownership of land is accepted as a traditional principle to be preserved. Land and chieftainship are, however, very closely related. When the British wanted to introduce a private land ownership the chiefs were seen as an ally in the struggle against the British. The main line taken towards chiefs was that these should have their power decreased. This was a principle with which the British colonial power agreed in the late 1930s. *Lekhotla-la-Bafo* as well as the more elite-oriented BPA supported this line.[53]

Later the *Lekhotla-la-Bafo* changed its strategy and supported the chiefs' demands to keep the land allocation system and strengthen its collective aspects, when the British colonial government suggested that private ownership of land should be introduced. Retaining the land allocation system whilst urging the chiefs to listen to the advice of village committees became the strategy of the *Lekhotla-la-Bafo*. This strategy has been adhered to by the BCP.[54]

Josiel Lefela was the founder of *Lekhotla-la-Bafo* in 1913. But it was only after the war in 1919 that the organization spread and became active. From the late 1920s and onwards, about a thousand members were active within this organization. It was spread in the lowland and foothill parts of Basutoland and had its centre in Mapoteng in the Berea district. During the 1930s Lefela was no longer the leader of the *Lekhotla-la-Bafo*. He was its International Secretary, communicating with organizations and individuals all over the world, campaigning for the recognition and acceptance of the oppressed people of South Africa and Basutoland as arbiters of their own destiny. In spite of his not being considered the leader by his own organization, the British colonial government chose Lefela to represent it in the National Council when it finally responded to the demands for representation. The National Council earlier consisted of only chiefs and their advisors and the colonial officials.

Lefela criticized the British with reference to agreements signed
between Great Britain and the people of Lesotho. He argued that
according to these agreements, the country had never been colonized.[55]

During the second world war Lefela was put in prison together
with other leaders from *Lekhotla-la-Bafo* for campaigning against
military recruitment of Basotho for the battlefields of Europe.[56]

When the war was over the imprisoned members of *Lekhotla-la-Bafo*
were released. Lefela's critical statements in the records of the
National Council are interesting to read. They reveal the insights
of informed participants in the politics of the colony. But the
British colonial officials at the time were seldom present to listen to the lengthy speeches of Lefela.[57] On the 12 March 1957 the
Lekhotla-la-Bafo assembled at Thaba Bosiu, the place of the capital
before colonization. The organization then decided to dissolve itself and become part of the BAC.[58]

The ANC was the main political organization with which the migrants met when in South Africa. Koenyama Chakela, General Secretary of the BCP until 1976 (when the BCP split and Chakela became
the main leader) describes the origin of his party in the following
way:

> Those Basotho who worked in South Africa had already become more
> politically conscious than the people at home. The Basotho from
> Basutoland who already were members or held posts in the ANC
> tried to pull to organize a party for Basutoland. We who came
> to work in South Africa and met there came from different villa-
> ges in Basutoland and we agreed that when we came home to our
> villages we should make sure that when we left for South Africa
> again we would leave behind a few people who understood our
> political ideas and who could form a unit back home. That is
> how we spread the ideas of the ANC all over the country...
> Many Basotho were workers in industries and they were conscious
> as workers... Some of them received high posts within the ANC
> organization and leadership.[59]

During the entire 1950s, the BAC Annual Conferences were dominated by delegates from the Transvaal and the Orange Free State branches of the party. Later the number of members within Lesotho increased and eventually came into the majority. Many women were
members and made up the base of the party inside Lesotho. It was
common to hold dual membership cards for the BAC and the ANC. In
1959 this was forbidden. The reason stated at the Annual Conference
was that the BCP should keep out of the conflict that was developing
between the ANC and the militant break-away faction of the ANC
Youth League, formed in 1958 calling itself the Pan-African Congress (PAC).[60]

The BCP maintained relations both with the ANC and the PAC,
attempting to avoid close involvement with either of these organizations. Both the ANC and the PAC have at times criticized the BCP
for having relations with the other organization. For practical
reason the BCP was forced to co-operate with both of them at the
places of work in the Republic.

Mokhehle in 1975 argued that the PAC was on the way to becoming a
mass movement when it was banned in 1960, whereas the ANC was an
elite-oriented organization and was less active than the PAC in
mobilizing a following.[61] His opinion was that PAC's militancy in
organizational methods resembled those of the BCP and the BCP owed
much of its organizational experience to this movement.

But the political analysis of the PAC movement was less detailed,
and also less radical. The BCP owed much of its historical analysis
and social views to the socialist tradition within the ANC and the
Lekhotla-la-Bafo.

After the ANC and the PAC were banned in South Africa in 1960,
the BCP suddenly gained a strategic position. The BCP was organized
across the borders of Lesotho and had relations with both organizations. The BCP leadership was, however, criticized by both the
PAC and the ANC for its leader's "bossy" attitude towards refugees
and for its far-reaching aspirations. An example of the ambitions
of the BCP is given in a speech by Ntsu Mokhehle in Cairo at the
Committee of Twenty-four African States in May 1962:

> Our activities are not and cannot be limited to Basutoland alone.
> We are geographically surrounded by the Union of South Africa and
> live in the same political atmosphere as Bechuanaland and Swazi-
> land. Our political interests and activities extend into these
> territories. Political movements are only being started in Swazi-
> land and Bechuanaland and in the Union of South Africa the ANC
> and the PAC have been banned; the leaders of these organizations
> are bitterly persecuted - some are banned and restricted to
> small areas, some have been deported into the wilds of the coun-
> try, some are in jail, and some have scattered all over the
> world as exiles. The result of this is that the BCP today is
> the only liberation movement in the southern end of Africa that
> is freely, openly actively engaged in the liberatory struggle.
> As a result, we have become the object of attack by the imperia-
> lists and colonialists in all these southern territories.[62]

But the fact that BCP for a period was left as the only "liberation movement" allowed within South Africa led to attacks not
only from the "imperialists and colonialists". The ANC and the PAC
also increasingly considered the BCP as a competitor. In Basutoland
the situation was complicated; the ANC and the PAC competed with
the BCP in winning members, at the same time as the ANC and PAC
refugees depended on the BCP for their living expenses. The BCP
allowed the South African refugees to become organized politically.[63] It also supplied their living expenses through resources
provided by the Liberation Committee of the All-African Peoples'
Conference (AAPC) and later the OAU. The severe conflict between
the PAC and ANC, particularly in exile, made the situation even more
complicated. Suspicion developed between many of the refugees. This
situation was remembered when the BCP depended on ANC in exile
after 1970. PAC inclined Mokhehle was isolated politically in Lusaka.

During the 1960s in Basutoland, the BCP was criticized by the British and
South African governments for sponsoring communists. Kidnappings of refugees

were justified by the South African police with reference to the security risk
of having communists in the "heart of South Africa". The BCP was active
in reporting cases of South African kidnapping to the United Nations
and the AAPC. The British government did not protest against the
kidnappings until an international opinion was formed.[64] After the
BNP came into power in 1965 officially no South African refugees
were allowed into Lesotho for the period 1966-1973. In 1973, after
a case of South African kidnapping of refugees in Lesotho the BNP
government decided to change its policy. An agreement at the United
Nations headquarters was made between representatives of the BCP,
the BNP and the ANC that refugees from South Africa should be allowed to stay under the condition that they did not organize politically in Lesotho.[65]

The Communist Party did not originate from the BCP, but when the
Communist Party of Lesotho (CPL) was formed in 1961, its aim was to
act mainly via the BCP. It claimed to have about 600 members, but
their names were never disclosed. Only one member disclosed his
name, John Motloheloa, a refugee and former trade unionist from
South Africa. With reference to the active subversive activities of
the anti-communist neighbour country through the kidnappings by the
police, it was claimed necessary to work indirectly.[66] The CPL had
an extensive educational programme, which included courses in
marxism given to BCP members.[67] A party programme was published in
1961 and a newspaper was distributed. The CPL was banned in 1970.

Summary of the aims of the Communist Party of Basutoland, 1961[68]

1. A socialist republic of Lesotho.
2. Work for a united front with the BCP and all other progressive forces.
3. Full and immediate independence.
4. UN membership.
5. A national bank.
6. Own currency system.
7. Fight the common enemy, South African imperialism.
8. Maintain close and friendly relations with the progressive
   movements in the Republic of South Africa such as the South
   African Communist Party and the ANC.
9. Demand a re-arrangement with the mines and other South African
   employers to pay adequate wages, guarantee safety conditions
   and trade union rights.
10. Demand that negotiations be opened to provide Lesotho with an
    outlet to the sea in return for territories wrongfully inclu-
    ded in the Republic by British imperialism.
11. Organize on the basis of democratic socialism, collective and
    individual leadership and the subordination of the minority
    to the majority.

It is interesting to see that before the elections in 1965, when
Leabua Jonathan met the South African Prime Minister Verwoerd, one
of the questions discussed was the territories inhabited mainly by
Basotho in South Africa, referred to in point 10 in the CPL programme above. South Africa and Great Britain held discussions during

the early 1960s after a South African initiative about the appointment of commission which should specify the borders between Basutoland and South Africa. No decision was taken. Jonathan when discus-
sing with Verwoerd had not yet reached his position in government.
Still, he raised the question of the Eastern part of the present
Orange Free State which belonged to the precolonial state "Lesotho",
but was transferred by Great Britain to the boer republic. Verwoerd
declared that a small part of this area was to become a bantustan
for the Sotho population in South Africa, the QwaQwa bantustan. It
was not clear how many of the more than four million South African
citizens classified as Sotho by the tribal standards applied in the
South Africa. The Qwa Qwa bantustan might, however, in a distant
future be administered jointly with the future independent Lesotho,
according to what is known about what Verwoerd said at his meeting
with Jonathan. The meeting was much criticized and speculations
about both incorporation of Lesotho into South Africa and speculations about incorporation of the QwaQwa territory with its large
and poor population into Lesotho were expressed in Basutoland. The
discussion was dropped but the independent government of Lesotho
was approached by South Africa about the appointment of a Joint
Border Commission. The Lesotho government accepted only in 1975,
"in principle to the appointment of a Joint Boundary Commission at
a time and with terms of reference to be agreed between the Two
Governments". The United Nations had in 1974 supplied an expert in
international law and in 1976 supplied a justice to become Boundary
Commissioner. The two governments have sofar not agreed on the
terms of reference for the work of the Joint Boundary Commission
appointed.[69]

Support by Workers, Co-operative Farmers and Students

The BCP claims to draw its support from peasants and workers,[70]
but also obtains some support from the educated groups. "Only the
ignorant vote for the BNP" was one slogan used by the BCP supporters before the 1965 and 1970 elections. During the early 1960s
BCP was the party which was entrusted with the distribution of most
of the available scholarships.[71] According to the BNP this led to
a tendency for intellectuals and students to support the BCP during
this early period, a tendency which the BNP claims to have later
reversed partly through the BNP control of most of the scholarships, partly through the system of state employees being required
to belong to the BNP as a condition for keeping their employment.
A split within the educated group emerged. The educated, who still
support the BCP, are mainly those who have worked in South Africa.
Among them are trade unionists, who often are skilled workers and
carpenters, shoe-makers, tailors and clerks.[72]
    There are, as already mentioned, two powerful organizations col-
lectively affiliated with the BCP. These are the Co-operative Movement and the Basotho Federation of Labour (BFL), later called FLTU.
The former organizes mainly farmers and craftsmen, the latter workers, farm labourers and other employees in both Lesotho and South

Africa. Three of the four trade unions joined the BFL in 1960.
They were the Transport Workers Union, The Commercial Employees
Union and the Teachers Union. The General Workers Union joined
the BFL. The Industrial Workers' Union and the Mine-Workers' Union
were the most important within the BFL because of their large
membership.[73]

Many trade unionists stood for election to Parliament as BCP
representatives. Through this party they worked for better working
conditions for their members. But not all BFL organized people were
BCP supporters. During the period 1960 to 1970, the policies of the
BFL and BCP respectively were according to their own statements,
to support each other while remaining separate organizations. During
the post-parliamentary period, that is after 1970, it has become
more difficult to distinguish the work of the BFL from the work of
the BCP.[74]

In July 1973 the BFL held a conference where a declaration was
prepared with demands to the government, including the right to
organize politically. The system to require BNP membership cards
for employment, *"Liphephechana"*, was particularly criticized. The
BFL demanded that employment on political grounds should be forbidden. During the period 1970-1973 this system had virtually excluded all BCP members from employment both in government and in
private enterprise. The BFL also criticized the government for inviting foreign monopolies employing few workers from Lesotho and
for neglecting the problems of the continued existence of the migrant labour system. The BFL demanded that nationally controlled
enterprises should be established in Lesotho to curb the outflow of
labour into South Africa and enable Lesotho to be economically
independent.[75]

The BFL conference demanded frequent consultations with the
Minister responsible for labour affairs to review workers' problems.
The government accepted this demand two years later after large
demonstrations by the workers. Representatives of the BFL were accepted in bargaining with the Labour Department and with the employers union from November 1975 onwards. The BFL has used this
position to promote elements of the BCP strategy.[76]

In 1975 the BFL represented 13,000 members, whereas the trade
union organization, Lesotho General Council of Workers (LCW),
started by the government in 1970, represented only 1,500 members
according to its own estimates. According to the BFL, the LCW had
only about 400 members. An ILO mission to Lesotho in 1975 estimated the lower figure as more accurate.[77] In spite of the small size
of the LCW, the government attempted in 1974 to make this trade
union organization the only legal bargaining partner to the Employers' union of Lesotho. The United States educational programme
for trade unionists was only available to LCW unionists.[78]

The government decision to legalize only the LCW and not the
BFL was, however, never implemented. The BFL organized meetings at
larger places of employment to discuss which organization should
represent the employees. The meetings ended with declarations
urging the employer to force the government to accept the BFL as
a union representative of the employees.[79] The only two large pla-

ces of employment where the LCW had members were the Holiday Inn of
Maseru, although the BFL had more, and the Institute of Catholic
Publications in Mazenod, where the LCW was in the majority. Government and public enterprises were dominated by the BFL. The Employers' Union called upon the government to recognize both the BFL and
the LCW because of the likelihood of strikes.[80]

Political Ideas, Origin, and Support of the Basotho
National Party

The BNP was formed in November 1958 by a group of BAC members who
broke away under the leadership of Leabua Jonathan and Gabriel
Manyeli. It appeared as a mild and modest alternative to the increased radicalism of the BAC, later BCP. It criticized the BCP for
being too militant. The BNP itself is militant on one point: anti-
communism. It stressed from the beginning peace and harmony instead
of conflict, a Christian life instead of socialist ideas, and co-
operation within the present order also in relation to South Africa.

Ideas of Political Harmony and Economic Growth

Two sets of ideas have dominated the BNP during its entire history
and are therefore worth further study: 1) the idea of harmony and
chieftainship as an expression of the people's united will and
2) the idea of economic growth through inter-dependence with South
Africa and other "free world countries".
  The idea of chieftainship as an expression of the people's will
is mentioned in the BNP constitution, but not elaborated there. It
is an important element in the BNP policies as presented and interpreted in the village.[81] It is closely connected with a view of
society as harmonious, when undisturbed by foreign ideas of communism. The view of the "good chief" is another element in the belief
in chieftainship as an expression of the people's will. This concept has been developed by the frustrated ex-chiefs, deprived of
their jobs during the period 1938-1946, as mentioned. These village
chiefs, their relatives and their advisors were often members of
the BNP and their ideas had important implications for the image
of the BNP in relation to the voters. They worked for a return
to the social and political order that existed during the first
half of the 20th century, when they chaired a village *lekhotla*
and were backed by the government. When the BNP came into power
it was on a programme of giving these ex-chiefs their roles back.
According to the ideal, harmony and unity are gained through the
chief's constant dialogue with his people at the *lekhotla* and the
pitso. The chief is seen as the true representative of the commoners. A special advisor educated him in the art of listening to
the people. He was taught the customs that had evolved from the
relationship between former chiefs and the common people. The
balance between different groups was believed to have been settled

through successive compromises, through discussions at the *lekhotla*,
the village meeting place and court, chaired by the chief or his
advisor. The institution of *lekhotla* was abolished in 1938. Stimela
Jingoes, born in 1895, and an advisor to several chiefs and chief-
tainesses, remembered the *lekhotla* in the following way:

> Any boy growing up in Lesotho in my time absorbed knowledge
> about the laws of his country without conscious effort because,
> from an early age, he joined the men at the village *lekhotla*.
> There he would hear disputes being settled, points of law argued
> and customs discussed. There anyone, even a boy, could put
> questions to the disputing parties and their witnesses, and a
> boy was never to young to add whatever knowledge he had about
> the case before the *lekhotla*. ... In those days women did not
> accuse each other at the men's *lekhotla* when they had a dispute:
> they had a hearing before the headman's of Chief's wife, in a
> special women's court. It was a great shame for a woman to ap-
> pear in the men's *lekhotla*, so women either came to blows when
> they fought, or had to ask more senior women to settle their
> disputes.82

The BNP government did not, however, re-introduce the *lekhotla*,
but another institution of traditional character, the *pitso*. The
pitso in its present form was first introduced by Moshoeshoe I.83
According to C. D. Molapo the *pitso* was the best way to express
the people's will:

> The will of the people will be known at village level and at
> national level through the *pitsos*. The *pitsos* are unique and
> characteristic of Lesotho and we hold *pitsos* both at national
> and village level. Everybody is allowed to speak without party
> affiliation. ... Anybody can speak, without having been pre-
> pared first by a party group.84

The *pitso* is a meeting of all people in the area of a chief. It
is called together by the chief on special occasions, when he or a
representative of the government or aid organizations wants to make
a statement.85 As a general meeting for announcements by officials
the *pitso* seems to function well. The police usually call together
everybody in the village or larger area to be present. The presence of the police at the *pitsos* is, however, regarded by many
as a way to prevent criticism against the government.

The statement by C. D. Molapo above includes a critical reference to party politics. The *pitso* is seen as an alternative to
party politics. This negative view towards parties in general is
often expressed by representatives of the BNP. Their own party
is presented as a unit above parties, a national party to unite
different factions of the people.

Harmony, peace and unity have been often repeated ideals in
statements by BNP representatives. Other terms for vaguely the
same thing have been used over the years: "holiday from politics",
"reconciliation" and "Moshoeshoism" are terms used since 1970.

In March 1970, Jonathan declared, that there was to be a five-
year holiday from politics and blamed the parties for having caused
the state of emergency announced earlier the same year.86 Neither

the BCP and the MFP nor the Prime Minister's own party were, however, prepared to accept such a recommendation.

"Reconciliation" was another slogan declared by the BNP government in 1972[87] after a recommendation from the Catholic Archbishop
in Johannesburg. Catholic priests had taken part in campaigns a-
gainst BCP supporters during the 1970 emergency period.

"Moshoeshoism" was the new philosophy of the "National Government" announced by Jonathan in November 1975.[88] This government
was to include also minorities. Representatives of the small factions of the "BCP" and "MFP" in the Interim Parliament were appointed Ministers. "Unity and peace under one leader, Moshoeshoe the
Great" was an expression used already in the party programme of
1958. "Moshoeshoism" stood for methods of all kinds, both peaceful
and violent, to unite people in a period of conflicts. According
to the BNP, the BCP stood for party politics which was seen as a
major cause of conflict, whereas the BNP was "national" in the
sense that it wanted to unite the people in the present territory
of Lesotho by all means and also let minorities have a say in
government.[89]

Moshoeshoe's rule[90] was, according to Jonathan, well described
in a lecture[91] at Moshoeshoe Day in 1974 by Mosebi Damane. Damane
states that Moshoeshoe formed a Council of *Matona*,[92] advisors, to
whom he always listened before taking important decisions. They
were chosen by him to represent different sections of the population, also minorities. They were experts in specific areas of
society, cattle and agriculture, defence, foreign relations, education etc. Moshoeshoe felt free to call in new advisors whenever
new problems arose. The *Matona* were not his relatives and did not
necessarily agree with him on general matters. He used his relatives as subordinate regional rulers. They took orders from him
and the Council of *Matona*. The regional rulers were gathered at
national *pitsos* together with "their people", the advisors and
other interested people. These national *pitsos* were called in at
times of crisis, and when it was possible regional *pitsos* were held
in advance. The *pitsos* were held mainly to hear the reactions of people to specific proposals made by Moshoeshoe, after he had discussed
them with his advisors. People were expected to approve or dis-
approve. The reactions were well articulated, according to witnes-
ses, but the system did not allow much discussion of alternatives.

Jonathan's aim was, according to his own statement, to re-
introduce the system of rule as it was under Moshoeshoe. It is,
however, clear that he intended to play the role of Moshoeshoe
himself and not his prime advisor. In spite of this intention he
called himself from 1970 onwards *Tona-Kholo*,[93] prime advisor to
King Moshoeshoe II. The King was made a "constitutional monarch"
and restricted by a special Order decided by Jonathan's government after the constitution was abolished in 1970.[94]

Peaceful co-existence and inter-dependence with South Africa
are frequently stated as methods for the economic development of
Lesotho. In the campaign before the 1970 election, Leabua Jonathan
stated at Mafeteng:

Leave the problems of South Africa to the South Africans. This
accords with the principle of the sovereignty of independent

states. The safety of Lesotho and the Basotho lies in peaceful
co-existence with South Africa and other free world countries.
Where countries do not live in peace with each other bloodshed
results. We treasure the blood of our brother Basotho... Leso-
tho's safety lies purely and simply in the degree to which
Lesotho can maintain friendship with South Africa *now* and also
with the rest of the free world. In the coming elections the
Basotho will be deciding whether or not to live in peace with
South Africa. The safety of Lesotho lies with the Basotho
National Party.95

The BNP lost the election to the BCP in this constituency as
well as in the country as a whole.

According to the South African government, "separate development" was designed to provide a system of local government for
Africans by Africans, but under white guidance and control. Laws
in 1951, 1959 and 1963 provided for a system of separate territo-
rial "development" with Bantu authorities, all under white control. At that time these laws and the programme for "separate
development" included the Basutoland, Bechuanaland and Swaziland
territories as well as South West Africa and the Native reserves
of the Republic of South Africa.96

After the Sharpeville massacre in March 1960 against black people
demonstrating for the abolishment of the Pass Laws, international
pressure on the South African government hardened. In 1963 the
South African Prime Minister H. F. Verwoerd felt obliged to declare, at least ostensibly, his government's benign intentions.

> ... until now, I have always refrained from discussing the
> High Commission Territories in public. However, since we have
> to suffer abuse on our policies even within the United King-
> dom Parliament and elsewhere from its members and from re-
> presentatives of the British Government, I feel free to dis-
> cuss in public - although dispassionately - what in fact is a
> United Kingdom responsibility, but of great concern to us.
> ... Suppose these territories were South Africa's responsi-
> bility, and not the United Kingdom's what would the effect of
> our present policy be?97

Verwoerd then mentioned the Transkei as a model for future developments in the High Commission Territories and pointed to what he
called separate democratic development in the bantustans and in
line with South African policies:98

1. We would aim at making them democratic states in which the
masses would not be dominated by small groups pf authoritarians.
Instead, natural native democracy and its leaders coupled with
representative democracy - as in the Transkei - would lead the
whole population to democratic rule over its own country.

2. We would steer away from multi-racalism. Where whites would
be needed and must remain for some time they should vote in South
Africa just as the citizens of the High Commission Territories are
voters in their respective homelands when they work in South
Africa.

3. We would have the territories adjacent to us advance in
the economic sphere. To help them we would apply our border industries policy near the boundaries. ... For example this could
easily be applied close to the Basutoland-Free State border...
Employees would be able to spend their incomes within their own
states so that these can be built up.

Origin in Chieftainship and Anti-Communism

It is difficult to accurately trace the roots of the BNP, but there
are several different reasons given for the emergence of this party. The leader was from the beginning Leabua Jonathan, a former BAC
member. According to two pamphlets published in 1970 and 1972 by
the Lesotho Information Department it was:
    1. a reaction by "chief Jonathan" to the formation of the roya-
list Marema Tlou Party in 1957[99]
    2. a reaction to communism, which was dominating the main poli-
tical organization in Basutoland, the BAC led by Ntsu Mokhehle.[100]
    As we have seen, both the Marema Tlou Party (MTP) formed in 1957
and the BNP formed one year later broke away from the BAC because
of the hostile attitude of the BAC towards chiefs. The MTP and
the BNP however favoured different chiefs and were in conflict with
each other. The BNP was supported by ex-chiefs, who would have held
hereditary positions if the colonial government had not dismissed
the lower chiefs who were their ancestors. The MTP did not, however,
voice the interests of these ex-chiefs but favoured a strong position for the existing high-ranking chiefs particularly the Paramount
Chief. In the first of the two pamphlets mentioned above, this is
expressed in the following way:

> Chief Jonathan's interest in encouraging the Chieftainship
> hierarchy to acknowledge the voice of the people resulted in
> several clashes between himself and the ultra-conservative ele-
> ments of the Chieftainship. This led to his final break with
> these elements to found the National Party, which eventually
> carried Lesotho to final independence.[101]

In the second pamphlet another explanation is given as to why
Leabua Jonathan formed the BNP:

> Chief Jonathan found it necessary to form his new Party, when
> the only existing organization in Lesotho, the Basutoland Con-
> gress Party was beginning to have alarming and constant contact
> with Red China and the Russian Communists.[102]

This pamphlet also mentions that the person who convinced Jonathan to enter politics was a famous liberal and PAC representative Patrick Duncan. Duncan was a South African Liberal Party member who worked as Judicial Commissioner in Basutoland during the
1950s. He reacted against the racial discrimination applied in the
Civil Service then. Leabua Jonathan worked as his Assessor. Duncan
later settled in the Orange Free State and edited the Liberal Party
paper "The Contact". He favoured an anti-communist alternative for

an independent Lesotho and wrote much about the good qualities of
chief Leabua Jonathan, "a born diplomat". The Contact was active in
explaining to the South African progressive whites the ideological
reasons for supporting the BNP led by chief Jonathan. Duncan left
South Africa when the Liberal Party in the Republic was banned.
(He became the representative of the PAC in Algiers until he died
in 1967.)

Their version is supported by Bennett Khaketla, the General Secretary of the Marema-Tlou-Freedom Party. In his book[103] on the 1970
coup d'état in Lesotho, Khaketla mentions three groups which were
instrumental in forming the National Party (BNP):

a. Catholic members of the Conservative parties in Britain and
Germany.

b. The Conference of Catholic bishops in Southern Africa (SABC).
This met regularly and drew up policies of the churches in the region. The Bishop (later Archbishop) of Maseru was one of the participants. A Catholic Party formed in 1957 did not gain much support
and the Southern African Bishops' Conference (SABC) decided to
assist "the party of chief Jonathan" instead. A lawyer in Johannesburg formulated the party programme in line with the bishops' conference document.

c. The support of a few journalists in the Republic, particularly in the Liberal "Contact" and the still existing "Sunday Times".

Without the support of about a thousand frustrated lower chiefs
and their families it would have been difficult to build up a party
strong enough to oppose the BCP. The other groups had to rely on
these to oppose the BCP in the election.

The Catholic Church is very influential in Lesotho. It is dominated by the conservative order "Oblates of Mary Immaculate" (OMI).
The OMI priests constitute a core group within the BNP also through
individual financial sponsoring, through contacts with influential
sponsors in South Africa and through their positions as authorita-
tive speakers in the churches all over the country.[104] The policy
of the Pope through his Apostolic Pronouncio in Pretoria to Southern Africa has more recently been to reform the OMI from within.[105]

It seems as if the formation of the policy of separate development or *apartheid* launched by H. F. Verwoerd was influenced by the
possibility of a policy like that of the BNP.[106] The BNP was active
in explaining to people in Lesotho that friendly co-operation with
the South African government and the large firms of South Africa
could prove to be more economically rewarding than the policy of
the BCP. BNP, in contrast to the BCP, argued that a separate Lesotho in economic interdependence with South Africa would be the
final solution. The BCP argued instead that a restructuring of the
South African society was the ultimate goal for people in Lesotho.

The statement by Verwoerd in 1963 was later to be followed by
financial support to the BNP. The BNP leader visited Verwoerd before the elections in Lesotho in 1965. Their faces of smiling
understanding were portrayed in mass media throughout the world as
if to hail a new era in South African policy. The foreign policy
of South Africa was from this date called"dialogue" and "detente"
with black Africa.[107]

It is interesting to compare the 1963 speech by Verwoerd with
another speech made by his successor B. J. Vorster in 1974. Vorster
said that South Africa's basic strategy would be the creation of a
"United Nations of Southern Africa States". This would include not
only the Transkei and other bantustans to be declared independent
by South Africa, but also Namibia, Lesotho, Botswana, Swaziland,
Rhodesia, Zambia, Mozambique and Angola. One result would be a
South African Economic Community. Vorster's policy was favoured
neither by the independent states, nor by the representatives of
the liberation movements in South Africa and Namibia.108
But what common political ideas could be held by the white South
African Nationalist Party and the mainly black members of the
National Party of Lesotho? If we leave out the racial perspective,
there are similarities in the ideological images of these parties.
Both stress the importance of family traditions and the philosophy
that every individual has a right to be treated as a part of his
or her own ethnic group. Both are conservative in the sense that
they want to re-establish a political and social structure which
existed in the past and to give the members of their party a superior position in society. Both regard economic take-off, even at
great cost to people as the desired development strategy.109
J. Kotsokoane, Minister of Education and Foreign Affairs in Lesotho,
made this unexpected comparison in conversation and pointed to the
cohesiveness of the members of the *Broederbond*, the "inner circle"
of the South African Nationalist Party. He pointed out the "Sons
of Moshoeshoe" and the "Oblates of Mary Immaculate" (OMI) as being
corresponding groups within the BNP. All the groups mentioned are
small and hold secret meetings, they have a well-defined member-
oriented programme.110

Support by Allied Interest Groups of Priests, Traders and Village Chiefs

The BNP claims to have support mainly among the poor peasants of
Lesotho. The active members of the BNP are not peasants, however,
but almost all member of established groups like traders, priests,
teachers and chiefs. The former General Secretary of the BNP, who
has been a Minister in Jonathan's government since 1965, C. D.
Molapo, claimed in 1975 that:

> The BNP organizes only those who succeed in life. ... Instead
> of articulating grievances like people do who have failed in
> life and like Congress Party members do.111

The general character of the BNP organization is an election campaign machinery - functioning between elections mainly through
allied pressure groups. It never aimed at becoming a mass organization, like the BCP was, with a large number of permanent groups and
offices. It did not aim at covering most of the villages in Lesotho
and the larger places of work in the Republic, which was BCP policy.
A result of the ongoing discussion on a change in the party
structure was the appointment in February 1972 of Tom Mokotso (ex-

president of the Senate) and Justice Mofolo, both prominent members
of the BNP, as leaders of a party commission. Other members of the
same commission were P. Mabathoana, T. Kuoe and T. Molapo.[112] The
Mokotso/Mofolo Commission was appointed by the BNP party Executive.
Alleged malpractices of the government, misappropriation of funds
and gossip about Leabua Jonathan being out of touch with his own
party were also to be taken up by the commission.[113]

The Mokotso/Mofolo Commission recommended that the BNP Executive
Committee should not be nominated by the Leader of the party but
instead by the BNP Annual Conference. It also recommended that the
Annual Conference should have a say in policy formation. It recommended a reshuffle of the Council of Ministers in order to avoid
domination of the Council by the chiefs, as well as the re-intro-
duction of the suspended 1966 constitution. The commission also felt
that too much was being done for the relatives of the Prime Minister and too little for the common man.[114]

In May 1972 a BNP conference was held. The recommendations of
the Commission were tabled. On June 4, the Prime Minister announced
that both Mofolo and Mokotso had been dismissed from the BNP together with ten other members of the party. No reasons were given
and according to the BNP Constitution no reason was necessary
either. Later in the same month the BNP candidate of the Maseru
constituency, Dr K. T. Maphathe, resigned. He publicly announced
that he had resigned from the BNP, because he was concerned about
the repulsion of Mokotso and Mofolo.[115]

Only one month later, on the 24 July 1972, another prominent
member of the BNP, A. C. Manyeli, Minister of Works, Posts and Communications resigned from the government. He later wrote a letter
to the weekly Catholic newspaper *Moeletsi* alleging that he had been
the victim of a political plot and that he had been forced to resign.[116] In 1974 his brother Gabriel Manyeli, a former Catholic
teacher and one of the signatories of the original BNP constitution,
was also dismissed both from the government and the party. Several
other prominent members of the BNP left the government. Peete
Peete, Minister of Finance left in 1974 and Sekhunyana. Maseribane
Deputy Prime Minister left in 1975. Former civil servants with education from Europe and North America succeeded them.[117]

All the Ministers mentioned by name were subject to severe criticism particularly among BCP supporters in Maseru. Also the Mokot-
so/Mofolo commission recommended their dismissal. The Prime Minister therefore strengthened his position through the reshuffle. At
the same time he took the risk of becoming less popular within his
own party.

There have been no reports of an active opposition on a broad
basis from the expelled BNP members. They do not seem to have organized an oppositional following after the return to their villages.
The demand they have all put forward has been a demand for more
room for discussion. It is clear that they have also expressed opinions on changes in other policy matters, particularly on agricultural policy, for example in connection with conclusions from the
Leribe and Thaba Bosiu agricultural projects. Most of the mentioned
individuals who have been expelled or who have left the BNP during

recent years, had been active in the Basutoland Progressive Association (BPA) mentioned earlier. The policy of the BPA centred around
a demand for commoners to take part in the public debate. This policy became obsolete during the 1950s, when this demand was met by
the colonial government. After the 1970 coup d'état in opposition
to the restrictions introduced by government, the demand for public
discussion was revived by the former members of the BPA, who had
found their place within the BNP. But this group was silenced, at
least temporarily, after the expulsion of its most prominent members.

The BPA was formed in 1907. It assembled educated Basotho at the
mission stations and colonial camps. Most of the members came from
Paris Evangelical Mission schools. The BPA referred to liberal ideas
of self-government for the educated and was less militant than the
rural-based *Lekhotla-la-Bafo*. During the period 1930 to 1940, the
BPA had a following of about 3,000 to 4,000. From its earliest days
its members sat on the National Council (NC). The NC was an advisory council to the colonial government. It was appointed by the
Paramount Chief and dominated by chiefs until 1948. Few of the
followers of the BPA were religious but they opposed the policy
of the Paramount Chief Griffith. During his time as Paramount Chief
(1913-1939) Griffith favoured the Catholic Church, particularly
its schools, at the expense of all other denominations.[118]

Although the BNP was partly formed and sponsored by individual
Catholic priests and teachers, it was careful to state that it
appealed to members of all denominations. In the party organ
Nketu, famous Protestants active earlier within the BPA were mentioned by name as good BNP members.[119]

The BNP grew out of several different interest groups concerned
with opposition to the increasingly militant BCP. Groups like "The
Sons of Moshoeshoe", the Traders' Organization, the village chiefs,
the Party Youth organization and Catholic Teachers groups are
known to have exercised influence on the Prime Minister and BNP
leader. The method usually applied, when presenting demands to the
Prime Minister is called "interviews". These "interviews" are a
general method to influence government policy. Delegations representing loosely organized interest groups attempt to put pressure
on the government to take or prevent decisions.[120]

Although there is this sponsorship by Catholic priests, and Catholic groups are believed to have the Prime Minister's ear, there is
no definite tendency for constituencies dominated by Catholics to
vote for the BNP. Nor do Protestant-dominated constituencies vote
generally against the BNP. There seems rather to be a tendency to
vote against the BNP in constituencies where the Catholic mission
dominated traditionally. Whereas there was the opposite tendency
in constituencies where the Protestant churches dominated traditionally. The Catholic Church affiliation is however visible at top
level. Almost all BNP members in Parliament were Catholic teachers,
whereas many BCP members in Parliament were Protestants.

All except one of the groups sponsoring the BNP, the village
chiefs, are interested in a continuation of the social order prevailing at independence. These village chiefs want a return to the

Diagram 3.B. *Background of the BNP Leader Leabua Jonathan*

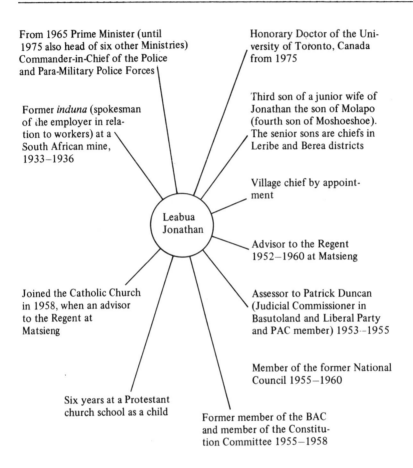

From 1965 Prime Minister (until 1975 also head of six other Ministries) Commander-in-Chief of the Police and Para-Military Police Forces

Honorary Doctor of the University of Toronto, Canada from 1975

Former *induna* (spokesman of the employer in relation to workers) at a South African mine, 1933–1936

Third son of a junior wife of Jonathan the son of Molapo (fourth son of Moshoeshoe). The senior sons are chiefs in Leribe and Berea districts

Village chief by appointment

Leabua Jonathan

Advisor to the Regent 1952–1960 at Matsieng

Joined the Catholic Church in 1958, when an advisor to the Regent at Matsieng

Assessor to Patrick Duncan (Judicial Commissioner in Basutoland and Liberal Party and PAC member) 1953–1955

Member of the former National Council 1955–1960

Six years at a Protestant church school as a child

Former member of the BAC and member of the Constitution Committee 1955–1958

social order existing in the decade before the second world war.
They were necessary allies to the other interest groups sponsoring
the BNP, who depend on village support to win elections.

Important groups behind the BNP are the white and Indian traders. During the time of the colonial government, the white traders had a monopoly on all the large-scale trading. Purchase of
wool, mohair, maize and wheat as well as the sale of groceries was
reserved for white traders. The competition from the BCP-sponsored
co-operatives was the first competition experienced by these white
traders. The traders were also threatened by the BCP programme
which included a demand to nationalize private trade. This caused
them to give their support to the oppositional BNP.[121] British
civil servants and aid personnel made up another strategic group[122]
supporting the BNP in government.

A new group with increasing importance were the educated government employees. These had neither grown up within the BCP youth ca-
ders, nor had they loyalities to the chiefs. Most of them, although
indegenious, were educated abroad and had become aware of the broad
sympathy for the ANC. As government employees they had to sign an
agreement with the BNP government, but rather influenced the BNP
in new directions than let themselves be influenced.

The old anti-communists within the BNP and the Catholic teachers
and priests were thus seriously challenged. The government implemented educational policies and family planning with assistance
from aid donors against the will of its old core groups. It also
slowly changed its foreign policy in opposition to the staunch
anti-communists. C. D. Molapo, Minister of Foreign Affairs and
uncle to Jonathan, was the most influential of the anti-communists
within the BNP.

Molapo left in protest to new diplomatic relations established
with several Communist countries in 1982, and formed a new party
to the right of the BNP. Thus the BNP in Government became more
radical and openly stated its support for the ANC and against the
South African government. This meant a complete turn compared to
the earlier policy, which was openly pro-South Africa.

A similar split had taken place earlier within the BCP in exile,
but with the opposite result. BCPs General Secretary Koenyama Chakela and his followers broke with their chairman Mokhehle in 1976. Chakela negotiated with the Jonathan regime via the Lesotho Embassy
in Mozambique. It had become known to Chakela that Mokhehle had
contacts with the South African government. Mokhehle was isolated
and frustrated in exile in Lusaka, because of his old ANC-anti-
pathy. He agreed to receive support for arming a guerilla to fight
the regime in Lesotho. The Lesotho Liberation Army, LLA, was based
in bantustans, neighbouring to Lesotho. The old BCP-leader and a
few hundred of his followers had become an instrument of the South
African destabilization policy, practiced in relation to Mozambique, Zimbabve and Angola.[123]

Chakela chose the less evil and started peaceful talks with the
old enemy Jonathan. He became one of several media of communication with the ANC and Chakela. Through his education in the Soviet
Union (Kiev) and his trade union contacts in South Africa, he saw

a possibility for Lesotho to get international backing, if the Lesotho government cooperated with the ANC and the pro-ANC followers of
the BCP. Chakela and his followers were given asylum and returned
to Lesotho in 1980. Only about one year later, in August 1981, Chakela was, however, shot dead on his way home in a mini-bus by an
unknown passenger. Several similar cases of murders occurred during
1981, ending with a bloody attack in December, by South African
security forces who shot refugees during nighttime in the middle of
Maseru.

This attack and the international support for the new anti-
South African and pro-ANC policy of the Lesotho government probably
gave the BNP-government new supporters from the old BCP-rank and
file. This was at least the interpretation given by Jonathan and
his Minister of Security and Information, Desmond Sixlise, when
general elections were time and again declared and later cancelled.
A serious attempt to hold general elections in September 1985 were
later declared unnessesary. No opposition party was ready to present 500 voters and 1,000 Maluti (Rand) for each nominated candidate within the short period of time required.[124] Thus the Jonathan
regime gained new supporters and lost old ones and managed to survive without general elections, which would be a risky undertaking
in any case with the increasingly polarized South African society
surrounding Lesotho.

Conclusions

The extreme dependence situation of Lesotho has certainly not resulted in a lack of political work. In spite of, or maybe because of,
difficulties such as poverty, migration and government repression,
political activity was intensive during the period under study.
There was, a decrease in the power base of the government. This was
expressed in the coup d'état of 1970, a few years after independence. Before independence, however, and the first years after, there
was probably rather an increase in the power base of the government
as a result of the colonial government handing over to a popularly
elected Parliament and a government chosen by Parliament. After the
coup the power base is less clear. We can probably characterize
the situation as an unstable one, where the government gets support
from different groups in different questions, but generally on a
narrow elite basis.

The basic political cleavage in Lesotho at independence corre-
sponded closely to the cleavage existing during colonial times.
This cleavage was basically between the heavily exploited social
strata - the migrant industrial and mine workers and their dependants - on the one hand and, on the other those deriving benefit
from the order prevailing during colonialism - chiefs, their advisors, traders, missionaries and the direct dependants on these
groups. The image of the BCP was a party of trade union activists
and radicals articulating the grievances of the exploited, whereas
the image of the BNP was a party aiming at peaceful resolution of

conflict for harmony between different social strata and for the continuation of the existing order, in which churches, traders and chiefs had a say in the promulgation of values.

The nationwide support of both the BNP and the BCP led to conflicts in almost every village. This illustrates that these parties were not limited to particular regions like the MFP, the CPL or the UDP. Whereas the different religious denominations were dominating each in a separate region, the parties did not follow the same pattern. The original affiliation of the BCP and BNP with the Protestant and Catholic churches respectively, existed at top level and it did not show as clearly in the voting behaviour at the 1965 and 1970 elections.

Each party appealed mainly to those groups which clearly supported one of the parties. Groups in the middle tended to be divided between the two parties according to economic, religious and political lines. Farmers and teachers are such groups in the middle. They tended to be split on extremist lines.

The people who identify themselves as mainly farmers, although peasants, are probably very few as we have shown. There are, however, some commercial farmers and some part-time subsistence farmers. Most of the farmers participate in share-cropping relations. The reason for taking a political line among these peasants as well as among the migrant workers seems to have more to do with education and social relations – with the type of experience of share-cropping and migrant work – than with the kind of occupation. There are examples of peasants supporting both BNP and BCP. Those depending economically on chiefs are believed to support the BNP. Teachers make up another stratum divided along party lines. Their stated political opinions often follow a religious background. After the coup d'état there has, however, been a tendency for the Catholic priests to be critical towards the BNP government. In 1973 part of salaries to qualified teachers was taken over by the government in spite of protests from the Catholic Church. A critical statement made by the Southern African Bishops Conference towards the Lesotho government strengthened the critics, but did not change the decision by government to increase its influence over the schools also through other methods.

This change might become one reason for a change in the earlier stable cleavage between the two largest parties. Otherwise there has been a tendency to stress the conflict through the alliances sought abroad by the parties. Sympathetic organizations tend to strengthen the conflict. The BNP allies with anti-communist organizations and generally conservative groups, whereas the BCP allies with socialist-oriented organizations and trade unions. The Organization of African Unity, OAU, has, however, attempted to function as a mediator between the two opposing parties in Lesotho, for example during 1975, when an attempt was made to make the BNP and the BCP form an alliance, although without success.

What potential did the two parties have to forward their party policies? The BNP leaders had access to government and, therefore, were in a better position to work for its policy. Since it had a weak party structure and there is little discussion within the

Diagram 3.C. *Political Parties in Relation to Some Social Strata*

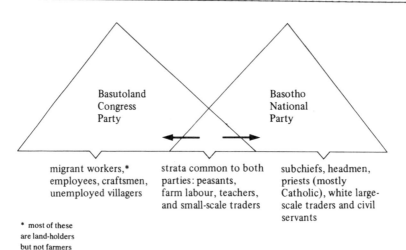

<table>
<tbody></tbody>
</table>

migrant workers,* employees, craftsmen, unemployed villagers	strata common to both parties: peasants, farm labour, teachers, and small-scale traders	subchiefs, headmen, priests (mostly Catholic), white large-scale traders and civil servants

* most of these
are land-holders
but not farmers
See chapter 2

party there were great difficulties in presenting a total strategy. The party strategy rests on articulated conservative ideas, but the support for concrete political actions often comes from one or more of the different small groups supporting the BNP. Nobody, not even the BNP leader, argued in November 1975 that the BNP was still existing as a party organization. The government policy of reconciliation has resulted in a weakening of the BNP. Also the BNP had internal conflicts between a militant minority, which after 1975 decided to take arms; under Mokhehle the Lesotho Liberation Army (LLA) was formed; whereas a majority trusted Chakela and his nonviolent methods of dialogue with Jonathan and in partnership with the ANC.

The very repression exercised by the government against the BCP has made many people compare the Lesotho government with the South African government. The BCP was seen as the main alternative to the oppressive policy by these people. Those who were critical of the South African government became just as critical towards the Lesotho government. But restrictions and oppression against the members of the BCP had hit the party organization hard. The BCP gained access to government mainly after 1980, although even during the 1970s there have been BCP supporters among high-ranking civil servants. The transformation of the BCP to an underground party had been implemented gradually. The BCP itself argued that it had been able to forward its policy even from prison and underground. There are many examples of bargaining between the government and imprisoned leaders of the BCP. There is also evidence of secret meetings with underground BCP members. BCP policies have later been imple-

mented by the government. The government emphatically denies that,
for example, the introduction in 1975 of the Deferred Pay scheme
had in any way been influenced by BCP pressure, although, this had
been a demand of the BCP during the entire 1960s, when Parliamentary debate had been allowed. Nationalization of wool and mohair
trade is another old demand by the BCP which was implemented in
1973-1974. Allowing refugees from South Africa, Namibia and Rhodesia (before independence), is also an example of an old demand met
by the Lesotho government.

This government strategy of meeting BCP demands has, however,
not been without problems for the BCP itself as a party. The BCP
leaders had the ideal that popular participation in policy formation is necessary. This made the party vulnerable to restrictions
on meetings and discussion. The party policy was that once aims
had been agreed upon, they should be stuck to until met. As long
as the government did not implement BCP ideas the old aims could
be repeated. But problems arose, when the BCP demands were met by
the BNP government at the same time as there were restrictions on
popular participation in discussions of new demands.

We can distinguish three different periods during 1950-1984
with regard to the type of political participation:

a) *The pre-parliamentary period:* During the 1950s there was a
rapid increase in the number of people who participated in the
organization of political action. The two large parties which
still exist in Lesotho emerged during this time. Both struggled
to take over the government from the colonial power.

b) *The parliamentary period:* From 1960 to 1970 there was a
national forum for political debate. The Village Committees and
District Councils played an active role during the early 1960s at
the same time as the Parliament was increasingly a common forum
for debate. At all levels there was an increasing conflict between
the more conservative BNP and the more radical BCP. At the same
time both parties increased their following. The BCP had already
during the 1950s built up a mass organization, whereas the BNP
built its strength mainly on contacts with established groups. The
difference in party organization was an expression of the difference in ideology. The deep cleavage between the parties was also
expressed in their different priorities in relation to the question of independence. The BCP argued that independence within the
framework of the South African government's Bantustan policy was
contrary to the ideology of the BCP and against the interests of
the groups supporting this party. But the BNP was anxious to gain
independence even if this meant the guardianship of the South
African government. It was in the interest of the groups supporting the BNP to keep the prevailing order and not make rapid
changes in the political and socio-economic situation of Lesotho.

c) *The post-parliamentary period*: After the coup d'état Leabua
Jonathan attempted to abolish all parties. This did not succeed
in spite of violent repression. The coup-government was not powerful enough to abolish either its own party or the opposition. A
reorganization of party work started. In 1973 Jonathan saw himself
forced to formally reintroduce an Interim-Parliament. This was

appointed by the government and did not manage to prevent political meetings outside the Parliament. A boom in political organization started instead and was met by police repression against the BCP and expulsion of party members within the BNP. After 1974, there was no longer an open climate of discussion. Political conflict was neither articulated in Parliament nor in the mass media. Trade union strikes, demonstrations and boycotts which were frequent already during the earlier periods now became the main method for political pressure. Several times Jonathan found it necessary to declare coming elections, which were however postponed.

There was a demand from migrant families for some kind of flexible organization giving them both a sense of belonging and an ideological alternative to the religious and other ideas provided by the establishment. Before the South African liberation movements were banned in South Africa in 1960, they also organized citizens from Basutoland. After 1960, the BCP through the BFL was the main organization covering the geographical area over which the migrants moved. This made the BCP different from the BNP, as the latter organization had no ambition to organize the migrant workers in South Africa. When the BCP was banned in Lesotho, (it was never officially allowed in South Africa) the trade union organization affiliated to the BCP, the Basutoland Federation of Labour (BFL), became a channel of communication for the migrants, their families and friends.

4 State Institutions

The character of state institutions is crucial for development. In Lesotho, the parties struggle to control the state institutions in order to control development policies. But, how are the state institutions organized? What laws govern them? Does the government control its own machinery? Have the popular demands for increased control been successful? In this chapter a closer look is taken at how the laws and state institutions have changed as a result of independence.

The Law-making System and the Laws

The position of Basutoland as a separate colony under British rule linked it directly to London in some respects. This is seen for example in the constitutional development after 1959. In other respects Basutoland was part of South Africa. This is seen for example in the practice of general laws.

The first Constitution of Basutoland was drawn up in 1959.[1] For the first time, half of the existing National Council was elected - although indirectly - via District Councils. The BCP obtained the majority of the votes as I have mentioned earlier, but 40 out of the 80 members of the National Council were chiefs, representatives of business, and church interests as well as the colonial administration. An Executive Council was divided in the same way. Already in 1964 a committee was appointed with the task to work out a new Constitution, and in 1962 a large Constitutional Conference was held.

This Conference instituted a British type Parliament to be directly and popularly elected. The Paramount Chief was to become a constitutional monarchy. The general election in 1965 gave the conservative BNP a victory in the House of Commons. The election results were, however, much disputed. Independence was granted on 4 October 1966, in spite of protests against the election procedure from the defeated BCP and MFP but in accordance with the wish of the BNP and the colonial power.[2]

The design of the Constitution was discussed at meetings held all over the country with the Constitution Reform Commission. Thousands of individuals articulated their opinions during these meetings and many of the speeches were recorded. The importance of popular participation at the local level was often stressed in these speeches.[3]

Popular participation in the control of the country's resources through popular participation in decision-making units at different levels of the political structure was explicitly defined as essential.

But the Constitution was based on the British model of a legislative and Public Administration, loosely adding elements of chieftainship and a system of Village Committees and District Councils. Popularly elected committees were to advise a chief at village level. At village level the chief had the final decision-making power, although, at the national level this was attributed to the Parliament. The Paramount Chief had no decision-making authority.

The practiced laws in Lesotho could be characterized as a mixture of Basotho customary law, British customary law and South African written "Roman-Dutch" law. The Basotho laws include oral traditional law as well as a collection of written laws called the Laws of Lerotholi. The latter were first written down in 1883.[4] The most important of these were the land law, stating that no private ownership of land was possible, and the trade law, stating that only traders following the rules set up by the Paramount Chief and the colonial government were allowed to carry on business in Basutoland. The strict application of these rules resulted in a total absence of white farmers and the monopoly of a few traders controlling the market in Basutoland.[5]

The British-South African law applied is the type of law that existed in the Cape Province in the colonial period before the 1880s. This was a mixture of British and Roman-Dutch law. The laws have changed since then, and are applied in Lesotho in their changed form. Few records have been kept from the Basotho courts and the judges often have to go back to the records of courts in South Africa in order to find cases of precedence.

According to the "Independence Order" of 1966 - later abolished - laws in conflict with the Constitution or Basotho customs should not be applied in Lesotho. All other laws should continue to be applied until they are changed by Parliament. A careful study by Palmer and Poulter of the legal system in Lesotho after independence shows that in practice law cases of South African and British courts are often quoted and applied in Lesotho. The racial segregation laws of South Africa are not applied, not even after the coup d'état of 1970, when the Constitution and the Independence Order were abolished.[6]

But after 1970 there have been no formal restrictions preventing South African laws from being applied in Lesotho. The coup government specified alternative emergency regulations in 1970. But unlike the Independence Order it did not specify that the South African laws were not to be applied in Lesotho. But there was not only a continuation of application of South African laws, new laws were drafted by a group of law experts sponsored by the South African Government. These experts made up Lesotho's Law Office. In 1976, after ten years of work, the laws of Lesotho also included modern South African laws.

Since 1966 jurisprudence can be studied either at the University of Roma in Lesotho or in Great Britain. Practical legal skill in

Roman-Dutch law was traditionally learnt either in South Africa or
through the leadership within Lesotho by law experts sponsored by the
South African government. These South African lawyers and judges
were considered experts on the laws as practiced in Lesotho.[7]
During the first period after independence not only the personnel
of the Law Office were South Africans, sponsored by the South African government, but also the Chief Justice of the High Court, the
Senior Public Prosecutor and the Appeal Court.[8]

The dominance of South African law experts and written South
African laws increased during the first decade after independence,
but already before that the British colonial power worked to integrate the practised laws in Basutoland with those of South Africa.

After the Parliament was dissolved in 1970 there was first little
discussion on the general problem caused by the introduction and
application of foreign laws in Lesotho. The Interim Parliament of
1973 has, however, raised the question of indigenization of legal
personnel within the Law Office and the Appeal Court. Lesotho's
Minister of Justice 1973-1975, C. D. Molapo (and Minister of Foreign
Affairs until 1983), has a South African law degree.
He answered my question about what his government thought (in 1975)
of the way South African laws were applied in Lesotho:

> In practice we do not apply the race discrimination laws of South
> Africa. I, however, consider the South African legal system as
> well as its lawyers among the best in the world.

But what was the content of the new laws made after independence?
What categories of laws were there? Before 1959, the High Commissioner and the Colonial Office in London applied a policy of non-
interference with the complex system of law practiced in Basutoland.
Few laws were officially promulgated for Basutoland after the end
of the 19th century. But after independence there was hectic
activity both to write down the commonly practiced laws and to make
new laws.

The Law Office drafted laws concerning two areas in particular:
business and the prevention of public violence: Reforms of the land
laws allowed so-called "institutional holdings" for tourism and
industry. (See table 1, Chapter 2.)

The following laws are examples given[9] by the Lesotho National
Development Corporation (a parastatal body started and developed by
businessmen from the Rupert concern in South Africa).[10] This was
established after a decision by the Lesotho government to encourage
foreign capital investment in Lesotho:

1. The Industrial Licensing Act
2. The Pioneer Industries Encouragement Bill
3. The Casino Act
4. The Companies Act
5. The Electricity Corporations Act
6. The Deeds Registration Act
7. The Mining Concessions Act
8. The Lesotho National Development Corporation Act

This legislation to actively assist foreign investment was appa-
rently compatible with the interests of the South African government, which provided development assistence particularly in the
form of experts on company law. During the colonial period, only
British - and not very much - capital was invested. Earlier, industrial development was inhibited. The laws, which prevented private
ownership of land were kept. On limited areas of government land
investments from Europe and the United States were allowed, however.

A general interest of the South African government is to introduce the same laws in the enclave as in South Africa itself. Some
of the South African laws made during the 1960s have, however,
been published in Lesotho only after the Constitution was abolished
in 1970. The South African Terrorism Act (1967) and the Supression
of Communism Act (1950) were introduced in Lesotho in 1970. The
Internal Security Act (1965), was introduced in 1974[11] in an even
more restrictive version than applied in South Africa. In 1976,
this version was, however, enforced also in the Republic.

In conclusion, we have seen that great changes were made in
the law making system during the years before and after independence. A legislature with formal powers to make new laws in
accordance with views held by the people of Lesotho was introduced
gradually throughout the period 1959-1965. Restrictions on the
application of South African law in Lesotho were introduced in
1966. Both these changes in the law making capacity were abolished
in 1970.

The British-styled constitution had become part of the political
heritage of the Basotho and not only through the educational system.
The short period of constitutional rule between 1959 and 1970 was
considered a positive experience by many people in Lesotho,
although criticism was directed against the lack of popular participation allowed by it. There was active opposition against the
abolition of the Constitution after the coup in 1970. Both the
MFP and the BCP demanded immediate reinstatement of the constitution.

Public Administration

The activity of the small South African group in the Law Office
had no parallel in the rest of the public administration. In the
following investigation of the changing character of the organization of the other parts of public administration, I shall deal
with cleavages within the administration and take a closer look
at recruitment and growth in state employment.

There have been many organizational changes in the state constitutions and these have taken place both before and after independence. But, what is the political significance of these changes?

Competition between Three Institutional Set-Ups

Before independence there were, in essence, three different institutional set-ups for public administration, each with its own political
background:

1. *The Colonial Administration in Maseru.* This grew out of the
Resident Commissioner's office. It included technical departments
like those of Health, Education, Agriculture and Works.

2. At the national level there were also *the Offices of the
Paramount Chief* with head-quarters at Matsieng. Since 1946 a Department of Finance has been located at Matsieng. The Paramount Chief
was formally the highest authority of the chieftainship with representatives in each of the more than one hundred areas into which the
country was divided for the purpose of land-distribution control.
The Paramount Chief was advisor to the Resident Commissioner and
had himself four advisors to assist in the linking of the people of
Basutoland with the colonial authority.[12]

3. *Local Government.* After the second world war a popular movement grew rapidly, demanding participation for the people in the
decision-making of government and administration. Groups of villagers took over the decision-making and administration of land from
the village chiefs already during the early 1950s. It is estimated
that, at independence in 1966, about half of the approximately
6,000 villages in Lesotho had Village Committees, which were popularly elected and actually controlled land matters. In the rest of
the villages the chief still had the final say but under pressure
of a tacit understanding that his responsibility could be taken
over by a Village Committee if he lost the confidence of the villagers or the government.

A transfer of responsibility from chiefs and central colonial
government was implemented. This was largely a result of the active
participation by large groups of people at district and village
levels. In 1946, District Advisory Boards were appointed by the
British District Commissioners in the nine districts of the colony.
The District Commissioner headed District Offices responsible for
tax collection. The mobilization of the BCP was implemented partly
through the involvement of villagers in the administration of their
own affairs via Village Committees, as we saw in chapter 3. To meet
the popular demands, the colonial government allowed popular elections at village and district levels from 1960 onwards.[13] After
1960, the Boards were succeeded by District Councils popularly
elected to 50 percent, which in turn elected half of the National
Council. The District Councils gained new responsibilities. They
became partly responsible for social services, economic development and some land questions.

The relation between the different institutional set-ups was
one of increasing competition and decreasing contacts. The election campaigns of 1960 and 1965 aggravated the conflict between
them. The distribution of administration and control between the
national and local levels was an issue of political party conflict.

The BNP, which based its support mainly on those who had profited from colonial rule before the popular reforms, supported the

first set-up. The public administration in the capital was to be
kept. All institutions at village and district levels constraining
chiefs, priests, and traders were criticized.

The BCP favoured a continued decentralization. The District Councils and Village Committees should be involved in decision-making
and administration. This was a strategic question for the BCP. The
party based its strength on the control and participation in decision-making at these levels. Wages deferred by the migrant workers
were administrated by the BCP-dominated District Councils and invested in development projects in agriculture and small-scale industry.[14] The BCP therefore, favoured the third institutional set-
up. The MFP, however, favoured the second, since it included a
central position for the Paramount Chief.

Co-ordination of these different set-ups of government became
difficult. A situation developed where the different parties favoured only one of them. In 1965, however, the BCP and the MFP agreed
on a common negative attitude to the selection of the first set-up,
favoured by an alliance of the BNP and the colonial government.
The BCP and the MFP referred critically to its foreign and colonial
background. They also criticized the domination of British civil
servants and their lack of contact with people in Lesotho. The geographical location of the colonial headquarters was also condemned.
This oppositional alliance was formed after the BNP won the election in 1965. It was very active and went to the extent of demanding
a delay of granting independence, with reference to the lack of
broadly-based state institutions.

The political conflict between the BNP government alliance and
the opposition concerning institutional set-ups also included per-
sonally based conflicts between the BNP and the MFP. Leabua Jonathan had three reasons to oppose the choice of the second institutional set-up mentioned above. Firstly, he saw the keeping of the
offices at Matsieng as an unnecessary strengthening of the position of the Paramount Chief. It was headed by a person who was un-
acceptable to the former regent Mantsebo to whom Jonathan had old
personal loyalties.[15] Secondly, the lower chiefs - who were powerful within this party - were anxious to regain their importance at
the expense of the high-ranking chiefs. Thirdly, in his capacity
of Prime Minister he had no interest in increasing the competition
from the Paramount Chief.

In 1965, the BNP government, which was the first generally elected government in Lesotho, agreed with the British representatives
on a policy of gradual abolition of the second and third institutional set-ups described above, concentrating most of the administrative decision-making to the former colonial civil service in
Maseru.[16] This was done in spite of the protests of the MFP and the
BCP.

Government in the Countryside after 1968

In April 1968 the whole District Council system and the Department
of Finance in Matsieng were abolished. All financial powers were
concentrated in Maseru. Tax collection had been the responsibility

of the Department of Finance in Matsieng, which had been assisted
since 1960 by the District offices. In 1968, a Ministry of Finance,
mainly with foreign civil servants, was established in the former
buildings of the Resident Commissioner.[17]

Hundreds of tax collectors, agricultural extension officers,
health officers, statistical surveyors and teachers were dismissed
after the coup d'état in 1970. The work of these officers was
partly undertaken by foreign aid personnel, by village chiefs and
by the police. But in most cases the posts remained vacant. Many
of the dismissed lower civil servants were returned to their home
villages under "village arrest". Those who had savings started to
build houses. In many cases they invested in farming.

The system of local government had functioned as a school for
civil servants and as an arena for political debate. According to
the defenders of the system, it had successfully mobilized people
and resources in the countryside.[18] According to the government
and its advisors, the village and district committees were a danger
to law and order as well as to the efficiency of the government.[19]
However, the expected law and order did not follow - on the contrary. The existing cleavage between the parties increased. It
strengthened the existing conflict between the capital and the
countryside. Violent conflicts occurred and dismissed state employees and local government participants spread disappointment
and suspicious attitudes towards Maseru officials. In the parliamentary debate, prior to the coup, the BCP stated that independence had not meant a real take-over of the government by the
people of Lesotho.

During the period 1968-1973, there was neither local government
nor any permanent representation of public administration in the
countryside, apart from the police stations and non-salaried
village chiefs. The only exception was that village committees in
many areas (possibly half of the villages) continued their meetings
without reference to the central government.

Decisions had been taken by the government to introduce two
new types of authorities in the villages, but were not generally
implemented: 1) development committees 2) advisory land distribution committees. Both of these were to be appointed by the chief.

1. The system of village development committees was described
in the First Five Year Plan of 1970. The Plan stressed the necessity
of contacts at village level to increase the efficiency and
implementation capacity of the development projects decided at
national level. Assistant Ministers in the Prime Minister's
office took over the responsibility for law and order in the
Districts. In 1970 these became the chairmen of the newly
established Development Committees, which were intended to have
the responsibility for implementing development projects. The
system was, however, not introduced universally, but only in
areas where foreign aid projects operated. These are scattered
mainly over the north-western part of the country and loosely
connected with the mentioned Assistant Ministers. Their main
responsibility was to co-ordinate the projects of different technical Ministries. However, both the Assistant Ministers, and the

Central Planning Office had weak executive positions, and implementation of development schemes was left to the Ministries represented
by foreign field personnel and chiefs in the countryside.

2. The system of advisory land distribution committees was decided
by the government in 1973 and by the Interim Parliament in 1974, but
again it was not universally introduced.[20] This system was criti-
zised by the existing popularly elected Village Committees, already
advising on land distribution, and by those chiefs who still had the
responsibility of allocating land in their areas.

At the BNP caucus meeting in July 1975, which consisted of the
Supreme Council and some trusted members, the question of village
committees and land distribution was discussed. There was criticism
of two kinds against the government's decision to accept the committees in the villages: a) against the interference of commoners into
land distribution matters b) against the election of committee members among BNP supporters on the basis that it was difficult to
find people to fill the posts in some areas.

The following statement by one of the chiefs present at the caucus meeting is an illustration of the second problem, mentioned
above:

> In one of the villages in my area of responsibility there are
> as far as I know only three supporters of the BNP. I have appoin-
> ted them all, although, it is a bit strange to appoint exactly
> those. People do not like it. But how should I fill the rest
> of the vacant posts in the committee of my village?[21]

The offices of foreign aid projects in the countryside of Lesotho
became new centres dominating the surrounding villages. In the large
agriculture projects of Thaba Bosiu and Leribe, for example, there
seems to be no differentation between the following five decision-
making units: a) the committee appointed by the chief to advise on
distribution of land, b) the committee to co-ordinate development,
c) the committee appointed by the chief to represent villagers in
the aid project, d) the district board and e) the board of the
development aid project headquarters. They are all believed to be
the same. The same people take part in all of these committees.
The resources controlled by the committee at the project offices
are used by the committees at village and district levels appointed by the chief. In the rest of the villages in the district,
the older system of Village Committees still exists, but without
resources.[22] Not only does this make it difficult for the villagers to distinguish between the different kinds of committees,
but new groups have taken over responsibilities from the committees in which the villagers themselves participated.

New Roles for the Chiefs

After winning the general election in 1965, the BNP, partly based
on ex-chiefs, demanded the reintroduction of the positions that
these had held earlier. After 1968, the government found itself
dependent on the village chiefs and police for information from

the rural areas on law and order. This strengthened the village chiefs in their positions as a link between the government and the rural areas.

There is, however, a split within the chieftainship hierarchy. The chieftainship has been "beheaded", since the Paramount Chief was divested of formal powers. The 22 Principal Chiefs are split in two factions, according to political party lines. Sixteen favour the King (and the MFP) and six favour the Prime Minister (and the BNP).

According to election results in 1970 the higher chiefs - who dominated the indigenous representation at the national level, particularly during the last two decades of colonial rule but also in the Interim Parliament of 1974 - have almost no popular support. The lower chiefs could be said to have gained in relative importance within the chieftainship hierarchy. But they have not succeeded in regaining their former powers based on land alloca-tion, since the income of the villagers is based less on land to-day. Another reason for the reduction of their power is that Village Committees, ministries, foreign aid projects and para-statal bodies now intervene frequently and have the final say. Today a foreign aid expert of a state employee has the responsi-bility for these community affairs, although the chiefs should still be formally informed before a decision is made.

In 1975 the Prime Minister, Leabua Jonathan, defined the roles of the present chiefs in the following manner:

> I would say that the chiefs are not as important any more...
> But the institution of chieftainship is an important arm of
> government. It is responsible for peace in the rural areas.
> We have a very small police force and it cannot cope with law
> and order. The chiefs work on behalf of government. To keep
> order is a function for which the chiefs are paid. If a chief
> does not fulfil this function he is dismissed.[23]

Asked how the chiefs are paid, the Prime Minister answered that most chiefs were paid "on traditional lines". They had more land than others and could until recently sell reeds for roofing and wood for fire.

It is unclear how the chiefs are recruited today. According to the Prime Minister, they were and still are the heads of each group of related families, and every larger village has a chief, "a chief is a chief by the right of birth".[24] The government, however, only accepts chiefs if they follow its policy. A chief is therefore chosen among related candidates on mainly political grounds, and can be dismissed also on the same grounds. Although most of their original powers have been lost some village chiefs have increased their influence for three reasons: (1) The aboli-tion of local government and the Paramount Chiefs offices in 1968. (2) Their involvement in the winning BNP after 1965. (3) The deve-lopment budget for selected areas was increased via aid projects which needed a contact in the rural area that was trusted by the government.

Their new role as a linkage in the flow of development aid resources in the countryside and as the only universally functioning
government representation beside the police has given the chiefs a
potentially important position. They might therefore emerge as a
new kind of elite similar to the new kind of chiefs in the so
called black states declared sovereign by South Africa, the "Bantustans".

State Employees

To analyze the changes that have taken place in the state institutions during the years before and after independence, it is
important to study the recruitment to these institutions of individuals and groupings. The background of the state employees is
particularly important during a period when there is a general
uncertainty about what laws and regulations to apply.

In the decades before 1950, the Basotho were recruited to lower
posts of the civil service. The presence of black people in the
lower categories of civil service did not differ from the situation
in the Republic of South Africa. From the mid-50s onwards educated
Basotho in lower posts of the civil service had increasing success in their demand for access to posts formerly reserved for
British colonial civil servants. The demand was loud and well
articulated in newly established magazines published both in
English and Sesotho.[25] At the same time as censorship was applied
and the writers were being discriminated against, a gradual break-
through by Basotho into the higher posts of the civil service was
allowed. This had no parallel in the Republic.

Slow Growth of Employment

In the Republic of South Africa there was direct discrimination
against black people. Increased security control directed particularly against black activists in the Republic resulted in an
influx to Basutoland of politically active black people. Most of
those who fled to Basutoland already had a knowledge of Sesotho.
Some of them were citizens of Basutoland. Most of them were people
who would under otʰ.ʳ circumstances have emigrated to the Republic.
A wave of organizational work took place, partly led by these
"returners". Well-organized strikes involved thousands of employees in Basutoland. An important demand was non-discrimination in
recruitment to government employment. This strengthened the
demand for access to the higher Civil Service posts for black in
general, including the Basotho.

At independence in 1966 only about 300 posts out of about
6,000 were held by foreigners in the Lesotho Civil Service, i.e.
about 5 per cent.[26] Most of these were higher civil servants.

Table 4.1. *Number of State Employees in 1962, 1971 and 1984*[27]

	Absolute figures	Change percent	Percent of internal recorded employment	Employment in absolute figures
1962	5,860		40	14,744
1971	7,637	30	40	19,087
est. 1984*)	21,000	358	39*)	54,000*)

*) estimated domestic employment.

In spite of a rapid growth of the state budget and definite changes in the structure of institutional growth the increase in the total number of government employees was only an average of 3 per cent per year during the period 1962-1971. The total number of state employees was 5,860 in 1962. This increased by 200 posts yearly, reaching 7,637 in 1971.[28]
British grants to meet current expenditure were given on condition that growth in the number employed by the state should not exceed 3 per cent a year. The reason for this condition being that the government of Lesotho was already employing 40 per cent of the economically active population which was considered too great a proportion of the labour force. Self-sustained economic growth was believed to be difficult to establish unless the proportion of state-employed people was reduced.[29]
In table 1 above we can see that internal employment in 1962 was only 14,744. Since about 150,000 persons were recorded as migrant workers the same year; this means that only 10 per cent of the total recorded employment was within the country and government employment only 4 per cent. In 1971, the proportion of state employment in relation to internal employment was still 40 per cent. Internal employment in that year was 19,887.[30] This estimate of total internal employment should be regarded with suspicion - particularly when it changes - since conditional aid might well have had effects on statistical recordings. Figures for state employment are probably more accurate since records of wages are kept.

A study of the distribution of the approximately 2,000 new posts over the period 1962-1971 reflects the general pattern of change in the priority given to certain state institutions:
1. Of the yearly increase of about 200 jobs on the average, 120 were for policemen. The para-military police received the greatest proportion of these police jobs.[31]
2. A few posts were for higher Civil Servants in the Office for Central Planning and Development, which dealt with foreign aid. Many of the posts in this new part of the government were filled with foreign technical assistant personnel.[32]
3. The Ministry of Agriculture grew even larger. Many of the higher posts in this ministry were occupied by foreign aid personnel.[33]

4. A state-controlled radio was set up in 1965 and employed a handful of people under the leadership of foreign experts.[34]
5. A small Foreign Ministry was established at independence with about 10-15 posts under the responsibility of the Prime Minister. Not until 1974 was a separate Foreign Minister appointed.[35]

Two principles restricted recruitment to the public administration, both of British origin: 1) a person who was a chief was not allowed to keep his position at the same time as he held a post in the Public Administration, 2) a civil servant was not allowed to be a member of a political party.[36] In Great Britain these principles were applied to assure the neutrality and autonomy of the Public Administration in relation to the elite groups. The consequence in the colony was, however, that few educated Basotho were allowed to be employed in the administration. During the period 1960-1970, the restrictions no longer prevented participation in politics. Few Basotho civil servants were then silent about their opinions. They stated their support frequently and openly, mostly in favour of the BCP.[37] After violent police repression in 1970 and 1974 against BCP supporters, this climate of open political discussion changed.[38]

"Indiscipline" and Dismissals

What interest and possibility did the government have to control its public administration? According to the Constitution 1960-1970, a Public Service Commission with executive powers guaranteed the autonomy of the public administration in relation to the government. The government was not allowed to recruit or dismiss civil servants freely. This law was implemented efficiently and, during the years before and after independence, the government had little possibility to make its public administration obey orders if the civil servants were not prepared to obey.

Technical departments are difficult to control in all countries, since they are their own experts as well as advisers to the government. The BNP government in office at independence was inexperienced and met with active opposition from large parts of the public administration. Both lower and higher civil servants were active supporters of the BCP. The newly recruited higher civil servants had, as mentioned earlier, got their education via the BCP.[39] The BNP had access to scholarships for higher education via the colonial administration, which favoured the BNP and refused scholarships to BCP supporters. These colonial scholarships were, however, very few. On the contrary, the BCP received many scholarships from OAU-countries like Ghana, Tanzania and Egypt, and also from Eastern Europe.[40]

The active African civil servants' organization was dominated by the BCP. Now and then it enforced its view on decisions by the Public Service Commission.[41] An indigenization of posts held by British civil servants was demanded by all groups of Basotho civil servants, even in the lower ranks. Most of these lower civil servants were considered to be supporters of the BCP.

Irregularities in the voting procedure had been discovered and
reported in the press in 1965. In two cases the BNP was found
guilty of such irregularities when these were taken to court. The
parties in Parliament had almost the same size and the government
would have had to resign if two opposition members had not crossed
the floor. The British principle of "majority in one-man-constitu-
encies" was severely criticized by the opposition. The opposition
had gained about 60 per cent of the votes in the election but did
not get more than 28 out of the 60 seats in Parliament, as already
mentioned in chapter 3. Gifts from the South African government and
the Catholic church to the BNP leader were stated publicly by the
opposition as examples of corruption and foreign intervention. All
these different circumstances led to a situation where BCP supporters among the civil servants saw the government as illegitimate.
It was called a "South African puppet regime". Foreign civil servants were considered "South African-minded", unless they openly
criticized the governments of Lesotho and South Africa. Government
orders were delayed indefinitely. BNP supporters as well as many
foreign state employees and aid personnel were treated as non-
existent.[42] This situation resembled an election campaign. It was
in fact a well-organized campaign of disobedience and continued
without interruption until a few months after the coup d'état in
1970.

Those in the central public administration who were most loyal
to the BNP government were the former British colonial employees.
In 1969, there were only about 60 of them left. Another 50 South
African government-sponsored employees were also considered loyal
to the Lesotho government.[43] In the countryside, village chiefs,
white traders, priests and teachers in Catholic missions assisted
the government.

There was undecisiveness at the national level and few decisions were taken as a result of the unstable parliamentary situation and the openly negative attitude of BCP supporters at all
levels of the public administration. Walter Coutts, A British
official, investigated the government structure and suggested
reforms to achieve more effective administration. He concluded
his report in 1966:

> All of these proposals will be politically difficult to carry
> out, but unless the nettle is grasped I can see no real hope
> for Lesotho. Your service has almost ceased to function at all
> for a variety of reasons. There is indiscipline at all levels
> which is almost unbelievable. Government instructions are
> either obeyed or ignored according to the whim of the reci-
> pient.[44]

The fact that Basotho civil servants and villagers supporting the
BCP opposed every act of government and reacted through civil disobedience in accordance with the BCP policy was not mentioned in
the report, but was nevertheless common knowledge in the country.

Action taken by the government to remedy the situation was
mainly of three kinds: (1) decision-making was centralized as far
as possible and more responsibility was given to the posts filled

by foreigners "neutral" to party conflict, (2) recruitment abroad
via foreign aid donors was rapidly increased, (3) police action was
increasingly used against disobedient civil servants of Basotho
origin.

We have already mentioned the centralization which took place
through the abolition of all administrative offices and governing
elements in the countryside. The necessity of foreign experts was
considered common to all underdeveloped countries by aid agencies
in Europe and the United States. The Lesotho government only had to
refer to the scarcity of educated citizens. There was, however, a
large number of citizens with formal education in Lesotho, who were
not acceptable for security reasons. Government reports on employment among secondary school leavers and university graduates indicate no scarcity. There was a rather high unemployment among educated citizens, and state employees who were citizens of Lesotho
often held posts below their qualifications. Others were given
less responsibility than their experience and education warranted.
The handful of Basotho civil servants trusted by the government
were overwhelmed with work.

After the coup d'état in 1970 the Lesotho Public Service Commission was controlled directly by the government. State employees
were dismissed for political and security reasons, and in the
Ministries of Health and Agriculture, the government did not even
fill the vacancies after dismissals. However, new posts were
created within the police force. The BCP had secured the majority
among the rank and file of the police force in 1970, according to
the separate poll taken the day before the general elections.
Supporters of the BCP and MFP left their jobs after the coup
d'état. Some of them joined guerilla groups operating in the
mountains without support of their parties. Others were dismissed
and their jobs were filled according to a system of BNP membership
card requirement. Memebership of the government, *Liphephechana*,
became an absolute requirement for recruitment in all parts of the
public administration. After much pressure inside the country and
criticism from the ILO in a special report on trade union rights
in June 1975, the government stated that this system had been abolished.[45]

Recruitment for Police Repression

The BNP government generally stresses the importance of law and
order in its public statements. The increased importance of the
repressive functions given to the state institutions is expressed
also in other ways. It is seen, for example, in the priority
given to the police forces when new posts are established in
state employment.

The number of policemen suddenly started to grow in 1965 and
almost doubled in five years. According to a policy statement by
the Commissioner of Police in 1967, the police forces should be
fully expanded by 1970.[46] This policy was changed after the coup
d'état as the state of emergency required more police personnel
than ever before. The establishment of new posts within the police

was again doubled within twelve months. The expansion of the police
forces continued, with particular emphasis on the military police
and the Police Mobile Unit (PMU).[47] There is no indication that the
police force is intended for the purpose of defence, and the technical facilities would be of little use in warfare with another
country. The figures should therefore, according to the Commissioner
of Police, be compared with army figures in other countries despite
the fact that the PMU has been used only against the population of
Lesotho.

Table 4.2. *Number of Policemen Related to (de jure)* Population in
1965, 1967 and 1970*[48]

	Absolute number	Citizens/Policemen
1965	823	1,150
1967		932
1970	1,230	600

* with citizenship in Lesotho including absentees.

How can we explain the priority given to armed police? The Jonathan regime had several reasons for strengthening the police force.
Possible reasons were:
    a. Earlier the British army or the South African army could be
called in on occasions of public violence. This was no longer
possible.
    b. Leabua Jonathan and his party had been elected by groups in
favour of law and order and status quo.
    c. The police was the best organized and most efficient of the
state institutions at all levels, and the only state institution
individually and directly under the control of the Prime Minister.
    d. Aid donors and foreign companies asked for a better control
generally in the country and for the personal safety of their staff.
The largest aid donor, Great Britain, did not try to counteract
this strengthening of the police but instead supported it by providing the top personnel.
    e. There was a strong and well-organized opposition in Lesotho
and the government was protected by the police on many occasions
when its members were threatened with hostile demonstrations.

The two reasons given by the Commissioner of Police in 1967 for
the recruitment of a large number of policemen at lower levels were
the increase in "public violence" and the higher incidence of
"stock theft".[49] In December 1966 according to police estimates,
about 30,000 people made their way to Thaba Bosiu, the historic
mountain and capital of Moshoeshoe I, to protest against the government. The government forbade the opposition leaders and the young
Moshoeshoe II to be present and the Commissioner of Police - acting

on the order of the Prime Minister - ordered the mounted policemen
to stop people going to the mountain.[50] The people, who had already
arrived were fired upon and ten were shot dead and others were
wounded. In the annual police report for 1967, reference was also
made to "attacks at several police stations". The police stations
of Leribe and Butha-Buthe are mentioned specifically. At Leribe,[51]
"the police, who had been warned, repulsed the attack and dispersed
the mob. One man was shot dead during the exchange of shots."
Eighteen men were arrested afterwards and charged with public violence.

Police Co-operation with South Africa

The South African police demanded active co-operation with the
police forces in the neighbouring countries. The leading British
policemen were openly willing to meet this demand.[52] The close co-
operation which already existed between the criminal investigation
departments in Basutoland and South Africa was not regarded as
adequate. In 1967, the co-operation was strengthened through the
establishment of a "Stock Theft Unit" and a "Diamond Branch" in
Lesotho. Their work in Lesotho was described as follows by the
British Commissioner of Police:

> A sound liaison between this unit (the Stock Theft Unit)... and
> its counterpart of the South African Police has been built up
> in order to combat this mutually disturbing crime.[53]

South African police statistics were referred to. The number
of stock theft cases in the Orange Free State had increased from
1,393 in 1961 to 3,588 in 1966.
The diamond branch at the headquarters of the Lesotho police
was intended:

> to protect the diamond industry of Lesotho... Once again there
> has been close liaison between this branch and its counterpart
> in the Republic of South Africa.

The reason for the co-operation was not specified. During the colonial period, the South African police had often crossed the borders
to look for stolen cattle or for people suspected of political and
criminal offences. Several kidnappings of political refugees from
South Africa, who were hiding in Basutoland had been reported.[54]
When Basutoland became independent the South African police could
not have continued to cross the borders as easily as before if
formal co-operation had not been established. With the creation
of a Lesotho Stock Theft Unit, South African policemen could travel around the countryside after reporting at a police station in
Lesotho.
The fact that South African police cars could be seen in the
mountains of Lesotho even after independence was stressed by the
BCP as evidence that "independence was false". [55] Frequent police
raids were made allegedly in search of stolen cattle but with

arrests for security reasons as a result. These are considered to
have been one important reason for the swing from the BNP to the
BCP by voters in the mountainous areas bordering the Transkei in
the 1970 election.[56]

Conclusions

The 1960s was a period of increased popular control of the state
institutions through parties and local government. After the abolition of the local government in 1968 and severe restrictions on
party involvement in 1970, a new period of decreasing popular control of state institutions started. The legitimacy of state institutions decreased in the rest of the society at the same time as
the remaining state institutions increased their efficiency in a
narrow sense. That is, orders were obeyed, the employees followed
the rules etc.

The government attempted to increase the efficiency of the state
institutions in this sense during the first decade after independence. Its decision-making capacity increased through the abolition
of local government, the centralization of decision-making, increased control of recruitment and, most important of all, through
the abolition of Parliament. This increased efficiency was largely
in line with the advice given by Great Britain to its former colony
and was also generally in line with the planning philosophy introduced through aid agencies, particularly the World Bank.

State institutions which were efficient in the same sense existed also during the colonial period. But they disappeared during
the decade preceeding independence. This was largely a result of
a higher level of political consciousness among the inhabitants,
including the state employees. Conflicts between different aims
became conflicts within the state institutions. Education and
recruitment had become largely BCP-controlled. This was seen as
one of its greatest problems by the BNP government when it came
into power. "Disobedience" through strikes and decisions contrary
to government intentions were frequent within the state institutions during the 1960s. After the coup of 1970, state institutions
were still inefficient and "soft" in the sense described by
Gunnar Myrdal for South Asia. Disobedience now met the government
mainly outside its state institutions. Government decisions were
difficult to implement. Companies did not pay taxes, the elite did
not obey new laws etc. But there was softness not only in relation
to the economically established groups. Government decisions contrary to the aims of the mass party, BCP, were impossible to carry
out. Occasionally the government met this problem with police repression. The repressive machinery was expanded in order to make
the inhabitants obey the government.

The existence of South African law inside Lesotho illustrates
how Lesotho is tied to South Africa: Since the Republic of South
Africa is an extremely legalistic society, changing its written
laws in accordance with the government policy, the new laws pre-

pared by the expertise provided by the South African government are of particular interest. We have seen that the kind of laws introduced were largely security laws and laws allowing for capital investments in Lesotho.

The growth of state institutions expected with a dependence approach did not occur as fast as expected in comparison with other post-colonial societies. Recruitment of state employees was slow, only 1-2 per cent. This can be explained partly by the British aid conditions. Another restriction was also noticeable. The majority of the educated inhabitants supported the opposition parties and were therefore considered security risks by the government. "Disobedience" in the civil service made the government suspect even its own state employees. Important decisions were prepared by advisers from outside and from foreign companies and governments. The relative ease with which the government was able to recruit technical assistance abroad resulted in an increase of the proportion of foreigners inside as well as outside the state institutions.

The most remarkable change affecting the character of state institutions after independence was the rapid increase in financial resources at the disposal of the government. Most of these resources came from foreign aid agencies. Drastic changes in the organization of public administration also occurred. In the countryside, aid projects tended to dominate the surrounding areas as all resources were concentrated on projects. Chiefs, foreign aid personnel and policemen controlled larger and larger areas in the countryside at the expense of the villagers, who had earlier participated in the control via co-operatives and elected committees.

But there was a marked increase of the number of subject areas in which the post-colonial state institutions were involved. However, labour recruitment and wool/mohair exports were still outside the control of the government and the people in Lesotho. These areas are - as we have seen in chapter 2 - the sectors which mainly define the relation between Lesotho and the rest of the international capitalist system. They are largely controlled by multinational companies based in South Africa and Europe.

5 Government Development Policies under Conditions of Unequal Integration

Many scholars define public policies as "whatever governments choose to do or not to do".[1] This definition has, however, been criticized: "In spite of what is often believed in the discussion ... governments do not choose their strategies".[2] This implies a view where public policies are determined by historical and structural conditions. In this case study, public policies are viewed as the result of both historically determined structural conditions and of the government's efforts to change these conditions, giving priority to self-chosen values. These values are of course also the result of historical and structural conditions. We have already discussed these conditions and the resulting political ideas. The aim of this chapter is to investigate the developmental priorities and actions of the government as well as the reactions to government development policies. Particular references are made to changes in foreign control of resources and administrative procedures. The present chapter contains a discussion on the declared development policies of the Lesotho government followed by two examples of their implementation.

Emphasis on Foreign Private Investment and Aid

After independence the government gave priority to security and the increase in state revenue. These activities are seen by the government as part of its development ambitions. The poor and stagnating economy in Lesotho is seen as the result of the limited economic relations with the outside world,[3] together with government restrictions on private investment.[4] Since independence the government has sought to create conditions favourable to foreign private investments.[5] Donor agencies provide a major part of state revenue and is channelled into fields which foreign private enterprises find profitable.

The government aims at economic independence and economic growth. Economic independence may be achieved through widened and diversified foreign economic relations. Economic growth is maintained through the actions of individuals. The government defines its own role as passive, stimulating the inflow of foreign private capital, and providing additional funds and know-how from donor agenices via its public funds to whatever opportunities private foreign capital finds profitable. It is claimed that social justice is secured via the land tenure system. Maximum domestic employment is sought through the natural growth of the economy, the indigenization of foreign posts in government and labour intensive so-called Food Aid Projects.[6]

In line with its general belief in non-interference with individual economic investment initiatives the government rarely publicly declares its development policies. The Five Year Plans are, however, often quoted in government speeches all over the country. We have, therefore, to turn mainly to these plans to find documentation on the declared aims of development. Tim Thahane, head of the Central Planning Office during the period 1970 to 1974, replied in the following way, when asked if the Lesotho government has any development policies of its own:

> Yes, of course. The government has accepted the Five-Year Plan. Every year we publish an evaluation of the year before and a list of the projects we are going to implement the coming year. The Development Plan is thus formed into concrete projects. We do not have policies stated except for the Five-Year Plan, but the Plan is very detailed and the projects are selected and implemented to fit the Plan.[7]

Although there were attempts to formulate a five-year development plan during the first four years after independence, the first plan was not published until December 1970.[8] This plan was mainly formulated by foreign advisors, but it was in line with general targets set in the BNP manifestos of 1965 and 1969.[9] This first plan became mainly a detailed recommendation on what further technical studies were needed, but contained also general priorities and a few detailed projects aiming at reaching the targets which had been given priority.

The government consciously attempts to avoid discussion of its priorities. The experience of public opposition during the first years of independence has strengthened the already existing inclination to present development as a technical matter, possible to delegate to experts rather than politicians.[10]

The government has met the internal opposition to its development policies by referring to foreign expertise. The Second Five-Year Development plan, published in 1975, states also: "Competent consultants on development possibilities and priorities have given their recommendations".[11]

During the first plan period the government had succeeded in reaching the targets of "raising more government revenue" whereas it failed in "providing more jobs in Lesotho and increasing local incomes".[12]

This is partly the result of conscious allocation of time and expenditure. High-ranking state employees travelled around the Western part of the world to raise more funds, whereas remaining state employees gave service to foreign missions visiting Lesotho to study possibilities of extending credits and technical assistance. In consequence the implementation of such projects tended to be neglected.[13]

Overall economic growth, planned to be 5 per cent per year, did not materialize according to unofficial estimates by the World Bank. There was, however, some growth in the sectors where foreign private capital chose to establish itself: in tourism, construction and commerce.[14] In its first plan, the government stressed that public funds to the agricultural sector would create employment. It stated that it expected "10,000 to 15,000 new employment opportunities mainly in non-agricultural activities".[15]

The target of job-creation was not reached. It was, according to the critics, not even planned for. Much was hoped by the government from a co-operation with the Republic of South Africa on building a hydro-electrical and/or irregation scheme, at the Malimabatso river in the North-West of Lesotho, serving South Africa with water. The government also hoped much from its pilot agricultural projects. The evaluation of such projects would give recommendations on what agricultural policies to follow.[16] The Leribe pilot project would, according to government declarations, not only give employment through new income earning possibilities, but also illustrate how productivity could be raised and production increased.[17] This turned out to be unrealistic.

The implementation of the Leribe project was left to the Food and Agricultural Organization (FAO), who financed the project together with the United Nations Development Programme (UNDP), later the Swedish International Development Authority (SIDA). The two principal chiefs were appointed by government to participate on the board of the project. They agreed with FAO on introducing scientific farming via this pilot project.

An increase in the cash crop part of production in Leribe was reached, and this was an old BNP aim, expressed in its 1965 manifesto. But employment in the project area decreased when productivity increased. More people migrated from this area than from other parts of Lesotho.[18] In 1973 and 1974 there was widespread and organized opposition among the villagers to the low degree of participation they were allowed. Village committees were not heard. Decisions concerning the villagers were taken by the project board and new farmer associations.[19] The villagers went to court to accuse the chiefs and a few others who had become "contractors" as part of the project. According to the villagers these contractors were getting a larger share in the existing share-cropping system than was rightfully theirs.[20] The villagers were given rights in a special investigation commission appointed by the government in 1974.[21] In its second development plan the government had second thoughts and gave up its plan to create more jobs in agriculture:

Employment will have to come in industry, commerce and tourism.[22]

These sectors of the economy are, however, to be left to the initiatives of future private investors from abroad. The government states again its intention to assist interested firms:

Everything possible will be done to foster expansion of private enterprise.[23]

The Lesotho National Development Corporation (LNDC) was given about half of the public funds, 80 out of totally 145 million Rand, for the period 1975 to 1980.[24] Leabua Jonathan declared in April

1975, at an aid donor conference in Maseru:

> We have always welcomed the participation of the private sector
> in the development of this country and the representatives gathe-
> red here can assure any potential investors that it is certainly
> not our policy to nationalize private investments.[25]

Jonathan also assured that "investors are by no means required
to use the services of the Corporation". LNDC has its prime target
to give service to interested foreign investors.[26]

Only lately has there been opposition from national capital.
The Basotho Traders Associations[27] reacted critically towards an
LNDC attempt in 1975 to establish a wholesale store in Maseru without their participation.[28] The government met this opposition with
a decision to establish a Basotho Enterprise Development Corporation (BEDCO) under the leadership of LNDC, and by ordering LNDC to
train interested Basotho to become managers and enterpreneurs in
LNDC subsidaries.[29] Since such managers generally have incomes
higher at present than most local enterprisers, it seems as if the
opposition was thus successfully met.

Lesotho, an Open Economy

At independence, Lesotho possesed an unusually open economy with
almost no restrictions on the flow of money, goods and labour
(see chapter 2). Subsequently, the government's policy has been
to increase the openness of the economy. Partly as a result of bargaining with South Africa, existing capital restrictions in connection with the lending of funds on the South African money market
have been lifted. Lesotho today lends out more money than ever
before to the development of the South African economy.[30] The government has also attempted to increase the security and favourable terms for foreign investors to establish themselves in Lesotho. In chapter 4 we saw that South African law makers were invited
to modernize the laws to bring them in conformity with company
laws performing in South Africa.

The country is not only integrated into the South African economy, but also into the Commonwealth and, as an associate member
since 1975, into the European Economic Community (EEC). The situation has been described as follows by the LNDC in one of its many
booklets published to attract private capital investment from
abroad:

> Lesotho has the entire South African market on its doorstep. It
> shares with South Africa the South African Rand... Lesotho has
> common customs tariffs and agreements with South Africa. There
> is no problem about repatriation of capital and profits, few
> immigration restrictions on staff... As a member of the British
> Commonwealth it can trade with all of Africa and the world on
> Commonwealth preference terms.[31]

In its ambition to apply a liberal policy, the government has
invited large efficient companies with a long tradition of techni-

cal skill and know-how at their disposal to compete with the few
local enterprises established during colonial rule, mainly in
commerce. The indigenous enterprises receive less favourable taxa-
tion and establishment terms. The Lomé Convention with the EEC
allows associated countries to protect their infant industries.
But the possibility to protect infant industries is more limited
according to the Customs Agreement with South Africa, Swaziland
and Botswana. Protection has only been efficient in handicraft.
The laws thus allow for greater protection also for other infant
industries.[32]

In relation to the Republic of South Africa the policy has
been to take up for discussion one area of formal decision-making
after the other. Where there was earlier only tacit understanding
of the principles, explicit bargaining rules have now been established. This policy may not have increased the powers of the
Lesotho government directly, but it has probably had the effect
of raising the level of consciousness. Earlier power relations
have been more openly confirmed. Examples of these are the Customs
and Excise Union agreement of 1969,[33] the Monetary Union agreement of 1974,[34] and also a whole range of agreements at lower levels of inter-government consultations concerning maize, wool,
mohair, wheat and other production levies, soil conservation
plans and labour recruitment.[35] The conclusion is that the Lesotho
government has established itself as a formal decision-making unit
accepted by the South African government within its regional
plan.[36]

It is interesting to make a brief comparison of the Lesotho
development plan with that of South Africa. The South African
plan is more specific, more authoritarian and more sophisticated
than the Lesotho plan. It also covers areas of consequence for
the neighbouring nations. The Lesotho plan is written, it seems,
to fit into this broader framework. It stresses particularly the
regional decentralization aim of the South African development
plan. Peripheral regions should, according to the South African
development plan, be given the chance to have industries and become integrated into the dynamic and expanding part of the South
African economy. Encouragement to private investors who want to
establish industries is given in much the same way as the Lesotho
plan indicates. Thus, the plan states, more jobs might be created
while keeping the same broad aims at the South African government.[37] Actual developments in Lesotho demonstrate that employment has not increased. The protectionist and regulatory orienta-
tion explicit in the South African plan is, however, not part of
the Lesotho plan philosophy. As already mentioned, the Lesotho
government considers regulations as obstacles to development po-
tentials in Lesotho.

Cheap black labour is a basic comparative advantage for the
South African economy in relation to other industrialized countries. The Lesotho government argues that it attempts to utilize
the same advantage.[38] Still, this is a major argument in LNDC
pamphlets. But a low wage policy in Lesotho is in contradiction
with its industrialization aims, since there is not enough labour

in Lesotho at the present low wages. Since wages are higher in South Africa there is an economic incentive for workers to migrate additional to all structural obstacles mentioned.

A low-wage policy in Lesotho is, however, in line with the South African plan. The risk of a shortage of labour is stressed as being dangerous to the low-wage policy in South Africa. In planning for the continued supply of low-wage labour, the South African plan counts on Lesotho as a source of migrant labour. Its plan stresses particularly the danger of a shortage of skilled labour.[39] The Lesotho plan includes a plan to increase training of its own people, but since there is no plan for absorbtion of trained people within Lesotho it seems as if they were planned to be exported to South Africa.

During the period 1973 to 1976 the South African employers who depend on foreign migrant labour have shifted areas of recruitment. This has been a strategy enforced by political changes in Mozambique and Angola and a reaction to the stoppage of labour migration from Malawi to South Africa.[40] Lesotho has grown in importance as a labour reserve, at the same time as total recruitment of foreign migrant workers has decreased. Wages increased as a result of increased recruitment within South Africa.[41] Mine labour recruitment within Transkei increased with the same percentage as within Lesotho.[42] Thus, we can distinguish a new pattern of labour reserves.

The Lesotho government policy has been to refer to the advantage of the increase in wages in South Africa.[43] In practice it has encouraged more of its people than ever to work in South Africa. Lesotho and Transkei have become the two most important reserves for mine labour. South African mining industry has thus increased its dependence on these two areas, at the same time as it attempts to slowly change to more capital intensive production.[44] South Africa lets the Lesotho state pay the costs of education, health and pensions, while taking advantage of the increase in the economically active population. In this way the Lesotho government expenditure is accomodated to suit the South African mine interests. Now a larger amount of money is passing via Lesotho as a result of compensations according to the Customs Union Agreement (1970), the Monetary Agreement (1974) and as a result of the Migrants' Deferred Pay Agreement (1975), without, so far, increasing local incomes or employment.

The Lesotho government has not interfered with the system of labour recruitment which has existed almost since colonization. South African recruitment firms recruit workers within Lesotho via a large number of offices and agents.

There are no published statistics on where migrant labour from Lesotho works, nor in what· capacities, although such investigations are in progress. The following list of recruitment firms includes the South African organizations with offices in Lesotho. These keep statistics of the numbers officially recruited mainly to the mines.[45] No Lesotho based recruitment organization is operating and individual job seekers are not recorded.

Table 5.1. *Recruiting Organizations in Lesotho*

	ACRO*	ARC	NCOLA	MLO (NRC)
Name of broker	African Central Recruiting Organization	Amalgamated Recruiting Corporation	Natal Coal Owners Labour Organization	Mine Labour Organization (Native recruiting corporation)
Type of employment	Coal mines Coal industries in Orange Free State	Gold and manufacturing	Coal mines and coal industries in Natal	Mines in the Johannesburg area

* Before 1963 the organization was called FRO, Frasers' recruiting organization.

Source: Lesotho Telephone Directory

As in Transkei, the mine workers are recruited via a network of offices with agents in every village. These agents are often miners themselves on home leave between contracts. At the offices there are health controls, passport and contract arrangements.[46] Since 1974 the government requires the recruitment firms to pay a small fee per contracted worker. This will be discussed in the next section of this chapter.

The largest employer in South Africa and also the largest employer of the officially recruited mine workers from Lesotho (estimated at about 80 per cent) is the Oppenheimer group.[47] Anton Rupert's Rembrandt group is another large employer. It is in fact believed to be one of the largest in South Africa, but does not publish any figures.[48] The Rembrandt group, containing for example breweries and textile firms, is believed to employ a large number of workers from Lesotho under the exemption rules from the apartheid laws.[49]

Multinationals as the Motor of Economic Growth

The Lesotho government has sought to reach its aim of economic growth through increased contacts with large and expanding firms. From 1967 onwards, tax shelter is given to foreign firms that want to establish themselves in tourism, construction or manufacturing. The tax shelter provides for

a. Complete exemption from company income tax for the first six years of operation or

b. Deduction of specified allowance from company income for the purpose of calculating company income tax. These provisions allow a manufacturer to deduct from his taxable income 145 per cent of the cost of machinery and equipment brought into use and an immediate

deduction of 75 per cent of new building costs with an additional
5 per cent during the next 20 years of cooperation. Other deduc-
tions relate to the cost of new housing for employees, wages paid
to Lesotho citizens, educational expenses, water, sewerage facilities, transport and iron and electric power.[50]

The reasoning behind the government's decision on a tax shelter
- and the establishment of the LNDC - was that the government considered the lack of economic growth during the colonial period to
be due primarily to a lack of capital and private enterprise. This
was blamed on interference from the governments of Britain and
South Africa. The Lesotho government is therefore determined to
let private foreign capital expand in whatever sector is considered profitable.

The interest to invest in Lesotho has been extremely low in
spite of the efforts exerted by the government to attract foreign
capital. Anton Rupert, the leading Afrikaaner industrialist has
written:

> In the belief that the multinational corporation even more than
> the geographically confined "local" business undertaking, has
> responsibilities far beyond the mere attaining of profit objec-
> tives, the multinational entrepreneur seeks to establish brid-
> ges of partnership, such as those erected by our group between
> capital and educations, capital and sport, capital and art,
> capital and culture. For these reasons too we are seeking ties
> of better understanding with our neighbour states.[51]

The results of the contacts established between the Lesotho
government and multinational corporations have been joint ventures,
where the government provides most of the capital and the multinational provide management, know-how and wider international contacts.[52] Both the Rupert and the Oppenheimer groups are, for example, in the vanguard of the South African government's "outward
looking" policy. They are in turn recipients (in the Republic of
South Africa) of large foreign capital investments from the United
States and Western Europe. They also have investments in many other
countries of the world. Although, South African-based, they do not
depend on strictly South African capital.[53] Still there are very few
cases of actual capital transfer from large private firms to Lesotho.

There is, however, another interest expressed by the Lesotho
government when tu   g to the managers of large multinational
firms. These are seen as powerful personal friends and advisors,
useful as partners in bargaining with the South African government.[54] In 1970 the managers of the Rupert-Rembrandt and the
Oppenheimer groups were mentioned as "friends who have stood by
in times of crisis".[55] In this case, and possibly also in other
cases, the support from these firms has been used against the
radicals among the people of Lesotho.

There is in Lesotho a tradition of playing off different interests in Europe and South Africa against each other to gain fa-
vours for Lesotho. Leabua Jonathan refers to Moshoeshoe the Great,
when arguing that more contacts with Europe strengthens Lesotho
in relation to South Africa. After independence in 1966, the

government saw its main conflict in relation to Great Britain.[56]
The conflict concerned the degree of priority that should be given
industrialization. Britain wanted to give Lesotho aid for infra-
structural development mainly, whereas the Lesotho government
wanted to start industrialization immediately and much faster than
the British aid administrators thought wise. Representatives of the
British government aid agency, Overseas Development Agency (ODA),
criticized particularly the invitation of South African businessmen as advisors to the Lesotho government.[57]

A reason for deteriorating diplomatic relations between Lesotho
and South Africa during the 1970s has been the question of setting
up industries in Lesotho. According to the Minister of Finance,
E. R. Sekhonyana, and the managers of LNDC several incidents have
occurred where foreign industrial giants wanted to set up subsidiaries in Lesotho, but were rejected because of pressure from
South Africa.[58] The examples of such incidents given are: a Japanese motor assembly plant, an Italian shoe factory, a West German
television assembly plant and a mill.[59] Exactly how this pressure
was applied is not easy to determine. Telephone calls from the
Ministry of Planning in Pretoria to the head of LNDC and the Ministers in the Lesotho government are mentioned as channels of
communication.[60] South African security interests are mentioned
as reasons for the South African pressure, but it is possible also
that firms experiencing competition in South Africa have protested
via the South African Ministries. The case of the Japanese investment application is interesting, since the government of Japan
has forbidden investments in the Republic of South Africa, because
of apartheid. If one firm had been allowed into Lesotho, possibly
many firms would have followed.

There are, however, a few multinational corporations with investments in Lesotho. Two of these established themselves prior
to independence; The *Anglo-American/De Beers* corporation recruiting mine workers from Lesotho long before independence and in-
vesting in diamond mining in 1975; and the *Fraser and Son, Retail
and Wholesale* with a near monopoly in commerce. The *Rembrandt
Corporation* is another important multinational after independence.
It supplies managers to LNDC subsidiaries and has ownership in the
Economic Development (Bank) for Equatorial and Southern Africa
(EDESA) established in 1973 in Lesotho. Neither EDESA nor the
Rembrandt group transferred capital to Lesotho.[61] *Holiday Inn* had
the monopoly in the rapidly expanding tourism sector from 1970
until 1974, when the government signed an agreement with the
Hilton Corporation.

The main similarity between these firms is that they are large
and belong to companies that expand in Southern Africa. With
the exception of Hilton and Holiday Inn they each control a distinct sector of the Lesotho economy and therefore do not compete
directly. They all have frequent and cordial contacts with the
government of Lesotho through personal visits by their top managers.[62]

The relation between the government on the one hand and the
companies of Anglo-American/De beers and Rupert-Rembrandt on the

other will be partly illustrated in the section where the imple-
mentation of the government's development policies is examplified.
Here I will, however, mention the expansion of Frasers and Holiday
Inn.

An Expanding Multinational in Trade

By far the biggest retail trader with a monopoly of wholesale
trade in Lesotho is the British multinational Alex Fraser and Son.
The Fraser family established themselves in diamond mining as
early as the 1870s in Kimberley, in the Boer Republic, but expanded in commerce mainly. Frasers was one of many trading companies
established in Basutoland during the colonial period.[63] Only during the 1960s did this firm manage to buy out several South
African based traders - Nolan, Hyland and others.[64] During the
1970s Frasers have expanded also by controlling hundreds of cafés
earlier owned individually by Basotho.[65] Frasers has about 300
large stores in the Republic of South Africa. About 60 stores in
Lesotho are organized under separate subsidary under the South
African subsidiary of the British Frasers.[66] Frasers in Britain
also have the largest share in a large assurance company, Protea,
with a South African subsidiary,[67] which in turn established a
branch in Lesotho as early as 1930.[68]
   In 1973 and 1974 the government nationalized trade in wool,
mohair, livestock and crops. This was done after the South African
government decided on the same policy change.[69] (See chapter 2.)
In Lesotho it was, however, presented as an isolated government
initiativ. Earlier, Frasers and other travelling South African
brokers had earned quite large profits, 30 per cent, on buying
agricultural produce and giving credit on food and manufactured
goods to the producers.[70] In Lesotho the Ministry of Agriculture and its Livestock and Crop Marketing Corporations act as the
main brokers. The agents of these state corporations can offer an
higher price than the private traders used to pay, according to
their own estimates.[71] Frasers and other private traders immediately increased their prices on manufactured goods and food to com-
pensate for losses caused by nationalization.[72] Inflation of about
20-30 per cent was experienced in Lesotho as well as in the Transkei
and other mainly black rural areas where the same reaction from
traders followed the take-over. The inflation in these areas was
5-10 per cent higher than in the urban areas of South Africa.[73]
The expected increase in rural incomes was thus consumed by
higher living expences.

An Expanding Multinational in Tourism

The tourist sector was the fastest growing sector of the Lesotho
economy during the 1970s, mainly due to the opening of Holiday Inn
and Hilton Hotel in Maseru, Hilton was invited to compete with the
Holiday Inn. 110,000 tourists visited Lesotho in 1972, compared

with 3,000 in 1968.[74] Both multinational firms had changing share-
holders on the international bond market. Both have drawn mainly
on Lesotho government capital.[75] Examples of such government in-
vestments with foreign management in addition to hotel bedrooms
are:
- Casinos, restaurants, conference rooms, cinemas, boutiques
- Travel bureau, taken over from a British firm
- One old hotel with a restaurant and bottle store
- A shopping centre in Maseru (a joint venture with the South
  African insurance company Sanlam)
- Housing for its foreign employees
- Investments in the old Maseru club
- Lodges at Oxbow, the "mountain road" and the Senqonyane falls.[76]
  The expansion of the tourist sector has resulted in rapidly in-
creasing imports.[77] The government revenue from tourism has been
mainly its share of customs on imports.[78] But a change in policy
was decided in 1975, when a levy on the casino incomes was introduced.[79] The increase in employment during 1970 to 1975 as a result of the expanding tourist sector is estimated at 1,200 including employment in construction.[80] This was in fact three quarters
of the total number of new jobs created during this time period.
This represents an increase in comparison with the first years
after independence and should be offset against the more than
corresponding decrease in the number of those employed in agriculture and diamond mining.[81] (See appendix II.)

Increased State Revenue and Aid

A remarkable increase in state revenue took place after independence, as mentioned earlier. But what changes took place in the
distribution of the sources of state revenue?
    The Lesotho government accounting system differentiates be-
tween capital and current revenue. Fifty-eight per cent of current accounts revenue in 1971/1972 were derived from the country's
share in the customs revenue pool. In the same year 90 per cent
of the capital revenue accounts were derived from foreign aid.[82]
(See also table 5.3 p. 112 for 1974/75.) In his budget speech over
the radio in 1971, the Minister of Finance, Peete Peete, said
that the position of his government was determined largely by
the financial and economic policies of the Republic of South
Africa and by the international economic fluctuations, over which
Lesotho had no control. There was, however, a reduction in the
budget deficit from 6 million Rand just after independence in
1966 to 1 million Rand four years later. This was, according to
the Minister of Finance, "an achievement which deserved publicity".[83]
    What are the tendencies in the structure of state revenue
during the years before and after independence? Until 1957/1958
the government budget was balanced. In that year overall expenditure matched domestic revenue at the low level of 3.5 million.
No additional financial resources from outside the territory
were provided.[84] Thereafter, demands to increase welfare for the

inhabitants became louder and these were gradually met with increased expenditure. Preparations for independence were made. State expenditure for administration and infrastructure also increased and
expenditure now exceeded domestic revenue.[85]

The domestic revenue of the government remained at a low level
in real terms after the 1950s. During 1966 to 1972, it was possible
to counter inflation by more efficient tax collection methods and
slight increases in tax rates. There were at least two reasons for
the stagnation of domestic revenue:

1. The wages of the migrant workers in the Republic did not increase in real terms until 1971/1972, after demands from the workers' representatives had been put forward. Large strikes among
the migrant workers in the mines and industries in 1973 and 1974
resulted in another wage increase. But the increases although real
(not only nominal) were only marginal.[86] They were mainly a compensation for the rapid inflation during the preceding five year
period. In 1975, the wages of state employees in lower categories,
teachers and technicians, were increased in Lesotho. This was the
first general increase since independence.[87]

2. Prices of the biggest export products (wool, mohair and diamonds) fell on the world market. The decreases did not stop until
1972-1973, when a stable floor price was set by the new producers'
cartels established during these years.[88]

The three largest sources of revenue for the state, foreign
aid excluded, are customs revenue, taxes from migrant workers, and
levies on wool and mohair. The levy is received via the South
African Wool and Mohair Boards as a percentage on sales at the international market of Port Elizabeth. The customs revenue is decided in negotiations with South Africa and the other members of
the Customs Union.

During the last five years of colonial rule and the first eight
years of independence, Great Britain compensated Lesotho for the
decifit between increasing expenditure and stagnant revenue. Before
independence this was done through an automatic system of compensation to cover the deficit, whatever size it was. The deficit
continued to grow during the first few years after independence
and was then covered by the Overseas Development Agency (ODA) in
London. This system was called "grants-in-aid" and remained until
1973/1974,[89] when the state budget was again balanced - at a
higher level - through increased shares in the customs revenue.
This was administrated by the Republic according to an agreement
signed in 1970.

During the first full budgetary year after independence, in
1967/1968, the overall budgetary deficit amounted to 9 million
Rand, which was 65 per cent of the total expenditure.[90] Looking
at the revenue side, we find that the customs revenue, which is
distributed after yearly meetings between the Customs Union
partners,constitutes a sum of 10,6 million out of a total expenditure of 13,5 million Rand. Thus, almost 80 per cent was administered via South Africa.[91] Part of the remaining 20 also were
channeled via the Republic since the tax collection office for
migrant workers was situated in Johannesburg, but administered

by Lesotho state employees. The wool and mohair levy was paid via
the Republic's Wool and Mohair Boards until a reform in 1975, when
it was paid directly to the Ministry of Agriculture in Lesotho.

The possibility to increase domestic revenue by fiscal measures
was limited, according to the government's economic advisor in
1966, Professor Owen Horwood from the University of Durban[92] (In
1975 he was appointed Minister of Finance in the Republic of South
Africa). Well-to-do people were few and none were extremely rich
and an increase in tax rates was not considered possible. The government depended on this small group for support and administration.

In 1970, a more efficient tax collection procedure - "pay as
you earn", similar to the system introduced later on for the blacks
in the Republic - was applied in Lesotho. This was done on recommendations by Professor Horwood and experts from the International
Monetary Fund (IMF). The procedure was well implemented and helped
the government to survive when the British Labour government delayed its aid to the country for a period of nearly six months
after the coup d'état in 1970.[93]

But tax revenues in relation to the total state revenues are
small in Lesotho. The revenue from company tax is particularly
small. The tax rate is 37.5 per cent compared to 45 in the Republic. The foreign enterprises established in Lesotho after independence enjoy very favourable terms including eight years of
"tax holiday". In fact, many of the old enterprises do not pay
any taxes at all. They have not been punished for this so far.[94]
The revenue from company tax is exceeded by the revenue from income tax in Lesotho, which is unusual for an African country.
Another reason for this situation is the fact that the economy
of Lesotho is based on wage labour to an extremely high degree.

I have mentioned earlier that the BCP-controlled District Councils administered voluntary funds of migrant labour savings for
investment in their respective districts until 1966, when the BNP
government abolished these funds.[95]

In 1974, the government agreed with the South African mine recruitment companies in Lesotho that these should pay a fixed
amount of money per contract worker to the government. In 1975
the amount was ten Rand per contract, but this figure has increased since then. Thus the government received a new source of income.[96] For 100,000 contracts a year, the government receives at
least one million Rand. Even if the fee per worker is low, this
income is not negligible in comparison with taxes, customs and
aid.

A crucial increase in state revenue resulted from a re-negotia-
tion of the Customs Union Agreement originally reached in 1910.
In 1965, negotiations took place between the Republic and the colonial power which resulted in a decrease from 0.92 to 0.5 per cent
in Basutoland's share of the customs revenue pool administered by
the Republic. In 1969, new negotiations were held and a formula
was set up to make the income fluctuate with the imports of the
customs union partners. This resulted in a large increase in Leso-
thos's share from 1970/1971 onwards.[97]

According to the formula agreed on, the more Lesotho imported
from outside the Customs Union, the more it earned from the Customs
Union pool. However, Lesotho did not directly control its customs
revenue on imports into the country. This control was exercised by
South Africa at the borders. Very delicate bargaining goes on between the Customs Union partners, the main principle being that the
small neighbour countries should prove in figures the compensation
they are entitled to from the common pool of customs and excise
collected by the Republic. Better record-keeping of imports at the
borders of Lesotho and closer co-operation with Botswana and Swaziland resulted in another increase of revenue for Lesotho in 1972/
1973.[98] In the following year compensation for incorrect calcula-
tions during earlier years resulted in yet another increase. The
formula for dividing the shares between the partners was complicated. Each partner country presented its own records on actual imports. Therefore, there was room for bargaining each year. In the
period after 1974, a totally new and unpredicted effect of the
formula was experienced by Lesotho.[99] The denominator of the formula contains an estimate of South African imports, which suddenly
increased more than the imports of the neighbour countries. This
disproportionate growth was due to a rise in oil prices as well
as rapidly increasing imports of arms in connection with the war
against the MPLA in Angola. The cumulative result was an adverse
effect on the Lesotho share of the customs revenue instead of the
increases expected earlier.[100]

Lesotho, Botswana and Swaziland experienced similar decreases
in their shares according to the Customs Union formula agreed upon
in 1970 by all the Customs Union partners. These three small countries co-operated in the bargaining process in 1975.[101] Skilful
bargaining and this co-operation were the probable reasons for
the more favourable terms obtained that year. The general political situation during the South African war against Angola and the
risk for opposition against the war from the Customs Union partners might have been other reasons why South Africa admitted more
favourable terms than the formula allowed for.

On the other hand, there is always a possibility for the Republic to neglect the demands and delays or refuse to pay out the
shares to smaller partners in the Custom Union. The government of
Lesotho has obvious difficulties in planning revenue in advance.
This results in difficulties to plan expenditure and makes the
Lesotho government vulnerable. Often unpredictable revenue from
foreign aid agencies has the same effect. The South African
"strings" attached to the Customs Union revenue payments are
difficult to pin-point because of the confidential nature of the
bargaining process.

The customs revenue estimated for 1973/1974 was 14.6 million
Rand.[102] But the revenue actually received was only slightly
higher than the year before, 8.9 million Rand. The reason for
the decrease in 1973/1974 was a 17.5 per cent devaluation of the
common currency and an inflation of 10-20 per cent. In 1974/1975
the estimated customs revenue was 10.9 million Rand, but the
actual revenue now rose to 17.3 million Rand. In 1975/1976, it

Table 5.2. *Government Budgetary Position, 1957/58 to 1980/81 (in Millions of Rand and Maloti)*

Current revenue	1957/58	1965/66	1974/75	1978/79	1980/81
Current revenue	3.2	10.3	26.7	80.5	104.3
of which Customs and Exise Taxes	–	–	12.2	–	50.3
(Transfers from abroad including Customs and Exise Taxes)	(0.4)	(6.7)			
Current expenditure	2.3	8.5	17.6	47.2	104.6
Current deficit/surplus	+ 0.9	+ 1.8	9.1	33.3	
Capital expenditure	0.9	2.4	5.6	19.3	62.2
overall deficit			3.5	– 6.0	– 62.5
Financing deficit/surplus	0	– 0.6			
Grants			3.2	11.5	21.2
External loans			1.4	2.5	14.3
Internal loans			0.6	0.6	27.0
Change in Cash balance (increase-)			– 8.7	– 8.6	–
Total current and capital expenditure	3.7	10.9	23.2	86.5	166.8
Capital Revenue	0.3	0.7	10.0		

Source: National Accounts of Lesotho, July 1983

unexpectedly dropped again to the level of 1973/1974.[103] This was immediately re-negotiated with a better result.

The same irregular pattern can be seen in the revenue from foreign aid agencies. In 1970, after the coup d'état, aid from Great Britain and the Scandinavian countries was not payed out due to the unstable political situation. It was delayed for almost six months. A slow increase in aid started in 1972. In spite of the continually unstable political situation in 1974, a large increase in aid from international agencies and governments in Europe and North America started from that year onwards.

Information about the coup d'état that prevented the winning party in the election from taking power in 1970 was spread not only inside the country, but also via mass media in Europe and the United States. In 1974, however, the news about uprisings and violent repression in Northern Lesotho were efficiently silenced abroad.[104] Even within the country, these events were not officially discussed. All foreign journalists were prevented from entering the country unless they had a special permit from the Prime Minister's secretary. Local journalists were either censored or arrested if they did not follow censorship rules. About two months later did a South African journalist report via the BBC about shooting that had taken place at Mapoteng, Peka and two other villages. More than 200 people had been killed by the police. This information was at first denounced as South African propaganda by the Lesotho government, but later admitted.[105]

Foreign aid increased from 500 million Rand in 1973/1974 to 10 million Rand in 1974/1975. In the following year, it rose to 30 million Rand. The government of Lesotho has shown a remarkable capacity to obtain aid during a period when violently repressive methods were applied against the majority party. The BCP had conducted anti-government protest campaigns within the country without success. After 1975, the BCP started a campaign in exile to demand that aid to the Lesotho government should be frozen.

Observers both within and outside Lesotho have been surprised at the surplus money available in Lesotho as a consequence of successful revenue raising and expenditure saving policies of the government during the first decade of independence.[106] However, there is still little noticeable change in living conditions as a result of government expenditure. The government was anxious to cut expenses. This hit particularly general social welfare and infrastructure in rural areas with the exception of certain roads. Much money is spent on hotels, government buildings and financial transactions abroad to increase yields on state revenue.

The increase in state revenue from sources abroad is a result of the amount of time spent by state employees on contracts with donor agencies. This allocation of time enforced by the government has its causes but also its effects on development policies. Some obvious causes are:

1. The political weakness of the government makes it difficult to raise state revenue internally.
2. The political weakness makes it difficult to change expenditure policies. Activities by state employees to spend public money mostly meet opposition.

Both the weakness of the government and its general ideology work for revenue raising abroad. Some effects of this are:
1. The government tends to widen its contacts abroad, particularly when faced with internal opposition.
2. The government tends to accept conditions set for increased revenue. Changes in the expenditure pattern have occurred as result of such conditions.

The government strategy has been to get aid from as many Western countries as possible to diversify the risk of foreign political mobilization against donations to Lesotho. The table below gives a picture of the agencies involved in giving aid to Lesotho. They are ranked in their order of importance.

The government's change in foreign policy towards closer co-operation with liberation movements of Southern Africa and the frontline state governments had effects on donor aid. Not only Scandinavian donors and East European governments started to give aid. Also the US and the UN agencies slowly increased development aid.

Maybe unintentionally this reorientation of the Lesotho government was strongly backed by the youth of Lesotho particularly young miners and other migrants with similar experiences as the Soweto young protesters.

From being described as an anti-communist, ultra-conservative regime in 1974 it was possible to describe it as completely the opposite ten years later. Still, this foreign policy image was isolated from practical internal development policies.

Table 5.3. *Percentage Distribution of Foreign Official Assistance (disbursements) to Lesotho from Different Donors 1975, 1979 and 1983*

	1975	1979	1983
United Kingdom	45	22	9
Sweden	7	5	1
Canada	5	6	3
United States	5	14	27
Denmark	4	6	1
Germany, Fed. Rep.	2	6	5
Rep. of South Africa	2	?	?
International Organizations	30	31	52
Other bilateral Donors		10	2
Total Percent	100	100	100
Total Rand	11,9		
Total US$		65,3	223,8

Source: UNDP and Planning Office Maseru, and OECD/DAC Figures

Two Examples of Implementation of Government Development Policies

So far we have discussed the declarations of the government on its
development aims and some decisions taken in line with these declarations. The government's greatest problem is no longer a lack
of revenue or information. It is a lack of implementation of its
policies. We have seen earlier that this problem of implementation is crucially related to the lack of political support for
the government. This is seen also in the following two examples
of the government's development policies. The two examples are
financial institutions and *diamond mining*. The government considers its policies in these two areas as generally more successful
than in other areas. The diamonds in Lesotho are the largest
known mineral resource, and money is a resource created by the
government's policy of revenue raising. Both examples are therefore strategic parts of development policies. I do not, however,
claim to give examples of average development policies in Lesotho.

Financial Institutions

Lesotho is not a poor country from the point of view of money.
There is a lot of money in circulation. The savings of individual
wage earners, co-operatives, commercial enterprises and government, are considerable and progressively growing. But, there is
"nowhere to invest it" according to the commercial bankers' estimates. The deposits collected by financial institutions in Lesotho are transferred largely as investment to South Africa. [107]
Since there are hardly any institutional arrangements for long-
term credits, it is difficult to estimate the potential for a
higher return on capital in Lesotho. But lack of savings is not
an obstacle to development. It is not the reason for the lack of
investment in Lesotho and probably never has been. Capital was
also present before independence, but it was transferred mainly
to South Africa.
    Only in 1974 did Lesotho, on IMF recommendation, introduce
legislation on financial institutions. Earlier, banks and other
financial institutions operated without reference to any laws. [108]
The existing regulations dated from 1865 and 1879. They were
generally considered outmoded and unenforceable. An IMF-sponsored
Registrar of financial institutions was appointed by the government in 1975. According to him "it will take another ten years
to modernize the financial laws of Lestoho, just as lengthy a
period as it has taken the South African government-sponsored
experts on company law to modernize Lesotho's business laws". [109]
    Lesotho had no Central Bank and shared as mentioned a common
currency until 1980 (when a Monetary authority was decided and
the "Maloti" was exchanged for the "Rand") with the Republic of
South Africa and Swaziland. Botswana decided to introduce its
own currency in 1976-1977. It was not until 1974 that an agreement was signed between the partners in the Rand Monetary Area.

Still, however, the Customs Union partners are highly dependent on the Rand monetary unit. According to this agreement Lesotho is compensated for the losses made through sharing its currency with the other countries.[110] Lesotho still transfers most of the deposits in the Lesotho banks. Not only the savings of residents in Lesotho but also the funds provided by aid agencies, customs union revenue funds and other funds are transferred to the Republic for investments there. This tendency existed already during the colonial period, but the funds lent out to South Africa are much larger today.

The bulk of deposits in Lesotho is with the three commercial banks: The Standard Bank, Barclay's Bank (both international banks with headquarters in London), and the Lesotho Bank. The Standard Bank established an office in the country during the 1930s and Barclay's Bank set up an office during the 1950s. Both banks were divisions under the Orange Free State branches of the South African Banks. Only after 1973 did the Lesotho divisions of these banks become separate branches under the British mother banks. This was as a result of a new South African law, which forbade foreign divisions of national banks[111] and was not a demand of the government of Lesotho. The new Lesotho branches of the British banks still continued to have most of their contacts with the respective branches in South Africa. The government of Lesotho uses the Lesotho Standard Bank for its deposits. Government revenue includes quarterly customs revenue compensation and the above-mentioned compensation for sharing a common currency as well as aid donations and loans from Western countries and international organizations. Barclay's Bank is the second biggest bank and receives savings from traders and individuals.

In 1972, the Lesotho Bank was appointed by the government to become a Development Bank for long-term credits to develop trade, industry, tourism, mining and agriculture. It never started because of lack of management. In 1974 the government changed its decision. The policy was now to establish a purely commercial bank, including provision for foreign currency operations. The government provided R 1 million in addition to funds transferred from the former Post Office Savings Bank.[112]

The reason given by the government for the new decision was that there was a need for competition in the field of commercial banking. The most profitable operations were to be found on the short-term money market. Such a market had been provided by the Monetary Agreement, which allowed the partners in the Rand Monetary Area to offer short-term credits on the money market of Johannesburg.

In December 1974 the government decided on a law of a "Deferred Pay Fund" (DPF). This system was planned to start immediately, but was delayed a year since there were forceful protests from the mine workers, who were concerned by the decision but not consulted. According to the law suggested by government, the mine workers would be forced to save 60 per cent of their wages in the Lesotho Bank. It was unclear who would get the interest on the money saved, but the savings should be deposited under the contract period and then put at the disposal of the wage earners. Before the decision on a Deferred Pay Fund was taken, the migrant mine workers had on the average saved 60 per cent of their wages, if both the compulsory and the voluntary part of the savings were counted but the voluntary part varied widely. The mining companies administered the compulsory part of the savings which made up about 30 per cent of the wages. Neither the government nor the workers themselves received interest on this money. As partial compensation for this interest-free loan the mining companies provided health and social services to the workers. These services were stopped immediately as a result of the Lesotho government decision to introduce the DPF system.

When the DPF was announced by the government, the 4,000 workers went home on a week's strike. A 26-man delegation presented a petition to the Minister of Industry and Labour, Joel Moitse, containing the demands of the workers. They demanded:
 - A lower compulsory share than 60 per cent.
 - An interest not lower than the commercial banks gave and that the money should be lent only to projects approved by the workers representatives, giving employment for wages acceptable to repatriated miners.
 - The Lesotho Bank should be separated from the LNDC (the government had planned to make the LNDC a co-owner of the bank and have a common board for the two public enterprises).
 - No Deferred Pay Funds were to be lent out to LNDC projects.[113]
 - The workers should be allowed to take out their money whenever they wanted.

The suspicions of the workers were not without foundation. The LNDC had existed since 1967 and had during the eight years of its existence given new employment only to 700 Basotho, according to the estimates of the BFL, at low wages and with an extremely high capital/employment ratio.[114] According to the LNDC itself the increase in employment was 2,000.[115]

In spite of heavy government subsidies, several undertakings had gone bankrupt and managers were accused of having left the country with the cash of the companies. Only a few of the remaining enterprises ran on a profitable basis.[116] Several profitable and more labour intensive firms closed down as a result of repression from the government and competition from subsidized LNDC firms.[117] Paradoxically enough, these demands from the workers favour the generally high demand for capital in South Africa.

Since the workers had to pay costs of health and other services themselves they were forced to save individually or via insurance companies.[118] The Deferred Pay money is lent out by the Lesotho Bank on the Johannesburg short-term money market, to make it possible for the Bank to pay the miners the rate of return which they demand. The Lesotho Bank is forced in practice to lend 100 per cent of the Deferred Payments Fund at an interest rate above that paid for savings deposits. The Lesotho Bank management has not yet invested in projects giving employment at wages acceptable to the workers. The government has interfered for reasons of security. The Bank's suggestions that money should be invested in co-operatives of the kind started by the BCP was tur- ned down. These co-operatives were closed for political reasons by the government during the late 1960s and in 1970.[119] But the number of credit cooperatives increased steadily, some 85 such cooperatives were registered in 1985.

Table 5.4. *Miners Deferred Pay Fund (MDPF) with the Lesotho Bank 1975-84 (Rand and Maloti millions)* [120]

	Deferred Pay Deposits
Oct 1975	5.7
March 1981	22.8
March 1984	53.1

Source: Figures by Head of Lesotho Bank for 1975, and IMF report for 1981 and 1984.

Deposits in the Lesotho Bank did first not increase by more than a tenth of the expected increase. Estimates made by the Lesotho Chamber of Commerce before the DPF was introduced was that a total deposit of about 50 million Rand would be available at the end of 1975. In October the total DPF was only 5.7 million Rand.[121] Not until 1984 did the Miners Deferred Pay Fund reach 53.1 million Maloti (=Rand). One reason why the DPF was lower than expected was that the workers had success in their demand that employers should make wage payments quarterly, instead of the earlier nine months. Another reason was the strongly articulated opposition against all government activity which led to suspicion towards the Lesotho Bank. The workers transferred their savings to the Standard and Barclay's Banks, which increased their deposits. The "time deposits" in these banks give higher interest rates than the DPF. The workers got higher wages in cash as a consequence of successful strikes in the mines in 1973, 1974 and 1975. There was already a relatively wide spread habit to place money in long-term savings. Deposits of longer than ten years duration are not unusual.[122]

The three commercial banks lend out an average of 30 per cent of their deposits to residents in Lesotho. The Lesotho Bank cre- dits amount to a total of 50 per cent of the deposits, excluding the DPF. But since 100 per cent of DPF is transferred as credits

to South Africa, the average for the Lesotho Bank is 30 per cent,
the same as for the two international banks during the 1970s.[123]

Table 5.5. *Lesotho: Consolidate Commercial and Bank Statistics.*
(in thousands of Rand)

Assets	Dec 73	March 74	June 74	Sept 74	Dec 74	March 75	April 75	May 75	June 75
Reserves	1,162	422	498	514	1,667	606	689	451	707
Foreign assets	14,599	13,633	12,207	14,865	14,645	9,596	11,408	11,506	12,283
Claims on statutory bodies	946	1,129	1,936	1,383	1,568	1,412	1,429	2,186	2,096
Claims on private sector	5,741	6,933	7,562	8,008	9,209	10,229	10,410	10,396	10,616
Liabilities									
Demand deposits	4,710	3,599	4,165	5,311	6,018	5,668	5,336	5,784	6,785
Savings and time deposits	13,386	14,632	14,412	14,491	14,920	15,115	15,469	15,792	15,730
Government deposits (net)	1,222	2,532	4,009	5,087	6,142	337	728	1,391	1,355
Foreign liabilities	4,706	1,774	74	374	513	12	603	729	972
Other items (net)	1,576	420	457	495	504	711	1,770	843	860

Source: Registrar of Financial Institutions

Insurance companies and building societies, all South African
based[124] but with agents in Lesotho, invest almost 100 per cent
in the Republic even after 1973, when insurance companies were
allowed to invest in Lesotho after a change of law in South Africa.
Largely due to the companies own rules requiring that investments
should be made in privately owned land, the change in South African law had no effect. The South African private building societies have stated that once a change in Lesotho's land tenure law
is enacted, funds will immediately become available. Loans to
individuals are at present given for the purpose of urban residental construction. The same practice is applied by the commercial banks. A large number of individuals and co-operatives in
Lesotho place their savings in the above-mentioned insurance
companies and Building Societies. There are no figures on the
size of this kind of deposit but the head of the Lesotho Standard Bank Branch estimated them as "quite substantial".[125]
    This general tendency to invest outside the country was not
followed by the Co-operative Credit Unions, which lent out 80
per cent of deposits locally. In 1972 the credit co-operatives
had 14,225 members with about R 300,000 in deposits. There were
46 Co-operative Credit Unions in 1972.[126] In 1975 the number of
credit co-operatives considered as viable had increased to 75.
They had joined in a Co-operative Credit League. The exact a-
mount in deposit in 1975 is not known, but according to the
Financial Registrar it could not be more than 1 per cent of
total deposits.[127]
    Basil Muzorewas' detailed study of financial institutions in
the period 1968 to 1972 shows that the co-operatives differed
from the commercial financial institutions in their credit pattern. The co-operatives lent out 80 per cent locally to rural
inhabitants. They also offered long-term credits to a greater

extent. They gave credits to productive activities within the
country as well as to housing.

Table 5.6. *Lesotho Co-operative Credit Union Loan Distribution
by Purpose*

Purpose	1970		1971	
	Amount (Rands)	% of Total	Amount (Rands)	% of Total
Agriculture	7,323	27	6,393	22
Trade and Transport	5,381	20	5,082	18
Building	2,489	9	4,244	15
Education	2,114	8	4,494	16
Medication	1,582	6	1,473	5
Food, Clothing, Furniture and Household Articles	4,446	17	3,293	12
Marriage	1,635	6	1,749	6
Repayment of Depts elsewhere	942	3	1,016	4
Miscellaneous	999	4	681	2
Total	R26,911	100	R28,425	100

Source: Muzorewa, B.[128]

Muzorewa draws the conclusion that these Cooperative Credit
Unions are the kind of institutions that should get more support
from government if its intention is to increase production and
incomes within Lesotho.

While 40-50 per cent of the credits from commercial banks went
as stock credits to South African Based traders, mostly Frasers
and café-owners, who aquired their stock from Frasers, the Co-
operative Credit Union channelled credits to housing, small-scale
business and agricultural improvements in the rural areas. Although the decision has not yet been taken, the government has
declared its intention to take over the control of the Co-operative Credit Union as soon as possible and establish an Agricultural Bank. It remians to be seen if this bank will manage to
distribute credits in the same manner and get as many peasants
to participate.

Another financial institution not often mentioned is EDESA-
Finanz, registered as an investment corporation in Zürich in
1972 and owned in turn by the EDESA-bank in Luxemburg. This investment corporation was initiated by the South African industrialist Anton Rupert, who also initiated the LNDC. Rupert is
the largest shareholder, but a number of West-German and other
banks as well as the Anglo American Corporation are co-owners.
The former Minister of Finance in the German Federal Republic,

Karl Schiller, is the chairman of its board. The former head of
LNDC, Wynand van Graan, is the head of EDESA's African branch.
After internal opposition against the initial decision of Leso-
thos's government to let EDESA have its Africa office in Lesotho,
this was established in Swaziland.[129] EDESA does, however, have
an agent in Lesotho, a former Civil Servant and veterinarian in
the Ministry of Agriculture, N.N. Raditapole.[130]

The purpose of EDESA is "to foster economic development in
Equatorial and Southern Africa by stimulating private enterprise
through provision of finance and know-how".[131] Its policy is to
work in partnership with governments and parastatals only to a-
void the risk of nationalization.[132] EDESA participates in local
enterprises through shares and arranges loans. It expects to have
representatives on the board.[133] In Lesotho it is only interested
in joint ventures with the LNDC. In November 1975, it still had
not participated in any projects. But its main interest was in
the mohair export industry.[134] The LNDC signed an agreement with
a British-Swiss company in April 1975. According to the agreement
signed by F. Schneider, a mohair product importer in Zürich, and
R. Seal, owner of mohair processing plants in Bradford (Great Britain), greasy mohair and tops would be imported to Europe and in
the near future a processing plant was to be set up in Lesotho.
According to the Lomé convention, Lesotho is allowed to export its
mohair duty free to the EEC, while for example South Africa has to
pay 30 per cent duty.[135] South Africa is the largest mohair exporter in the world and Lesotho the fourth. France, England and other
EEC-member countries are the main importers of this mohair.[136]

Although the other parts of the agreement with the British-
Swiss company have been fulfilled, no processing plant had been
built in 1977. The possibility of channelling South African wool
and mohair export via Lesotho's exports to the EEC might be a
good reason for the agreement. The government's aim to have a processing industry was, however, not met, nor are there so far any
indications that the production from Transkei (South Africa's region for wool and mohair) is being registered as Lesotho's produce.

The existence of the EDESA Bank is difficult to explain. No
operations have been registered after the investment bank was
established in 1973. One possibility is that EDESA has been set
up to secure the continuation of the favourable attitude towards
foreign private en   rise and continued exports of foreign currency to South Africa. The foreign currency earned via Lesotho
has already become important for the Rand monetary area. In
situations of balance of payment crisis in South Africa, this importance increases. A crisis is already envisaged. Severe shortage of foreign currency has started as a consequence of the
rapid increase in imports of armaments in connection with the
wars in Angola, Zimbabve and Namibia, at the same time as the
exports from the Republic are less in demand. Lesotho's foreign
currency earnings via aid and better prices on wool and mohair
are thus considered important. According to IMF estimates this
had positive effects on the Lesotho government's bargaining potential in relation to South Africa and its industries.

Diamond Mining and Prospecting

According to official statistical sources the deposits of mineral resources in Lesotho are small. The only mineral deposit which has been found worth exploiting is diamonds. UN Statistical Yearbook figures for 1974 show Lesotho as being the 20th largest diamond producer in the world. Zaire, USSR and South Africa are the top three.[137] These countries account for about half of the world's total diamond production of 46 million carats a year. Botswana, Ghana, Sierra Leone and Namibia are also large producers of diamonds.[138] Botswana, a new-comer to the diamond producer's league, produced almost nothing in 1969 but reached a better position in 1974 than Ghana, which in 1969 was placed number four. In 1969, Lesotho was ranked number 13 with an output of 30,000 carats against the world total of 3 million carats. Although Lesotho's diamond exports are small by international standards, they make up an important part of the country's total exports, with only livestock, wool and mohair contributing more.[139]

The government's policy has been to quickly establish a modern diamond industry.[140] However, one multinational company after the other has left after prospection, declaring that it is not worthwhile commencing large-scale mining operations. The small restricted areas where the prospecting has been going on are situated at an altitude of about 3,000 meters in the northern mountainous districts of Mokhotlong and Butha-Buthe. The machines, spare parts and fuel necessary for industrial production require better communications than the present landing strip and the gravelled road, inaccessible at times. Snow covers the area for about three months of the year.[141]

The diamonds are, however, easily transported to the outside world and do not suffer quality deterioration during storage. Almost all registered diamond exports have so far been produced by individual licensed miners, many of whom are women. They dig for the diamonds using a technology which is well adapted to the conditions prevailing in the area. Their tools are pickaxes, spades, water pumps and rotary pans produced in Lesotho. According to a UNDP mineralogist this technology was innovated during the 1960s by one of the surface miners.[142] These diggers operate as private entrepreneurs and pay a licence fee of about three rand annually. The government issues the licence in the form of a contract. It earlier delegated the responsibility of signing contracts to the LNDC. In 1973, however, the government increased its control and transferred the responsibility of signing contracts to the Mining Department within the Ministry of Finance.[143] The LNDC is an independent corporation, although sponsored by the government. The market value of the diggers yield is taxed at a rate of 15 per cent. The individual miner's earnings vary over time from a bare subsistence level to about 100,000 rand per annum in individual cases. One group of 82 miners have joined to form a co-operative and profits are shared between the members. In another case one miner has been able to aquire more tools and a number of self-constructed machines. He has employed about twenty workmen. The rest, both men and women, either work alone or in smaller groups.[144]

Multinational companies have prospected without finding diamond resources worth exploiting. In the very same areas the surface min- ners find enough to get an income and enough to give Lesotho a sub- stantial export income. How is this possible? There are many pos- sible reasons and here I will discuss four of them:

1. The capital intensive techniques applied by the large compa- nies are less profitable in Lesotho.
2. The type of diamond deposits existing in Lesotho are diffe- rent from those generally found elsewhere and therefore re- quire a different technology not yet developed by the large companies.
3. The companies do not prospect as the contracts require, but mine without registering their production.
4. The companies sign prosepcting contracts in order to restrict competitive companies and control production so that diamond prices are kept at a high level.

The first explanation is plausible since alternative wages for the licensed individual surface miners are low. The costs of their technology are also low. Therefore, they compete successfully with the giant diamond producing companies, although these companies have more capital and larger organizations.

According to a recent UNDP report, the second explanation also holds true. The kimberlite pipes in Lesotho contain many medium and small diamonds. These are found in soft material easily wor- ked by labour-intensive techniques, whereas the machines used by the companies miss many of the diamonds. The technology of the surface miners, therefore, is superior under the prevailing local conditions.[145]

The third explanation was given by a select parliamentary com- mittee, which in 1960, at the request of the BCP, investigated the diamond legislation and contracts with prospectors. A con- tract had been granted by the colonial government in 1955 to Jack Scott from the General Mining and Finance corporation in Johan- nesburg. The committee concluded that Scott had prospected for diamonds from 1955 to 1959 without reporting his finds. a) Scott was using his prospecting licence to exploit diamonds, b) during prospecting he had made a net income of no less than 20 million pounds per annum, c) Scott did not report his findings, d) the government exercised no control over Scott's activities. Scott had left without being charged.[146] Many other companies have pro- spected after Scott. They have been active without reporting any finds. Legislation has changed to give the government increased mineral rights. But according to rumours circulating in Lesotho, other prospectors succeeding Scott are also mining without supervision.

The fourth explanation might, however, be the crucial one, since international market conditions seem to support it. The mul- tinational companies attempt by various means to restrict indivi- dual diggers' production, particularly at times of low demand, in order to keep the price of diamonds at a high and stable level.[147]

The prospecting contracts with Scott, Anglo-American, Rio Tinto, Lonrho, Newmont Mining, and other mining companies have all con- tained the same clause: the prohibition of mining hitherto carried out by successful surface miners in the area. In 1968, the year after the export of diamonds from the individual diggers had risen sharply, the British multinationals Rio Tinto and Lonrho, not specializing in diamonds but active in mining in general in Southern Africa, signed contracts with LNDC for the areas of Letseng-la-Terai and Mothae. These two areas had earlier been mined by the individual miners who accounted for all the export of diamonds. When Rio Tinto and Lonrho moved in, the diggers were expelled from the areas in question. They left, although under protest, for new areas - Kao, Liqhobong and Lemphane - to which they were directed by government.[148]

The Kao area turned out to be highly profitable for the diggers. Production and consequently exports soon rose again. In Kao alone there were about 3,000 active miners. The production in Kao and Liqhobong in 1969 was 30,000 carats, almost the highest in Lesotho's diamond history.[149] In 1970, only a month after the coup d'état, the government announced through the LNDC that a prospecting contract had been signed for the Kao area. A new company, Maluti Diamonds, had been established by the LNDC. Lonrho and the USA-based Newmont Mining owned half of the shares each in this company. For the second time, the LNDC ordered the individual diggers to move as soon as possible. The miners now organized a protest action. They occupied the office of the new company. The company's foreign staff left immediately.[150]

Other people in the surroundings of Kao were ready to join the protest. Opposition to the government was already widespread as a consequence of the coup d'état and several minor uprisings had taken place in other parts of the country. Thousands of people gathered at Kao to discuss and protest against the general policy of repression exercised by the coup government. The protest was, however, specifically directed against the government's policy of giving priority to foreign companies at the expense of thousands of families who lost their incomes. After the discussion people started to march towards Maseru, the capital, to present their demands to the government.[151] Hundreds of people joined the march and several police stations in Northern Lesotho were occupied by marchers, some of whom had armed themselves. The police intervened to stop the march. Hand grenades were dropped from small aircraft flying low over the marchers and the villages in the neighbourhood of Kao. Between 200 and 500 men, women and children were killed.[152] More people were killed in this incident than on any other single occasion during the violent year following the coup of 1970.

Not until the end of the following year did it become possible to carry out the evacuation of the remaining miners from Kao. They were given a once-and-for-all compensatory payment of about 15 rand each. They were directed to Liqhobong and Lemphane,[153] which now provided the total diamond production of the country; less than one third of the earlier diamond export income.

The diamond market is remarkably internationalized, as well as monpolized by the conglomerate of DeBeers. DeBeers was a company originally established by Cecil Rhodes at the diamond

Diagram 5.A. *Local and International Contractors in Diamond Mining and Prospecting 1964-75 in Lesotho. Source: Annual Reports of the Department of Mine*

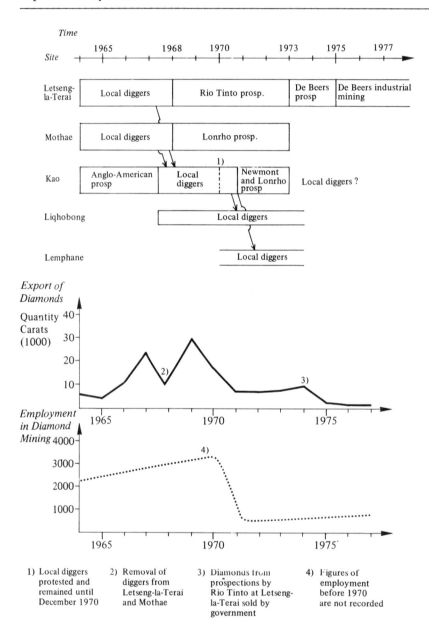

1) Local diggers protested and remained until December 1970

2) Removal of diggers from Letseng-la-Terai and Mothae

3) Diamonds from prospections by Rio Tinto at Letseng-la-Terai sold by government

4) Figures of employment before 1970 are not recorded

mines of Kimberly, in the 1870s. It was taken over by the Oppenheimer family which, during the period 1920 to 1959, expanded the
company and created the present world monopoly in diamonds. In
1959, DeBeers were successful in breaking through into the Rus-
sian diamond market and were able to control Russia's exports.[154]
By 1970 it was generally considered that the only appreciable
production outside the control of DeBeers and its Central Selling
Organization in London was the Venezuelan production and Russia's
production for its home market. About 80 per cent of the international diamond market was then controlled by DeBeers.[155]

A stable market price for diamonds is considered by DeBeers
to be the main requirement for a high profit margin. Price control is facilitated on the one hand by DeBeers co-ordination of
the output of several production companies scattered around the
world and on the other hand by marketing all products through its
own Central Selling Organization (CSO).[156] In its Yearbook for
1971 the CSO mentions that a problem had arisen with regard to
the attempts of some African governments to stop the "co-ordination" of the monopoly. In the words of the Yearbook:

> And of course, in the emergent and under-developed countries
> of Central and West Africa, where diamond production takes
> place, the guardianship of the CSO over the stability and
> health of the diamond market is of prime importance. The loss
> of revenue which these states suffer from illegal mining and
> smuggling causes their governments to turn increasingly to-
> wards the CSO as a body that will help them to get better re-
> turns from their local industries; and indeed recent history
> has recorded several instances where close ties have been
> established in order to consolidate orderly marketing in
> these countries. It is a special strength of the Diamond Cor-
> poration working in association with the CSO that it is pre-
> pared to take the full range of any organised production. No
> other buyer or potential buyer is so far as we know prepared
> to compete on this basis.[157]

The same statement holds true also for "emergent and underdeveloped countries" in Southern Africa, although diamond producing countries such as Lesotho, Botswana, Angola and Namibia are
not mentioned.

According to Harry Oppenheimer, the present chairman of DeBeers
Anglo-American and several other large companies:

> - A degree of control is necessay for the well-being of the in-
> dustry.... Whether this measure of control amounts to a mono-
> poly I would not know but if it does it is certainly a monpoly
> of a most unusual kind. There is no one concerned with dia-
> monds whether as producer, dealer, cutter, jeweller or custo-
> mer, who does not benefit from it.[158]

Those ready to accept the conditions of DeBeers and its Central
Selling Organization are thus considered to profit from it. However, the conditions are not stated and it is most unclear what
happens to those who do not accept the conditions of the monopoly.

The CSO admits that it has its critics. The pattern of world

production has become far more complex and tremendous changes
have taken place:

> In both old and new diamond areas politics and nationalism
> have modified the pattern of production and sales; and the
> participation of individual diggers has greatly increased.
> In the space of a few years a great world power has become
> a major diamond producer.159

The USSR is not mentioned by name. It is clear from the quotation that nationalism, participation of individual diggers and
the increasingly important role of the USSR both in diamond production and African politics are facts that have changed the
pattern of world production with adverse consequences for DeBeers
and the CSO.

> Through all this the CSO has 'kept it cool', modifying from
> time to time its tactics but not its aims and purposes.160

Another change of great interest to Lesotho is that industrial
diamonds which earlier had a lower price are now fetching the
same price as the gemstones, because of increased industrial demand. There is no longer a price differentation between these
types of diamonds.161 The years 1970 to 1973 were a period of
recession for the diamond industry. DeBeers acted swiftly to
integrate and control production in order to "save the market"
for diamonds. 162 In Sierra Leone, mining was checked by police
helicopter in co-operation with DeBeers and the government.
Several incidents of violence because of repression and uprisings were reported. In Lesotho, the government tried to stop
individual diggers by moving them to a less profitable area.
Whether this was in the national interest is, of course, dispu-
table.

The Lesotho government's policy is to allow the individual
diggers to operate only as a method of finding out where the diamond deposits are to be found. The 1970 Five-Year Plan states
that at Kao and Liqhobong:

> ... local diggers have been working these sites with some suc-
> cess; production from these two pipes in 1969 was nearly
> 29,787 carats valued at R 1,173,502. This has thrown doubt
> on the conclusions of the earlier survey, and it seems likely
> both these pipes could be mined on a mechanized basis by well
> capitalized companies...163

The diggings were not seen as part of the government's policy
to increase employment, and not as part of the government's
policy to increase participation in development. Nor was diamond
production seen as a way to increase export income, unless the
mining was undertaken by "well-capitalized companies".164 This
policy can be explained by the general reluctance of the government to exercise state control. Instead of controlling the individual diggers, it preferred to let a company exercise control.
This idea was strengthened since the diggers did not trust their
own government for political reasons. In government circles in
Lesotho the diggers are generally considered as "communists".

This label seems to have to do not only with their support of the BCP, but also with their alleged market relations with other dealers than those of DeBeers.[165]

The anger of about 3,000 diggers from Kao in 1970 was a political factor to be taken into account by the government. The prospecting at Kao never started in practice. When their contracts ended in 1973, Lonrho, Rio Tinto and Newmont Mining left the country. At Letseng-la-Terai, Rio Tinto had found some diamonds. These belonged, according to the agreement, to the government. They were found to have low value, and were not considered worth exploiting.[166] However, a few months later they were revalued and their value was now found to be much higher. The Department of Mining, which had now taken over from LNDC, announced that a new prospecting contract had been agreed upon with DeBeers for the Letseng-la-Terai site. Early in 1974, DeBeers also registered a production company and a marketing company in Lesotho.[167]

In answer to a question in the Interim Parliament late in 1973 about the diamond findings of Rio Tinto at Letseng-la-Terai the newly appointed Minister of Finance E.R. Sekhonyana stated:

> With the sudden increase in diamond prices and the revaluation of stones recovered during the Rio Tinto programme, there is possibly a more attractive mining prospect.[168]

DeBeers declared in March 1975 that they planned to invest 23 million Rand during the following five years in industrial mining at Letseng-la-Terai. 500 workers would get employment, when full operations started in 1977.[169]

This is the largest single private investment made in Lesotho. DeBeers became at once the largest private enterprise in Lesotho. The government holds 20 per cent of the shares and will derive about ten per cent tax from the yield, in addition to the customs on imported machines. According to the Second Five-Year Plan, the annual income from this mine could reach 12 million Rand. In 1976 one year after the mining had started, but before it came in full operation, the production had only increased slightly and was still only one-third of the 1969 production figure, when the individual miners at the two mines Kao and Liqhobong provided the total export.[170]

Let us consider for a moment what interest DeBeers could have in establishing a production and marketing company in Lesotho. Attempts from various competitive interests to put pressure on the monopoly is one possible reason. The underdeveloped countries have started to co-operate on the pricing of other raw materials like oil and copper, for example. The risk of similar co-operation in the diamond market is apparent. One possibility is, of course, that new deposits of diamonds have already been or may be discovered, which could make industrial production and the building of roads commercially viable. But it is also likely that other circumstances have been important for DeBeers' decision. The company regards the increasing uncontrolled production by individual miners as an irritating development, particularly since the international market is unstable and supply is generally larger than demand.

The existence of alternative employment for migrant workers is generally considered as negative by the employers in South Africa. These employers have an interest in keeping the wages of workers low. The low wages of migrant workers have for a long time been an efficient way of holding down the wages of black workers. DeBeers and Anglo-American employ about 80 per cent of the migrant miners from Lesotho.171 Control of alternative employment opportunities provided by diamond digging is therefore in the firms' interest apart from their interest in the diamond monopoly. Strikes in the South Africa by the migrant workers took place, as we know, throughout the period 1973 to 1975.

The Lesotho government's policy has also changed slightly since the diggers started organizing themselves and stating their demands. The government was for the first time, at least in the Second Five-Year Plan, ready to give the diggers a special site. The Kao area was to be reserved for 300 individual miners, beginning some time during the plan period of 1975 to 1980.172 For the first time the government had maximized the number to be allowed as diggers and for the first time the technology of the diggers was admitted to be superior, at least at Kao, where it was believed that the kimberlite pipes contained particularly soft material. The government had earlier provided the diggers at Liqhobong and Lemphane with loans totalling 22,000 rand for better equipment and water supplies. This small sum of money was to be paid back by the miners themselves.173 However, it was the first time that the right of at least some diggers had been admitted as part of the development plan.

The African governments have, according to DeBeers, a vested interest in prohibiting their subjects from competing with that company. Is this true in the case of Lesotho too? What made the Lesotho government conclude an agreement with the monopoly? Many people in government circles in Lesotho have a view of development which equates mechanized production with economic progress. They regard the selfmade rotary pans and other tools of the diggers as symbols of backwardness. They also estimate the loss of employment to be low.

It is considered more convenient for the government to let a large company take the responsibility for the co-ordination and security aspects involved. The possibility of getting state revenue (and customs revenue on imported machines) without the trouble of controlling the many small diggers is seen as positive. The diggers are also politically critical of the government.

Notwithstanding the government's sympathetic attitude to DeBeers, there is some opposition within the administration declaring itself to be in favour of independent diamond miners. By permitting diamond prospecting and mining over wider areas and by a virtually free-for-all issue of licences, it would be possible to provide income and employment to thousands of people in Lesotho.

According to a UNDP report there are probably many areas where diamond mining on the same small scale as at Kao would be profitable. One way of providing an income for thousands of the presently unemployed would be to open up much larger areas for exploitation. But this would not be economically viable from the point of view of DeBeers monopoly. A major question to be answered is how the dominating circles within the government, who argued for the agreement with the giant DeBeers concern, will in the long run react to the country's constantly growing problem of employment. How much room for maneuver for the government will remain after it has allowed the monopoly not merely to operate in part of the country but also to sell all the country's production of diamonds, including that of the 300 diggers allowed to operate individually.

Conclusions

The aim of economic growth has often been stressed by the Lesotho government in its development policy declarations. It is vaguely understood as overall growth in the Gross Domestic Product. Such statements have become less frequent than before and it has become clear that GDP probably has not grown in real terms during the first decade after independence. Instead, there is increasing emphasis on the expansion of specific sectors of the economy.

The strategy for development is 1) to demand aid from as many international organizations and donor agencies in Western Europe as possbile 2) to encourage multinational corporations to invest in the country 3) to work for inter-governmental procedures giving Lesotho a better opportunity to have a say in decision making concerning its development.

The aim of the Lesotho government's development policies has been to integrate Lesotho with the streams of capitalist expansion. Resources that were earlier left idle in Lesotho would be exploited by lifting restrictions on the flow of capital and labour. Some encouragement to multinational firms was, however, thought necessary.

The activity exercised by the government in foreign relations is not matched by activity in internal affairs. The government has declared its intention to remain passive in its public policies. This intention is reinforced by the forceful opposition that meets almost every attempt by the government to implement its policies.

The opposition reactions to the government's development policies have concerned neither its stress on expansion of foreign aid contacts nor its stress on increased state revenue. What is mainly criticized is the low priority given to jobs and the high priority given to capital as the motor of growth in production.

A clear change in the pattern of production in Lesotho's small internal economy that is consistent with declared government policies can be distinguished. Although the economy as a whole probably has not grown at all, growth has taken place in the sectors of tourism, construction, manufacturing and commerce. Productivity has increased in the production of livestock (including wool and mohair) and cash crops. Trade in agricultural pro-

duce has also become more efficient. Total agriculture production
has continued the steady decline that started as early as the
1930s. The export share of crop production has increased markedly.
The result has been that food aid and the import of foodstuffs
have increased rapidly.

Government development policies have not prevented a growing
share of the population migrating to work in South Africa.

Employment decreased after 1970, particularly in agriculture
and diamond mining, when the government stopped labour-intensive
mining and when measures taken to increase agricultural productivity started to give results. Employment has increased slightly
in tourism, handicraft, construction, commerce and a few small
manufacturing assembly plants. But this increase in production
has only been able to meet a small share of the demand for jobs.

The government has had success in raising state revenue. This
is an important economic condition for future development policies of any kind. There is more money in circulation: larger imports than before, larger donations and credits, larger customs
revenue, currency compensation and increased control of migrant
workers' savings. So far much of this new money reaching Lesotho
is not channeled into internal activities, but largely transferred to South Africa and Europe to give the government a high
interest on its money resources. This pattern, already established by the financial institutions during colonial times, is
becoming more pronounced as more money is being saved. Although
Lesotho did not have a currency of its own, the country was forced to place some reserves. These reserves are larger now than
they were during the post second world war period. At the end of
the first decade of independence, the government had aquired
skill in placing its money where the interest was highest.

Instead of starting a development bank which could have focu-
sed on longterm savings and investments within Lesotho, a commercial bank was established which was able to speculate on the
international market. At the same time as the government has been
cautious not to take any risks in creating employment within the
country, it has appeared as a skilled speculator in financial
affairs.

When the government attempted to raise more funds by forcing
the migrant workers to increase their savings in a special fund
in the Lesotho commercial bank, the workers protested. They turned down the government plan to give the Development Corporation
a fund for industrial investments in joint ventures with foreign
capital. The migrant workers did not trust their home government.
The most important effect of the establishment of a forced savings scheme in Lesotho is the fact that the government and the
workers are for the first time put in direct contact with each
other. As long as both the government and the workers prefer a
higher interest on their money than they can get through co-
operation with the other party and as long as they continue to
be suspicious of each other, the transfer of the workers' savings
to other countries will continue. The workers have no reason to
support joint ventures between the government and foreign capital that will not give them or other people in Lesotho better

living conditions. The government has no reason to support repa-
triation of migrant workers who are both opposed to government
and well organized.

Remarkably little of the new state revenue has resulted in increased local incomes. Corruption within agricultural projects is
a problem that the government has not yet started to deal with.
State employees and field personnel run tractors and spread fer-
tilizers and crops over their own and their neighbours' fields.
Who actually gains from this process remains to be investigated.

Lesotho had, already during the period described in this book,
embryonic elements of a national bourgeoise. This is rapidly
growing and is indeed worth a study. The only income possibilities outside migrant wage labour and state employment is livestock. In the parastatal sector of livestock and to some extent
crop exports we might find a group emerging with a national interest in conflict with foreign capital interests. Import trade is
monopolized by the British-South African firm Frasers. The government has taken over the export trade in line with a similar
policy change in South Africa.

It can hardly be argued that private foreign capital has expanded in Lesotho via investments to any large extent, the only
exception being diamond mining. Private foreign capital has expanded through the provision of know-how, technology and management, whereas the government of Lesotho has raised funds via
foreign and international aid agencies.

At the same time as some sectors of the economy have expanded,
they have increasingly come under the control of foreign private
capital. But the pattern is not the same in all sectors. Trade
in livestock remains to be more thoroughly investigated. Land is
still collectively owned and cattle is relatively evenly distributed among the citizens of Lesotho. The goods produced, however,
can only be marketed with the help of know-how and through the
markets controlled by foreign multinational buyers. The conditions of work of the many small export producers have changed
largely without the participation of the Lesotho government. The
three largest mohair and wool exporting countries have started
to co-operate. Although Lesotho does not participate, it has
gained from the results of this co-operation. More stable and
slightly higher prices are paid also to the Lesotho producers,
although higher costs of living have consumed this price increase for most of the small producers. In Lesotho the main interest of foreign capital is migrant labour. The country's role
as a labour reserve has become more important during the decade
after independence, since other important labour reserve countries such as Zambia, Malawi and Mozambique have gradually left
this market. Rhodesia is the new large competitor in the export
of labour to South African mines. Although the export of migrant
labour from the Transkei was large earlier it has also increased.
The South African mines have at the same time decreased their
general dependence on migrant labour. Wages in kind have been
transformed into wages in cash. Welfare services earlier provided
by the mines are now left to the Lesotho government. It is un-
certain if the large nominal wage increases have led to better

living conditions for the migrant workers.

One possibility for a government without internal political support to remain in power is to rely on external support. The Lesotho government has managed to get such foreign support. Although it has had little success in raising private capital it has been able to raise aid funds and to get support in the form of international political legitimacy.

The government of the enclave state Lesotho has estaliblished itself as a decision-making unit with its own interests and goals. The South African government has tolerated its continued existence not only because of the reactionary political ideas and minority character of the regime but also since increasing conflicts within South Africa itself and radical changes in other parts of Southern Africa have given the Lesotho government new scope for manoeuvering and bargaining with the South African government. There are areas of conflict between the Lesotho and South African governments, particularly concerning the speed and the type of industrialization in Lesotho. Multinationals in Taiwan and Japan are ready to establish labour intensive industries. Through what pressure against the workers will the Lesotho government be able to reach it aims to establish co-operation with these countries and their corporations? So far the migrant workers have not been ready to accept co-operation with their home government, and the government does not believe that it can control its labour force within the country.

6 Final Comments

The problem of dependence is one of the most pressing problems affecting development in Lesotho. In the preceding chapters the specific mechanisms of dependence in that country have been analysed in detail. The resulting internal conditions have created new conflicts in Lesotho, aggrevated by the whole Southern African conflict. However, conflicts do not prevent change, but often make up the very dynamics of change in the longer run. In Lesotho it is clear that the establishment is weak and maintained through forceful support from external sources. Thus, the Jonathan regime was established with the assistance of personnel from the Adenauer Foundation, British aid topping up salaries of policemen from Britain in charge of the Lesotho police at the time of the coup. Of strategic importance was also the assistance of arms from the Republic of South Africa as well as statements made from the Republic of South African Broadcasting System in favour of the regime in 1970. This positive attitude changed however slowly during the following decade, when it became clear that the Jonathan regime was able to defend an independent foreign policy.

The regime was maintained through sometimes violent repression. Such repression was not continued in the longer run. Instead a broader political base was established, both internally through dialogue with opposition groups, and abroad through international co-operation with countries outside the region of Southern Africa (both East- and West-oriented regimes).

Although the problem of dependence is extreme in the case of Lesotho and reproduced in new forms, this is not a problem that is unique to that country. On the contrary it is a problem that is an urgent one in all the underdeveloped countries of the Third World. Keeping in mind that there are distinct types of dependence relations, the labour export type of relation in Lesotho being one such type, we will now turn to the general questions raised in the introduction.

In the preceding chapters we have compared actual political conditions in Lesotho with six general tendencies derived from the theoretical literature applying a dependence approach to the study of underdevelopment and development. These six important tendencies have been selected among those upon which there is a measure of consensus among scholars applying a dependence approach. It is clear from the comparison that there is agreement between the expectations of dependence theoreticians and the reality of Lesotho.

On the other hand, it is also clear that the agreement is not total. One conclusion of my study is in fact that predictions gene-
rated by the dependence approach have to be qualified by reference
to historical periodicity and the political struggle in the country under study.

Which of the six tendencies were found to prevail in the case
of Lesotho during the period 1960-75? Table 6.1. should not be
interpreted as a schematic answer to this question. Each of the
points of comparison requires separate examination and comments.

The diversification of production has increased rather than
decreased and production has become rather less disintegrated
than before, mainly as a result of the government's attempts to
transform the structure of production. Since economic production
in Lesotho is extremely small, these tendencies resulted in minor
changes in society as a whole. It is important also to remember
that decreasing diversification and increasing disintegration of
sectors of production were noticeable during earlier periods in
history.

Table 6.1. *General Tendencies often Associated with Dependence
Compared with the Case of Lesotho, 1960 to 1975*

Tendency often associated with dependence	Found in Lesotho	Not found in Lesotho
1. Decreasing diversification of production		x
Increasing disintegration of sectors of production		x
2. Increasing inequalities in welfare		x
Increasing inequalities in income and wealth		x
3. Decreasing power base of the state	x	
4. Increase in the size of state insti- tutions		x
Increase in the scope of state activities	x	
5. Increasing foreign control of human and material resources	x	
6. Increasing emphasis on economic growth in government declarations	x	
Failing economic growth	x	

If we take a closer look at recent contributions to dependence
literature, these tendencies are described as typical of the periphery during an earlier period of world capital accumulation. On
the basis of my findings we can, therefore, raise the question
whether dependence during the specific period under study (1960-75)
is associated with tendencies in the structure of production dif-

ferent from those indicated in the main body of the writings of
the dependence school also in extremely poor and dependent countries. We can also raise the question whether Lesotho will find a
higher ranking position for itself in the international capitalist system if relations between capital and labour change in
Southern Africa. Opposition by striking workers from Malawi, South
Africa and Lesotho as well as political changes in Mozambique,
Angola, Namibia and Rhodesia have probably weakened the capital
side in relation to labour. Has this given Lesotho a more important role as a labour exporter and does this new role now include
the possibility of industrialization in Lesotho?

No definite tendencies of increasing inequalities in welfare
and income have been found during 1960-75. Such changes during
the following decade are, however, noticeable. Public services
have decreased in real terms. The structure of wealth distribution became for the period 1940-70 more equal than before, but
at a very low level. Land holdings and cattle were more equally
distributed. But because of populations growth each land holding
is smaller than before. As stressed particularly in chapters 2 and
5, those who had access to means of scientific farming and livestock production have been able to increase their agricultural
incomes, e.g. state employees with land holdings. Those without
this opportunity have been forced in increasing numbers to seek
their incomes in the mines and industries of South Africa.

Still, this conclusion has to be approached with considerable
caution. There is a possibility that the difference between the
wages of the migrant workers are much greater than is generally
believed. If, in fact, many Basotho work under exemption rules
as skilled labour in South Africa the income distribution is in
reality less equal.

The general socio-economic structure is, however, changing in
new direction. The pattern of income distribution changes slightly
if we include the fact that Basotho have replaced the earlier
high-income colonial officers and the fact that a growing number
of foreign technical personnel both of multinational firms and
international and foreign aid agencies are in Lesotho. The latter
are on short-term but favourable contracts. Earlier tendencies
in the direction of new bourgeois groups emerging were, however,
halted. We have seen, for example, that the commercial farmers
and the village chiefs were deprived of their incomes during the
1930s and 1940s as a result of successful demands from South
Africa's white farmers and mining companies. We have raised the
question whether the situation in Southern Africa has changed
so that the new bourgeois groups grow in Lesotho as in other
newly independent states.

The size of the power base of the government increased during
the period 1960 to 1965, but decreased again thereafter. This
conclusion can be drawn from the patterns of voting and popular
protests. Popular participation became more widespread than ever
before, at least since colonization. Support of the government
was rather broad until the coup in 1970, when a majority government was prevented from taking control. A coup government in

conflict with the majority party is - as we have seen - more ready
than a popularly based government to listen to foreign supporters.
We might pose the question, therefore, if there is a tendency for
foreign capital to support a minority government, since such a government might be more ready than a majority government to accept
conditions even contrary to the interests of the internal groups
supporting the government.

Surprisingly enough, state institutions did not grow in size
in the sense of an increasing number of state employees during the
period 1960-75. This is otherwise believed to be a political condition for foreign penetration through capitalist expansion.
During the period 1960 to 1973 British aid was given on the condition that the number of state employees should not expand. This
condition was set to safeguard the British taxpayers' money.
Similar lines have not been followed in other former British colonies but in Lesotho, however, they were both applied and carefully
followed. A large number of government employees, mainly field
personnel, were in fact later dismissed for security reasons and
their posts remain vacant. Although the number of policemen increased more than ever before, the total number of state employees
did not increase more than a few per cent yearly. The number of
state employees in relation to other local employees did not
change. State employment even decreased in relation to migrant
labour. The responsibilities of the state, however, grew quickly
after independence. Not only did the state intervene in new economic areas, nationalizing trade in livestock and crops, and participating in joint ventures with foreign interests in tourism,
mining and industry, but it also increased its responsibilities in,
for example, education and banking, fields which had earlier been
left to the missions and private financial institutions respectively. The scope of state activity grew as the state received
added importance within the society. The state also got increased
revenue.

Foreign dependence clearly increased, mainly via Western European aid assistance to the state budget, but also via increasing
control exercised by the management of foreign companies and subsidiaries of multinationals. Diamond mining was taken over by
De Beers, as late as in 1975. This was only after long and forceful protests from the thousands of diamond diggers. The diggers
had lost their employment already earlier as a result of the
take-over by Lonrho and Newmont Mining, other multinationals who
were allowed by government to prospect in the diamond areas. In
1975 De Beers got both mining and trading rights. The government
thereby in effect transferred its potential control in this important sector of the economy and at the same time lost an opportunity to increase employment. De Beers is not only the largest
diamond firm in the world and a near monopoly, but through the
interlocking holdings of De Beer and Anglo-American it shares in
the control of employment of Basotho labour in South Africa. The
Oppenheimer concern, including De Beers and the Anglo-American
Corporation, is by far the largest employer of workers from Lesotho as well as the largest South African company. Tourism, the

main expanding sector, was managed by multinational firms such as
Holiday Inn and Hilton. There are also other examples of transfers
of responsibilities to foreign firms and foreign aid agencies. In
some villages the committees and co-operatives were replaced by
aid project administrators and government-dominated representatives, often a village chief. Thus some of the chiefs were given new
importance in aid administration and food aid distribution in
particular.

There is a clear emphasis on economic growth in many government
declarations when development policies are specified. It is not
difficult to see similarities between government policies and the
policies demanded by foreign firms who want to establish themselves. It is, however, not clear if the similarity is the result
of pressure from firms wanting to invest in Lesotho. The causal
relation might well be the opposite. The Jonathan government, in
its attempts to find allies abroad and bring new capital to Lesotho, has attempted to formulate policies favourable to foreign
capital investment. Possibly we could say that declarations on
general economic growth as the main goal have become less frequent
and explicit during the period 1970 to 1975. This is partly a
result of political opposition and partly that of actual stagnation in the general output of production in Lesotho. During the
latter part of the period under study more emphasis is given to
economic growth in sectors which had experienced some expansion.
International acceptance has also been possible to find through
other diplomatic methods.

The clearly unequal conditions under which Lesotho was linked
to the capitalist international system were established successi-
vely through military intervention and colonial take-over of local
trade (1880s) and through the prohibition of agricultural production (1935) during the colonial period. The effect of this colonial intervention was a political and socio-economic structure
where British and South African traders, foreign missionaries and,
until the second world war, local chiefs, served colonial interests and controlled the other sections of the population. The
rest of the population served colonial interests by becoming migrant workers in South Africa, mainly in mining. After the colonial society was established they had few alternative income
possibilities at home, the main but limited exceptions being in
mohair/wool production, diamond mining and lately tourism.

Today there are fewer employment opportunities within Lesotho
than ever before. In actual fact, the workers have been forced by
their own government to continue to work in increasing numbers in
South Africa. During the period of 1960 to 1975 the workers have
been more active than before in articulating their views on the
policies of their home government. The government has adapted its
policies to the workers' demands but has not increased its legitimacy in the eyes of the workers. The development strategy was
criticized by the BCP and the trade unions as a strategy not
meeting the needs of the majority of the country.

When we take into account the atypical enclave character of
the Lesotho society and the political struggle going on in the

surrounding country, it is easy to understand that the struggle
for political rights is also a struggle for better living conditions in the long run. In the present case this involves a struggle
against the bourgeoise of South Africa and is part of an international movement. A change in the power structure in South Africa
will have crucial effects on Lesotho. But, on the other hand, a
change in the power structure of Lesotho would probably also have
effects on South Africa.

Throughout this study we have found signs of changes in the
structure of the political parties, state institutions and development policies. How have these changes affected Lesotho's dependence? Organizations covering only Lesotho have been centralized
and strengthened. Communication with foreign organizations thus
takes place increasingly at top level. The polarization of the
party conflict increased rather than decreased, although the situation has been less clear during recent years. After independence
the government reduced the effect of some of the earlier exploitation, in the sense that there is now good compensation for participation in the common customs and monetary union with South
Africa. Aid to the country is relatively very large. Without
changing the forms of the relation with South Africa, Lesotho has
increased its state revenue. New forms of money transfers from
Lesotho to South Africa have, however, been established. The introduction of a government-controlled migrant wages savings scheme
was one such form. The resources at the disposal (at least formally) of the government have efficiently been retransferred to
South Africa, with little resulting improvement for the inhabitants of Lesotho.

The relation between parties in Lesotho expresses the dependence of the country on South Africa. Lesotho is integrated into
South Africa on both sides of the conflict raging within South
Africa. The two largest parties in Lesotho are affiliated with
different sides in exploitative relations in South Africa: the
side with an interest in *status quo* and continuation of the migrant labour system and the side interested in social transformation including a change in the migrant labour system. The conflict
between the two large parties in Lesotho became increasingly polarized during the period under study. Neither party has allowed its
opponent to implement its development goals.

The development policies of the parties are related to their
attitude to South Africa. The BCP is clearly for a change in the
social structure as a condition for improvements in living conditions in the long run, whereas the BNP strategy is to let others
work to change the South African society and in the meantime work
for better living conditions, at least for a few, within the framework of the existing system. The BCP in turn considers such a
strategy to be in support of continued *status quo*.

Through its very character the enclave state of Lesotho is the
object of conflicting interests in South Africa, involving world-
wide interests i.e. those aiming at *status quo* in South Africa
and those aiming at introducing majority rule - the latter im-
plying transformation of the exploitative character of the apart-

heid system. The awareness among people in South Africa has increased so that it is probably no longer possible to introduce majority
rule without resulting in a radical change in the socio-economic
structure.

In South Africa the migrant worker is still an important factor
in the growth policy of the government, and thus the keeping of
migrant labour system is sustaining the present type of rule. A
growing awareness among the governments neighbouring South Africa
has resulted in their adoption of two different strategies:

1. Withdrawal step by step of the migrant labour force with the
   double aim of putting pressure on South Africa and meeting internal demands to employ the citizens of the country at home.
2. Increased migrant labour export exploiting the opportunity for
   government earnings, i.e. taxing the workers, forcing them to
   save their wages in their home country and if possible bargaining for higher wages with South African employers.

Lesotho and Transkei employ the latter strategy, whereas Malawi
and Mozambique have chosen the former. We can only speculate about
which one of the two strategies results in the greatest improvement in living conditions. There are strong indications that
"take-home" wages for the workers from Lesotho have increased and
employment in South Africa has increased, whereas the former migrant labour forces from Malawi and Mozambique are both lower paid
and risk unemployment in the short run. Clearly, if Lesotho had
followed the same strategy as Malawi and Mozambique, the economic
return for the workers would have been less. However, wage increases as well as the increased employment of workers from Lesotho are results of strategy 1 above, since strikes and withdrawal
of migrant labour were important reasons for the employers to increase wages. Another important reason was that the employers had
to increase wages to attract South African workers to the jobs
left by workers from Malawi and Mozambique. Strikes by workers
from Lesotho (not sponsored by the Lesotho government) also added
to the pressure put on South African employers. Thus in the short
run, the Lesotho government has slightly improved living conditions for its nationals, if these are measured in terms of money
and if the loss of compensations in kind the negative effects of
migration are disregarded. Consequently, strategy 2 is only applicable if strategy 1 is applied first. Strategy 2, however, coun-
ters the aims of strategy 1 since it weakens the pressure against
the South African economy.

The Lesotho society is now more efficient in the sense that
the mechanisms of exploitation and repression have become stream-
lined. The migrant labour character of the Lesotho society has
been accentuated, local leaders' have taken over the responsibility
for repression from the colonial government, and the resources
accumulated by the Basotho are transferred abroad through new
monetary channels. The Lesotho government is skilfully utilizing
the double aims of aid donors. The multinationals of the donor
countries with an interest in South Africa are anxious to remain
in South Africa while improving their image among critics. The

Lesotho government demands compensation for potential trade and investment boycotts, while inviting the subsidiaries of the multinationals in South Africa to move across the border to Lesotho but still remain within the same monetary and customs union.

Appendices

Appendix I: Results of the General Elections in 1965 and 1970

I a: Party Cleavages in Different Districts in Lesotho in 1965 and 1970 Elections.

Districts.								
	Number of constituencies.							
Party:	BCP		BNP		MFP		Total	
Year:	1965	1970	1965	1970	1965	1970	1965	1970
Leribe	8	4	1	5	–	–	9	9
Butha-Buthe	4	4	–	–	–	–	4	4
Berea (TY)	2	6	5	1	–	–	7	7
Maseru	3	9	6	3	4	1	13	13
Mafeteng	4	6	3	1	–	–	7	7
Mohales Hoek	2	3	5	4	–	–	7	7
Quthing	–	1	5	4	–	–	5	5
Qachas Nek	–	4	4	–	–	–	4	4
Mokhotlong	2	4	4	2	–	–	4	4
Total	25	36	31	23	4	1	60	60

Source: Bureau of Statistics 1970

I b: Votes and Seats in the General Elections 1965 and 1970

	Votes		Seats		Share of votes %		Change in share of votes	
	1965	1970	1965	1970	1965	1970	1965	1970
BNP	108,162	127,410	31	23	41.6	42.0[1]	+ 0.4	
BCP	103,050	151,868	25	36	39.7	51.0	+ 11.3	
MFP	44,837	16,582	4	1[2]	16.5	5.7	– 10.8	
BCP and MFP added					56.2	56.7	+ 0.5	
MTP and independents	5,776	–	0	–	2.2	–		
Independents		1,198	–	0		0.4		
UDP	–	564	–	0				
CPL	?	68	0	0				
Total	261,825	297,690	60	60	100	100		

[1] According to Macartney's figures the BCP got 49.8 percent of the votes
[2] The only constituency where the BCP did not stand for elections

Source: Human Rights Commission, Geneva 1975; and Macartney, W. J. A., The Lesotho General Election of 1970, *Government and Opposition*, 1973 Oct., p. 485.

Appendix I.C: Changes in Constiuency Boundaries and Election Results from 1965 to 1970.

General Elections in 1965

Constituencies 1965

1	Matsoaing	20	Berea
2	Hololo	21	Thaba-Moea
3	Tsime	22	Senqunyane
4	Lipelaneng	23	'Maletsunyane
5	Malibamatšo	24	Makhaleng
6	Kolberg	25	Thaba-putsoa
7	Pela-tšoeu	26	Thabana-li-'Mele
8	Mphosong	27	Thabana-ntšonyana
9	Qoqolosing	28	Matela
10	Likhakeng	29	Maama
11	Hlotse	30	Qiloane
12	Likhetlane	31	Qeme
13	Manka	32	Maseru
14	Phuthiatsana	33	'Masemouse
15	Koeneng	34	'Maliepetsane
16	Mosalemane	35	Mount Olivet
17	Khafung	36	Monkhoaneng
18	Malimong	37	Halinyane
19	Tšoanamakhulo	38	Qalabane
		39	Thaba-Phechela
		40	Tsoaing
		41	Hloahloeng
		42	Thaba-telle
		43	Qagatu
		44	Morifi
		45	Mohale's Hoek
		46	Mpharane
		47	Taung
		48	Qhoali
		49	Tšitsong
		50	Tosing
		51	Quthing
		52	Tele
		53	Makheka
		54	Tsoelike
		55	Qoacha's Nek
		56	Thaba-chitja
		57	Lihloahloeng-Matsoku
		58	Mokhotlong
		59	Popa-Linakaneng
		60	Khubelu

BNP   BCP   MFP

General Elections in 1970

Constituencies 1970

1 Matsoaing
2 Tsime
3 Pholonamane
4 Pela-tšoeu
5 Malibamatšo
6 Kolberg
7 Mphosong
8 Matlakeng
9 Qoqolosing
10 Likhakeng
11 Likhetlane
12 Manka
13 Kolonyama
14 Koeneng
15 Mosalemane
16 Malimong
17 Khafung
18 Maluba-Lube
19 Thupa-kubu

20 Berea
21 Thaba-Moea
22 'Maletsunyane
23 Thaba-putsoa
24 Senqunyane
25 Makhaleng
26 Matela
27 Maama
28 Thabana-ntšonyana
29 Koro-Koro
30 Boqate
31 Maseru
32 Qeme
33 Tsoaing
34 Thaba-Phechela
35 Qalabane
36 Monkhoaneng
37 'Maliepetsane
38 'Masemouse
39 Thabana-Morena
40 Mafeteng
41 Taung
42 Mpharane
43 Mohale's Hoek
44 Thaba-telle
45 Hloahloeng
46 Qaqatu
47 Morifi
48 Quthing
49 Tele
50 Tosing
51 Tšitsong
52 Qhoali
53 Qacha's Nek
54 Tsoelike
55 Thaba-chitja
56 Makheka
57 Mokhotlong
58 Bobatsi
59 Matsoku
60 Khubelu

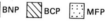

□ BNP   ◩ BCP   ▣ MFP

Notes

1. INTRODUCTION (p. 1 - 10)

1 Bodenheimer, S., "Dependency and Imperialism. The Roots of Latin American Underdevelopment", *NACLA Newsletter* (New York), Vol. IV no. 3., May-June 1970, pp. 18-27. Mikkelsen, V., "Imperialism og Studiet av avhangighet" (Imperialism and Dependence). *Politica* 2-3, 1976 (Århus), Senghaas, D., ed., *Imperialismus und strukturelle Gewalt. Analysen über abhängige Reproduction.* Frankfurt a.M. 1972. See also notes 3, 8 and 12 below.

2 *International Development Strategy for the Second United Nations Development Decade* (A/8124 and Add. 1) Item 42, 24 Oct. 1970, pp.39-49, 1883 plenary meeting. General Assembly-24 Session, Resolution no. 2626 (XXV). For elaboration on the measurement of levels of living see for example *Measurement of Changes in National Levels of Living*, Social Affairs Division of OECD. MS/S/67.126. and Russet, P.M., *An Empirical Assessment of Global Inequalities and Dependence*, Yale University, Sept. 1974 (mimeo), paper to Conference on Global Dominance and Dependence at Peace Research Institute, Oslo 1974.

3 Ewers, T. and Wogau, P.v., "Dependencia: lateinamerikanische Beiträge zur Theorie der Unterentwicklung", *Das Argument*, no. 3 1973.

4 Hobson, J.A., *Imperialism. A Study*, London 1905, see also Hobson, J.A. *The South African War*, London 1903, for a discussion of the Southern African subsystem during this early period.

5 See note 3.

6 Frank, A.G., *Capitalism and Underdevelopment in Latin America. Historical Studies of Chile and Brazil*, New York 1967.

7 Laclau, E., "Feudalism and Capitalism in Latin America, *New Left Review*", no. 67 1971, argues that Frank overestimates the impact of capitalism on the hierarchical structure of the international world order. The rapid increase in inequalities between the different parts of the international system are, however, well documented.

8 Amin, S., *Accumulation on a World Scale*, New York 1974.

9 For example Amin, S., *The Future of Southern Africa*, (mimeo) Introduction to a forthcoming book based on papers to the Conference on Socio-economic Change in Southern Africa, organized by IDEP and OAU, Dar-es-Salaam, 6-10 Dec. 1975.

10 Amin, S., *Le Developpement inégal. Essai sur les formations sociales du capitalisme peripherique*, Paris 1973, p. 174, see also *Accumulation...*, note 8, vol. 1, p. 15.

11 *Accumulation...*, vol. 11, Afterword to second edition, p. 603. Most of the critics of Amin have expressed themselves only orally at seminars, for example at the Dar-es-Salaam Conference mentioned in note 9, See also paper by Wuyts, M., *On the Nature of Underdevelopment: An Analysis of Two Views on Underdevelopment*, (mimeo) Economic Research Bureau, Dar-es-Salaam March 1976. There is also a political criticism directed towards regimes utilizing the results of the research done with a dependence approach, particularly research on trade and investment relations. The criticism is against the lack of distribution of the fruits gained in bargaining as a result of increased knowledge and thus not a criticism of the research itself.

12 Cardoso, F.H., *Current Thesis on Latin American Development and Dependency: A Critique* and *The Consumption of Dependency Theory in the U.S.*, papers for III Scandinavian Research Conference on Latin America, Bergen 17-19 June 1976.

13 *For example:* - Legassick, M., "Race, Industrialization and Social Change in South Africa", *African Affairs*, Vol. 75, No. 299 April 1976.
- Kaplan, D., "Capitalist Development in South Africa: Class Conflict and the State". (unpubl.) 1974.
- Wolpe, H., "Capitalism and Cheap Labour-Power in South Africa: from Segregation to Apartheid", *Economy and Society* 1, 1974.
Simson, H., "The Causes of Apartheid Revisted", *Studies on South African Imperialism*, Report No. 17 Part I 1977, Department of Peace and Conflict Research, Uppsala University, 1977.

14 About 100,000 were recorded as recruited only to the mines via the South African recruitment offices in Lesotho, in 1972. (*Annual Statistical Bulletin* 1975, Maseru). At the same time about 270,000 men were economically active (*First Five-Year Development Plan*, Maseru 1970). The proportion was higher in 1976 although the labour force had increased. See chapter 2 for details.

15 *Economic Development Programme for the Republic of South Africa* 1972-1977, Department of Planning, Pretoria 1972, p. XV.

16 Good, D. and Williams, M., *South Africa: The Crisis in Britain and the Apartheid Economy*, Anti-Apartheid Movement 6, London Nov. 1976, p. 5.

17 Potholm, C.P. and Dale, R., ed. *Southern Africa in Perspective*, New York 1972, p. 3-15.

18 According to *Proclamation 400* a state of emergency has been in force in Transkei since 1963. Other laws with an impact on political research are for example *Supression of Communism Act* no. 44 1950, *Unlawful Organizations Act*, no. 34 1960, *Terrorism Act* no. 83 1967.

19 *Bibliography on Lesotho/Basutoland by Centre for International Studies*, Ohio University, Athens 1966. World Bibliographical series Vol. 3, Lesotho, S.M. Willet and D.P. Ambrose, Oxford 1980.

20 Mafeje, Archie, (Institute of Social Studies, The Hague) in lecture at Department of Peace and Conflict Research, Uppsala University, Febr. 1974.

21 See note 19.

22 - Wallman, S., *Take out Hunger: Two Case Studies of Rural Development in Basutoland*, London 1969, and "The Modernization of Dependence in Lesotho", *Journal of Southern African Studies*, March 1977.
- Macartney, Alan, "The 1970 General Election in Lesotho", *Government and Opposition*, Ocotber 1973.
- Weisfelder, R., "Power Struggle in Lesotho, *Africa Report* vol. 12, no. 1, African American Institute, Washington January 1967, *Defining National Purpose in Lesotho*, Paper in International Studies, Africa Series, no. 3, Athens 1969, *Lesotho: An Unstable Irritant within South Africa*. Paper to meeting of African Studies Association. Boston 1970, *The Basotho Monarchy. A Spent Force or a Dynamic Political Factor*. Paper to meeting of African Studies Association, Denver 1971.
- Spence, Jack, *The Politics of Dependence in Lesotho*, London 1968.

23 Selwyn, Percy, *Industries in the Southern African Periphery*, London 1975.

2. SOCIO-ECONOMIC CHANGE (p. 11 - 35)

1 Wallensteen, P., *Dealing with the Devil: Relations between South Africa and its Neighbours*, Department of Peace and Conflict Research at Uppsala University, Uppsala 1971.

2 Väyrynen, R., *Some Theoretical Aspects of Subimperialism*, Tampere Peace and Conflict Research Institute, Tampere 1974.

3 Statement by Head of Chamber of Mines, *The Guardian*, 23 March 1973

4 *First Five-Year Development Plan 1970/71-1974/75*, Maseru 1970.

5 Ibid. p. 6.

6 *Agricultural Statistics* 1960, 1960 and 1965-70, mimeo, Bureau of Statistics, Maseru 1973.

7 *Interviews* with villagers in 1970 and 1975, Figures by Mannuku Mohale, Maseru District in 1970.

8 C. Hellman, *Leribe Pilot Agricultural.Scheme*, August 1974, and *Interviews* with Project Employees of Khomokhoana (Leribe) and Thaba-Bosiu Agricultural Schemes in November 1975, and Per Sörensen, FAO-employee 1970 in Lesotho (field worker), introducing fertilizer.

9 Document of International Monetary Fund (IMF), *Lesotho-Recent Economic Developments*, Washington May 28 1975, Table 9, p. 13.

10 Document of the International Bank of Reconstruction(IBRD) and International Development Aid Fund (IDA), *The Economy of Lesotho*, Report No. 331 a-LSO. 25 June 1974, p. 1.

11 See note 5.

12 See note 9, p. 12.

13 Figures given by Roger Leys, see also his paper *Labour Migration*, *Lesotho IDR*, D 75,1., Copenhagen 1975, p. 7.

14 See note 9, p. 101, Appendix I.

15 *Interviews* with BFL and Labour Officials, Maseru Nov, 1975.

16 *Thaba Bosiu Rural Development Project, Evaluation Study No 1*, Maseru April 1975 (Provisional Results, later confirmed), Table 3, p. 3.

17 See note 8, C. Hellman, figures confirmed by A. Lexander, Maseru Nov. 75. (Agricultural sociologist who has undertaken studies of for Thaba Bosiu (foothill), Thaba Tseka (mountain), and Leribe Khomokhoana (lowland areas).

18 Summary of *Annual Statistical Bulletins 1967/68-1971/72*, Maseru and IMF estimates.

19 Shaw, Timothy, *Southern Africa: Dependence, Interdependence and Independence in a Regional Sub-system,* (paper presented at a workshop on Southern Africa), Dalhouse Canada 1973.

20 4th Annual Report, 1 March 1969 - 28 February 1970, *South African Mohair Exports* (Cape and Basotho Mohair) and 9th Annual Report, 1 March 1974 - 28 February 1975, *South African Mohair Exports* (Cape and Basotho Mohair), *Interview* with Dr. Wacher, Lesotho Livestock Marketing Corporation, Maseru Dec. 1975.

21 *Second Five-Year Plan 1975/76-1979/80*, Maseru 1975, Introduction, p. 5, *Agricultural Census Report* 1970, Maseru 1973, p. 63. *Third Five-Year Plan 1980/81-1984/85*, (unpubl.).

22 *Annual Statistical Bulletin* 1976, Table 7, Bureau of Statistics, Maseru 1977.

23 The keeping of cattle is mostly considered as a medium of saving in underdeveloped and dependent countries. Since the mid-1800s Lesotho has exported wool and mohair to Europe. Purchase of cattle is considered as an investment by large groups in Lesotho.

24 IMF, see note 9, Table 10, p. 16.

25 Ashley, M.J., *Education and Social Change*, Report from Social Commission, No 44, The Study Project on Christianity in Apartheid Society, Johannesburg 1973.

26 Wilson, M. and Thompson, L. ed., *Oxford History of South Africa*, London 1969, Part II, p. 69

27 Germond, R.C., *Chronicles of Basutoland*, Morija 1967, p. 325. One bag (miud) contained 185 lb.

28 *Journal of the African Society 1903*, p. 209, Lt. Dryndale: "on entering Basutoland from the Orange River Colony, one is much struck by the ferti-

lity of the valleys", (quoted in Paul Spray, *The Economic History of Basutoland*, unpubl. 1975, Institute of Development Studies, Sussex).

29 *The Friend of the Free State*, quoted by *Leselinyana*, February 1870 and in Germond, R.C., see note 27, p. 319.

30 Ibid. p. 319.

31 Letter from P. Germond, Thaba Morena, March 1887, quoted in R.C. Germond, see note 27, p. 469.

32 See note 13.

33 Wilson, Francis, *Labour in South African Gold Mines 1899-1969*, Cambridge 1972, pp. 135-136 and 139.

34 In 1912 the Chamber of Mines established the Native Recruiting Corporation (NRC) to recruit labour and control wages for mine workers from South Africa, Basutoland, Bechuanaland and Orange Free State. This organization still exists and has the same function. After 1976 it is called Mine Labour Organization, (MLO). Already in 1900 the Chamber of Mines (itself founded in 1899) had established the Witwatersrand Native Labour Association (WENELA) to recruit from Mozambique, Malawi, Rhodesia and Angola.

35 Wallman, Sandra, "The Modernization of Dependence - a Further Note on Lesotho", *Journal of Southern Africa Studies*, 1977, pp. 102-107.

36 Chakela, K. Qalabane, *Review and Bibliography: Water and Soil Resources of Lesotho, 1935-1970*, Department of Physical Geography at the University of Uppsala, February 1973.

37 Mafeje, Archie, *Land Tenure and Development of Agriculture in South Africa*, FAO 1975.
   Basutoland, Bechuanaland Protectorate and Swaziland, History of Discussions with the Union of South Africa 1909-1939, December 1952, (kept at the Library, Roma University, Lesotho), Letter from General Hertzog to the Secretary of State J.H. Thomas, Pretoria 30 November 1932.

39 Ibid., Letter from J.C. Smuts, Minister of Justice in the Union of South Africa, 28 July 1933.

40 Ibid., "Aide-mémoire to the South African Ministry of Native Affairs" from W. Clark, the British High Commissioner to South Africa (administrating Basutoland, Bechuanaland and Swaziland, which were all called the High Commission Territories) July 1st 1935. See also Morris, Mike, *The Development of Capitalism in South African Agriculture*, Marxistisk Antropologi, Vol 2, Nr. 2-3, 1976.

41 *Financial and Economic Position of Basutoland*, (Pim Report), London 1935, and *Native Administration Proclamation*, No 61, 1938.

42 An attempt to give a more critical view of the history of colonization and the period before the arrival of the colonizers is found in Oxford History..., see note 26. This was published with 30 blank pages in South Africa.

43 Keen, Kerstin, *Two decades of Development in Basutoland 1830-1850*, Bulletin of Department of History, University of Gothenburg 1975.

44 See note 26, Part I, p. 131.

45 Mason, R.J., and van der Merwe, N.J., "Radio-carbon Dating of Iron Age Sites in the Southern Transvaal", *South African Journal of Science* 60, V, 1964.

46 *Wikar's Journal 1778-79* ed. Mossop, E.E., Cape Town 1935, see note 26 Part II, p. 153.

47 Casalis, Eugene, *The Basuto: twenty-three years in South Africa*, Africana Collectanea Series, Cape Town 1965 (Reprint from 1855, Paris) and Campbell, J., *Travels in South Africa 1820*, London 1822.

48 See note 26, Vol I, p. 154.

49 Ibid., Vol II, p. 142.

50 Ibid., p. 143, and Borcherds, P.B., *An Autobiographical Memory*, Cape Town 1861, p. 83 and 124 (The first written records of an eye-witness).

51 Livingstone, David, *Missionary Travels and Research in South Africa*, London 1857, p.50, according to which the communications with China were from at least the 12th Century, and *Missionary Correspondence 1841-56*, ed. Schapera, I., London 1961, p. 95.
52 Kresten, Peter, UNDP minerologist in Lesotho 1972-1974, *Report on assignment and interview* in Stockholm, February 1974.
53 Casalis, see note 47; Philip, J., *Researchers in South Africa*, London, 1828, ii. 132-6.
54 See note 26, Part I, p. 156.
55 Ibid., p. 158 and Damane, M., *The Statecraft of Moshoeshoe, the Great*, Moshoeshoe Memorial Lecture IV, Maser 12th March 1975.
56 Simson, Howard, *Historical Notes on South Africa*, Department of Economic History, Uppsala University 1975 (unpubl.).
57 Marquard, Leo, *Peoples and Policies in South Africa*, London 1968, p. 103.
58 Carter, G.M., Karis, Y., Stultz, N.M., *South Africa's Transkei - The Politics of Domestic Colonialism*, London 1967, p. 84.
59 Pim Report, see note 41.
60 *Native Courts Proclamation* No 62, 1938 (enforced in 1946), 1,340 courts led by chiefs were reduced to 122 courts, not led by chiefs. Basutoland Treasury, established in 1946, took over the responsibility to collect fines. This was earlier the responsibility of chiefs.

3. POLITICAL PARTIES (p. 37 - 76)

1 All recruitment firms with offices in Lesotho are South African. Most of these offices belong to the Mining Labour Organization (MLO) of the Chamber of Mines (former Native Recruitment Organization, NRC). Also the Labour Office, set up by the government in 1933 (*Basutoland 1935, and 1953* H.M.S.O. London) in Johannesburg, expanded after independence. This Office provides social services and communication facilities for migrant workers and their families.
2 Jacotett, E., *Growth of the Church in the Mission field*, Morija 1950 and Wellmer, Gottfried, Mission and Migrant Labour, *Ministry*, Vol. 10, No 1, 1970.
3 Haliburton, R., *Politics and Religion*, paper presented at Conference on History of Southern Africa, Gaborone 1973.
4 Estimation in *Urban and Rural Consumption Surveys*, (Figures from 1968), Bureau of Statistics, Maseru 1973 and 1983.
5 Election Statistics 1965 and 1970 (reported over the Lesotho Police Radio before the Coup), see Appendix I. Macartney, W.J.A.
6 Articles by G.M. Kolisang and others in *Leselinyana* (weekly newspaper in Sesotho), during 1974-1975 published by Lesotho Evangelical Church, Morija. Translated into English by the BCP Office, Lusaka and *OBS* (radio programme by Swedish Broadcasting Corporation, Margareta Gelbort and Leif Söderström) and complete taped interviews with group leaders in the Interim-Parliament.
7 Declarations at Annual Conferences of BAC in 1957 and BCP in 1959 published by the BCP weekly *Makatolle* and *Mohlabane* (The Warrior, edited by Bennett Khaketla) all kept at the Library of the National University of Lesotho at Roma.
8 *All-African People's Conference*, 5-12 December 1958; *Khaketla, B.M., Lesotho 1970. An African Coup under the Microscope*, London, 1971, p. 48.
9 Halpern, J., *South Africa's Hostages*, Harmondsworth 1965, pp. 145-146.
10 Ibid., p. 157.
11 See Appendix I.

12 Surfontein, J.H.P., *Sunday Times*, Johannesburg 8 February 1970.

13 See Appendix I, *United Democratic Party* (UDP) got 564 votes in the 1970 election in the three constituencies where it had candidates.

14 Statement by the General Secretary of the BCP to the Press, Stockholm June 1973.

15 *Interim National Assembly Hansards 1975.*

16 Collection of articles in Swedsih newspapers 1974 by journalists participating in journey to Lesotho, Botswana, Swaziland and Zambia. Republished by Swedish International Development Authority (SIDA), who also financed the journey. Stockholm 1975.

17 Ibid., see also note 6.

18 Table of Ministers in Breytenbach,W.J., *Crocodiles and Commoners in Lesotho*, Africa Institute of South Africa, Pretoria 1975, p. 103 and p. 118.

19 *Leselinyana*, "Manyeli gives Masupha a 22 day ultimatum", Morija, 27 June 1975. A.C. Manyeli former Minister in Jonathan's government was expelled from the BNP, Masupa Kathiso was General Secretary of the BNP, at the time.

20 A letter signed allegedly by Mokhehle, Mofolo and high-ranking police officials was published by the government in mid-December 1973, disclosing plans to overthrow the government. In the following week after the Annual National Conference of the BCP was to be held - the first publicly held since 1969 this conference was stopped and followed by arrests and intensified police raids in the countryside.

21 Funerals, weddings etc., when many people usually gather are now attended by more people than ever. They are openly used as pretext for political meetings. Many speeches are held and the BCP views are put into the mouth of the dead: For example: "The last words by N N" (name of the person who has passed away)... "were that the government should resign immediately". - Funerals of prominent members of the BCP, like Mr. Mou have drawn up to 5,000 participants, (*Leselinyana*, August 1975).

22 This translated version of the "Aims and Objects" of the BCP party constitution is published in *Readings in Boleswa Government. Select Documents*. Selection by Macartney, W.J.A., Roma 1971. The English version is not authorized by the party itself. The BCP Constitution is only authorized in its Sesotho version. The translation used in "Readings..." contains, however, the same words as a translation given by K. Chakela, General Secretary of the BCP, the only exception being that "fight" is exchanged for "struggle".

23 The "Aims and Objectives" of the BNP are copied from "Readings..." see note 22. The English version is authorized by the party.

24 *Interview* with C.D. Molapo, Minister of Foreign Affairs, Maseru November 1975. Opinions of Ruling and Exiled Leaders of Lesotho. Interviews by Winai Ström, G., Report No.14, Department of Peace and Conflict Research, Uppsala University Jan. 1976. Information given by Yugoslavian diplomat, Lusaka 1975 later confirmed by Khetla Rakhetla, Minister of Labour and Industry, Stockholm March 1976.

25 The BNP published a detailed programme for economic growth already in 1969, see "Readings..." in note 22.

26 When the BNP in 1983 established diplomatic relations with the Soviet Union, North Korea and China it actively cooperated with Communist countries and thus broke its anti-communist Aim under paragraph e).

27 A change in 1975 by Yugoslavia to support the BNP as well as the Chakela group of the BCP was crucial. Another event was the liberation of Mozambique in 1975 with which the BNP-regime established relations partly trhough contacts with the Chakela group.

28 This comparison of idelas is based on my own interviews with leaders and members of the BCP and BNP, as well as on the party constitutions.

29 Interview with C.D. Molapo in *Opinions...*, see note 24.

30 *Interview* with K. Chakela, Stockholm June 1974.
31 Disunity within the Executive in exile during 1976, which got wide publicity abroad has been caused partly by a challenge of the extreme financial powers kept by the Leader.
32 C.D. Molapo in *Opinions...*, see note 24.
33 *Halpern*, see note 9, p. 163. Halpern states that Mokhehle was actually elected for five years. According to BCP spokesmen he was not. The party constitution was, however, changed to allow for such a decision.
34 K. Chakela in *Opinions...*, see note 24.
35 The MFP suddenly also got large financial resources at its disposal before the 1965 elections. Joe Matthew, a former ANC refugee from South Africa who worked within the BCP, had as an individual been given assistance in the form of money and transport facilities. This assistance allegedly came from the Soviet Union to be used for the election campaign. Shortly before the elections Matthew walked over from the BCP to the MFP, taking the funds with him. The reason he gave for this action was that the BCP had in essence an anti-communist line. The BCP in turn criticized Matthew for being "elitist" and carreerist. After the 1965 election Matthew left Lesotho and settled in Botswana, where for a period he became Judicial Commissioner and later businessman. On finance of the parties see also Khaketla note 8, pp. 116-119, 239, 260 and Halpern, see note 9, p. 256; C.D. Molapo note 24 on sponsoring of the BCP until 1976.
36 Khaketla, see note 8, p. 30.
37 This analysis of the elections in 1965 and 1970 was often quoted in Maseru among intellectuals during 1970.
38 N. Mokhehle and K. Chakela in *Opinions...*, see note 24.
39 Ibid.
40 Ibid.
41 *Interviews* with BCP members in 1970 and 1975, see also the interviews in *Opinions...*, see note 24.
42 Wallman, S., *Take out Hunger. Two case studies of rural development in Basutoland.* Toronto 1969, p. 30. Information from Peder Govenius, former leader of Thabana-li-Mele Handicraft Centre, Lesotho, confirmed by S. Mokhehle, treasurer of the BCP and Khetla Rakhetla, Minister of Industry and Commerce in November 1975.
43 Information by Mr. Bamber, head of Barclays Lesotho Branch and board member of Village Industry Development Organization (VIDO), state-owned association for co-operative and other village enterprises; see also S. Mokhehle in *Opinions...*, note 24.
44 Halpern, J., see note 9, p. 148.
45 My summary of statement by *G.M. Kolisang, taped interview* Stockholm, July 1972. Kolisang was General Secretary of the BCP until 1960, when he was appointed Senator by the King. From 1970 to 1973 he was official spokesman for the BCP abroad. Since 1973 he has been member of the Executive of the BCP, and works as a lawyer (with the interruption of a few months in prison in 1975-1976).
46 Weisfelder, R.F., *Defining Political Purpose in Lesotho*, Ohio University 1969. Weisfelder is the political scientist who has in greatest detail studied the party debate in Lesotho. He notices that the BCP has sought to mobilize the discontent, grievances and suspicion abundant in Lesotho. He points out that for the BCP, "attaining power in Lesotho is seen as only a short-run intermediate objective since true national fulfillment can occur only in the wider context of a totally liberated African continent". Weisfelder criticizes the BCP for lacking a programme of action and considers the support given to the BCP as unrealistic. Since Weisfelder is interested in mainly national strategies he outranges the political discussion within the BCP in an artificial manner, according to my opinion. It is quite possible that the BCP

supporters are "realistic" when they mainly work for a change in South
Africa, when striving for better living conditions.

47 N. Mokhehle in *Opinions...*, see note 24.

48 Summary of issues raised during the parliamentary period 1965 to 1970,
as remembered by N. Mokhehle in *Opinions...*, this summary is not complete, but referred to here as a statement by the BCP leader of what
the BCP strategy included.

49 Weisfelder, R.F., *Early Voices of Basutoland*, paper presented at Conference on History of Southern Africa, Gaborone 1973. The figures given
are for the early 1930s. In the late 1930s and during the 1940s the BPA
had 3,000-5,000 members according to the same paper.

50 The leader of the BPA was Thomas Mofolo, who later became a prominent
member of the BNP, see note 113.

51 Both Halpern, see note 9, pp. 169-71 and Weisfelder, see note 49, pp.
12-16, give details on correspondence between representatives of
Lekhotla-la-Bafo and the South African Communist Party. Socialist
nationalism without reference to any specific tribe or geographical
area, was difficult to classify for these two authors. In comparison
with other early liberation movements at the time, the Lekhotla-la-
Bafo is not as odd as indicated in the footnotes of the paper by Weisfelder, who characterizes L-1-B as a movement centred around one person,
J. Lefela. This is probably incorrect. There were many self-educated
commoners of the same type as Lefela, who were, however, not chosen
by the British colonial government to represent the movement. Lefela
did not sign letters and declarations from the L-1-B during the 1930s
and 1940s. Particularly Jingoes, S.J., *A Chief is a Chief by the
People*, London 1975, pp. 204-205.

52 Preamble to the Constitution of Lekhotla-la-Bafo, translated in Haliburton, G., see note 3.

53 Weisfelder, see note 49.

54 Mokhehle and Chakela, in interview Lusaka October 1975, only partly
recorded in *Opinions...*, see note 24.

55 Haliburton, see note 3, p. 40: Lefela was born 1885 at Mapoteng, third
son of a commoner, he went to school for a few years, then to the
mines. But he did not want to go underground and left the mine. He met
Clements Kadale of the Industrial and Commercial trade union (ICU) in
South Africa. In 1910 he settled in Lesotho, married the first of his
three wives and opened a small bar and a butcher's shop. He died at
the age of 82. One of his sons and most of his neighbours in Mapoteng
were considered to be dangerous by the police, and were killed in a
massacre of 48 men at Mapoteng in February 1974 (*Star weekly* 12 March
1974).

56 Weisfelder, see note 49.

57 The *National Archive* of Lesotho contains the papers of Lekhotla-la-
Bafo. These records remain, however, to be organized. Records of the
discussions in the National Council are also kept there.

58 *Mohlabane*, Vol. 3. No. 6, pp. 15-16.

59 K. Chakela in *Opinions...*, see note 24.

60 Ibid.

61 Ibid, interview with N. Mokhehle, Lusaka, November 1975. See note 54.

62 Verbatim Record of the 49th session of the Committee of the Twenty-
Four, May 14, 1962, AC/AC 109/PU.

63 Some students affiliated with the BCP Youth League got their education
in the People's Republic of China during the late 1950s and early
1960s (altogether about 10, who were not allowed transfer through
South Africa on their way home, and were therefore not allowed back
to Lesotho), many more received scholarships via the ANC in Eastern
Europe, the Soviet Union and African universities.

64 Halpern, see note 9, describes these incidents in detail, pp. 3-50.

65 Information given by T. Thahane, head of Central Planning Office, Amsterdam August 1974.

66 See the summary of the party programme of the Communist Party of Lesotho in Halpern, note 9, pp. 176-168. Unfortunately it has not been possible for me to get a written copy of this programme. According to underground CPL spokesmen in Lesotho the summary made by Halpern is correct (although other information given in Halpern on the CPL is not, according to these spokesmen).

67 Information given by Elliot Mokoena, BCP spokesman in Stockholm November 1976.

68 Halpern, see note 9.

69 Ministry of Foreign Affairs' Note No. 5, 21.1.1975 and information from the Boundary Commissioner C.-G. Asplund in Nov. 1977.

70 N. Mokhehle in *Opinions...*, see note 24. No statistical survey on the voting of workers and peasants in Lesotho. Migrant workers are not allowed to vote unless they are at home both at the time of registration and at the time of the election. C.D. Molapo in *Opinions...*, see note 24, argued that almost all migrant workers support the BCP. The same is argued by K. Chakela in the same collections of interviews.

71 C.D. Molapo, note 24.

72 Education statistics do not indicate any difference between constituencies with a large BNP following and constituencies with a large BCP following. C.D. Molapo argues that university students earlier tended to support the BCP, and that this still is a tendency in spite of careful screening of students.

73 *Report of the Fact-finding and Conciliation Commission on Freedom of Association concerning Lesotho*, International Labour Office (ILO), Geneva 1975. *Interview* with Joel Moitse, (former Minister of Industry, Commerce and Labour), Maseru November 1975.

74 S. Mokhehle in *Opinions...*, see note 24.

75 Preamble and Resolution agreed on by the Annual Conference of the Basutoland Federation of Labour, Maseru, 2nd of July 1973. Copied from the original kept by S. Mokhehle (leader of the BFL) including correction made by hand on this original. On this document point (d) under resolutions are missing.

76 *Interview* with Acting Leaders of the BFL, N. Pekosela and R.M. Monese, Maseru December 1975.

77 ILO Mission estimates, see note 73.

78 *Labour News* monthly, Gaborone, February 1975 stated that the LCW was sponsored by the American-African Labour Centre, AALC, and was to be the sole bargaining partner to the Employers Union; See also Leselinyana, Morija November 1975. At the 1976 Conference of the Organization of African Trade Unions (OATU) in Tripoli May 1976, a statement was made that a Federation of both the LCW and the BFL should be supported.

79 See note 76.

80 Ibid.; and information given by acting head of Lesotho National Development Corporation, (LNDC), Ilmar Rostahl.

81 The BNP is characterized as the party of the lower chiefs by for example Frank, L., *The Basotho National Party - from Traditionalism to Neocolonialism*, Denver 1970 and by Devitt, P., *A micro-study of power politics at a village in the Roma Valley*. M.A. Thesis, Witwatersrand University, Department of Anthropology, 1969.

82 *A chief...*, pp. 216 and 218; Kowet, D., *Botswana, Lesotho and Swaziland*, (unpubl.), Department of Political Science at Uppsala University 1974.

83 As we saw in the Preamble to the constitution of *Lekhotla-la-Bafo*, the pitso in the form it had during the reign of Moshoeshoe I, and the first thirty years after colonization was not seen as satisfactory, since it did not express the people's will. The Lekhotla-la-Bafo and the BCP were critical to the optimistic view of the BNP on the pitso as a forum

for political discussion and decision-making.

84 C.D. Molapo in *Opinions...*, see note 24.

85 Ibid. and my interview with C.D. Molapo.

86 Speeches by his Excellency the Prime Minister Chief Leabua Jonathan on the Fourth Aniversary of Lesotho Independence 4-6 October 1970, p. 9.

87 *The Honorable Chief Leabua Jonathan*, Information Department, Maseru August 1970.

88 *Radio statement by the Prime Minister* in connection with the announcement of a National Government, 14 November 1975.

89 L. Jonathan in *Opinions...* see note 24.

90 Ibid. The MFP in Lesotho and the PAC of South Africa also often refer to Moshoeshoe I, as a great statesman, whereas Lekhotla-la-Bafo and most representatives of the BCP are much more critical.

91 Damane, M., *The Statecraft of Moshoeshoe the Great*, Moshoeshoe Memorial Lecture IV, Maseru 12 March 1975.

92 This word was used by Jonathan about his Ministers in the National Government he appointed on the 12 November 1975. See Opinions... note 24.

93 Emergency regulations 1970. *Tona-Kholo* was a term sometimes used also for the Prime Minister in Transkei Kaiser Matanzima, it was thus later omitted.

94 *The Order of the Office of the King*, December 1970. The King swore an oath to follow the rules decided by the government.

95 Khaketla, see note 8, p. 191, speech by the Prime Minister at Mafeteng on 6 December 1969, quoted in extenso.

96 *Summary of the Report of the Commission for the Socio-Economic Development of the Bantu Areas within the Union of South Africa* (Tomlinson), UG 61/1955; *Government Decisions on the Recommendations of the Commission for the Socio-Economic Development of the Bantu Areas within the Union of South Africa* (White Paper), W.P. F/1956.

97 *Dr. H.F. Verwoerd, on I. Crisis in World Conscience II. The Road to Freedom for Basutoland, Bechuanaland, Swaziland* Department of Information, Pretoria 1963.

98 Ibid., my summary.

99 *The Honourable...*, see note 87.

100 *Leabua Jonathan. A Tribute to the Prime Minister of the Kingdom of Lesotho*, Information Department, Maseru October 1972.

101 *The Honourable...*, see note 87.

102 *Leabua...*, see note 100.

103 *Khaketla*, note 8, my summary.

104 Catholic Directory 1975 of Southern Africa, Cape Town, pp. 319-339.

105 Ibid. p. 78 et.al. The appointment of P.J. Buthelezi (OMI and DD) in 1972 as auxiliary to Bishop Boyle of Johannesburg was a step in this reformist direction. The appointment of a well-known militant priest, Dean Desmond Tutu, from Johannesburg as Archbishop in 1976 is seen as another example of the attempts from the churches to change their image among black people in Southern Africa, *Star* 27 March 1976.

106 Africa Institute of South Africa, *South Africa's Development Aid to African States*. After a manuscript by Leistner, G.M.E., Pretoria 1970.

107 Leabua..., see note 100.

108 Legum, C., ed., *Africa Contemporary Records*, 1974, Vorster's statement was made to the diplomatic corps in Cape Town; economic assistance to Lesotho from South Africa has been given mainly in the form of small financial transfers from state-owned and private firms to joint ventures in Lesotho and border industries in the Orange Free State. The latter are mentioned in the speech by Verwoerd in 1963, see note 97 above.

109 These reference to the apartheid ideology are based mainly on party programmes of the Nationalist Party and pamphlets published by the Information Department of the South African Government. See also Simson, Howard *South African Fascism*, Uppsala 1980.

110 *The Sons of Moshoeshoe* is a gathering of the direct descendants to Moshoeshoe I, Oblates of Mary Immaculate (OMI) is a conservative Catholic Order, mentioned earlier. The missionaries in Lesotho are mainly from Canada and are French-speaking. There are 60-70 of them, many of whom settled in Basutoland during the 1930s.

111 C.D. Molapo in *Opinions...*, see note 24.

112 Breytenbach, see note 18, p. 107, Tomas Mofolo and Justice Mokotso were both leaders of the Basutoland Progressive Association, BPA.

113 *The Star*, Johannesburg, 1 April 1972.

114 *The Drum*, Johannesburg, 22 August 1972; *Mareng a Meso*, Johannesburg September 1972, p. 3.

115 *Rand Daily Mail*, Johannesburg, 22 June 1972.

116 *Moeletsi*, weekly, Mazenod, 12 August 1972.

117 *Leselinyana*, weekly, Morija, 27 June 1975.

118 see note 49.

119 *Nketu*, Vol. 3, No. 8 (1967), p. 8. quoted in Breytembach pp. 67-69.

120 *Interviews* with BNP rank and file members in 1970 and 1975; also said by C.D. Molapo and Leabua Jonathan in *Opinions...*, see note 24.

121 Information given by Chamber of Commerce, and discussion with traders, December 1975.

122 In articles in *Rand Daily Mail*, *Star*, *Friend* and other newspapers during February-June 1970 and information by G.M. Kolisang (BCP), K. Chakela (BCP) and C.D. Molapo (BNP) on a period of interparty discussions broken in September 1975.

123 First, R., ed., *Black Gold; The Mocambican Miner, Proletarian and Peasant*, Brighton 1983, is a good description of peasants who are migrant mine workers, and whose families do not live from agricultural produce since decades back, pp. 183-194.

4. STATE INSTITUTIONS (p. 77 - 94)

1 *Report on Constitutional Reform and Chieftainship Affairs*, Maseru 1958.

2 Report of the Basutoland Independence Conference 1966, supplement to Gazette no 3538, London, June 1966, published in *Readings in BoLeSwa Government*, Select Documents. ed. W.J.A. McCartney, UBLS printing unit, University of Roma, 1971.

3 See note 1 and 2. My own interviews support the official documents.

4 Laws of Lerotholi, Theal, G.M., *Basutoland Records*, Cape Town 1883.

5 Legassick, M., Race, Industrialization and Social Change in Southern Africa, *African Affairs*, April 1976, p. 228.

6 Palmer, V. and Poulter, S., *The Legal System of Lesotho*, Charlottenville 1972.

7 Catalogues of the University of Botswana, Lesotho and Swaziland at Roma, Lesotho, in 1970 and 1975, and interviews with law students.

8 *Africa Contemporary Records*, ed. Legum, C., London 1974.

9 Prospects published by Lesotho National Development Corporation, *The sky is the limit* 1970, and *A Small country, but what a market* 1973.

10 Anton Rupert has a special position in South African business. He is a member of the Broederbond (inner circle of the Nationalist Party) and Director of the Reserve Bank (Central Bank) of the Republic. He

is also one of the first successful businessmen of Afrikaaner extraction. He owns breweries, cigarette companies and food processing firms with investments in many other countries than South Africa.

11 *Repressive Legislation of the Republic of South Africa*, United Nations on Apartheid, New York 1969; *Focus on Political Repression in Southern Africa, Annual Survey of the South African Institute of Race Relations*, Johannesburg June 1976.

12 *Lesotho, 1967*, Maseru Department of Information 1968, p. 223.

13 Report of the Basutoland Independence Conference 1966, see note 2. In May 1966 the resolution requesting independence for the British colony Basutoland was passed by the Parliament with 32 votes for the resolution and 28 against. The members of the BCP and the MFP, representing 60 per cent of the votes, were against the resolution.

14 See note 2 and *Report on the Structure and Administration of the Lesotho Government*, Coutts, W., Cabinet Circular Notice no. 20, Maseru, 1966 p. 7.

15 *Judgement of Mr. Justice Landowne in Mantsebo v. Bereng 1943.*

16 See note 2, p. 10.

17 *Interviews* with dismissed employees of the Department of Finance at Matsieng.

18 *Interviews* with BCP supporters and leaders, April 1970 and November 1975.

19 *Interviews* with BNP supporters and leaders, April 1970 and November 1975, see also note 14, *Report...*, p. 7.

20 *Land Administration Act 1973*, accepted by the Interim Parliament in 1974.

21 Confidential interviews with participants in this meeting.

22 *Interviews* with villagers at the Thaba Bosiu project buildings November 1975 at Ha Nsi, Maseru district.

23 *Opinions of Ruling and Exiled Leaders of Lesotho*, Report no. 14, Interview with Prime Minister Leabua Jonathan, Department of Peace and Conflict Research, Uppsala 1975.

24 Ibid.

25 The most well-known writer is Bennett Khaketla. In his newspaper *Mohlabane* (The Warrior) Khaketla criticized the colonial government, particularly its recruitment policy. He was politically active in the BCC/BCP 1954-1960, Freedom Party from its inception 1961. He then joined the MFP in 1962.

26 *Lesotho 1966*, Her Majesty's Stationary Office, London 1967.

27 Figures given by the head of the Planning Office in 1973, based on *Basutoland 1962* and figures from the Bureau of Statistics. See also Walter Elkan *Report to the Government of Basutoland on the Manpower situation*, ILO/TAP/Basutoland R1, and Anthony Beattie *1971 Public and Private Sector Manpower Surveys in Lesotho*, Overseas Development Agency, London, November 1971.

28 *Government Staff Lists* and *Annual Reports of the Commissioner of Police*, Maseru 1968 and 1972.

29 Document of the IBRD, *Economy of Lesotho*, Report No. 331a-LSO, Washington 1974.

30 See note 27.

31 *Lesotho 1967*, Department of Information, Maseru 1968, and *Annual Reports of the Commissioner of Police*, 1968 and 1972.

32 UNDP reports in 1970 and 1975 on United Nations and other personnel assistance.

33 Ibid.

34 South African and later West German aid personnel.

35 Figures given by Percy Mangoaela, who worked in the Foreign Office in 1966-1968 and Lesotho Radio 1968-1970.

36 The 1964 Constitution confirmed the rules practiced.

37 *Interviews* with British civil servants, leaders of BNP and BCP, also mentioned for example in Breytenbach, W.J., *Crocodiles and Commoners in Lesotho*, Africa Institute, Pretoria 1975.

38 *Interviews* with civil servants about the climate of discussion in 1975, as well as my own general comparison with the atmosphere after the coup d'état in 1970.

39 Interview with C.D. Molapo in 1975, confirmed by BCP leaders, see note 23.

40 The People's Republic of China also provided about ten scholarships. The students who studied in China were, however, never allowed to return to Lesotho via the Republic of South Africa.

41 *Interviews* with the leaders of the organizations of civil servants: Percy Mangoaela, Khetla Rakhetla and Sam Montsi.

42 *Interviews* with both BNP and BCP supporters in the public administration and *Report on assignment to Lesotho* by Percy Selwyn, Institute of Development Studies, Sussex 1971.

43 See note 38.

44 Report, see note 14.

45 Report of the *Fact-finding and Conciliation Mission on Freedom of Association Concerning Lesotho*, International Labour Office, Geneva 1975.

46 Annual Report by the Commissioner of Police, Maseru 1968,

47 Lesotho 1967 and Lesotho 1971, Information Department, Maseru 1968 and 1972.

48 Ibid.

49 See note 46.

50 Khaketla, B.M., *Lesotho 1970 an African Coup under the Microscope*, London 1971, and my interviews with two persons in "the crowd" in 1970.

51 Head of the Leribe police district was Fredric Roach, appointed Commissioner of Police in March 1970, dismissed 1973.

52 There were about 30 British policemen in top posts within the police force. Their salaries were paid by the Lesotho government and they received additional salaries, so-called topping-up, from the Overseas Development Agency in London.

53 See note 46.

54 Halpern, J., *South African Hostages*, Harmondsworth 1965, pp. 3-51.

55 *Interviews* with BCP leaders and supporters in 1970 and 1975 and article in Cape Argus, February 1970, (quoted in Weisfelder, R., *Political Struggle...*, Ohio University 1970).

56 Macartney, W.J.A., "The Lesotho General Election of 1970", *Government and Opposition*, October 1973.

5. GOVERNMENT DEVELOPMENT POLICIES UNDER CONDITIONS OF UNEQUAL INTEGRATION (p. 95 - 131)

1 Dye, Thomas, *Understanding Public Policy*, Englewood Cliffs 1972, p.1.

2 Hettne, Björn, *Utvecklingsstrategier i Kina och Indien* (Development strategies in China and India), Göteborg 1971.

3 *BoLeSwa Government Readings*, collection by Macartney, W.J.A., vol. two: Lesotho, p. 264, BNP Manifesto 1965.

4 Thahane, T., quoted in Winai-Ström, G., "The Influence of Multinational Corporations on Lesotho's Politics and Economics". *The African Review*, vol. 5, no. 4, 1975 (Dar-es-Salaam).

5 See note 3, p. 263, "The Government of the Basotho National Party will spare no pains to maintain the peace of Lesotho so that it will be possible to develop a tourist industry. This can only be possible under a peaceful atmosphere".

6 *Second Five-Year Development Plan 1975/76-1979/80*, Maseru 1975,
  pp. 20-21; Donor Conference Minutes, CPDO, Maseru June 1975, p. 22.
  (Localization is the Lesotho term for indegenization.)
7 *Interview* with Thahane, (head of CPDO in Lesotho from 1970 to 1973) in
  Stockholm July 1973.
8 *Budget Speech by the Minister of Finance*, Maseru March 1967 and *Speech
  by the Prime Minister, moving the 1968/69 Development Fund Expenditure
  in the House of Assembly*, March 1968.
9 See note 3, BNP Manifestos for 1965 and 1969.
10 An exception to this line is a statement by Leabua Jonathan early in
  1973, *"Towards Self-reliance"*. This was an attempt to unite the parties
  in Lesotho. Speeches afterwards ressemble the earlier line taken.
11 *Summary and objectives of the Second Five Year Plan*, CPDO Maseru 1975,
  (mimeo), and the Third Fice-Year Plan, CPDO Maseru 1979 (unpubl.).
12 *First Five-Year Development Plan* 1970/71-1974/75, Maseru 1970, see
  also note 6 pp. 18-19.
13 This is my impression during many visits to different parts of the
  state institutions in 1970 and 1975. It holds true particularly for
  the Ministries of Agriculture, Finance and Planning, and the Ministry
  of Industry, Labour and Commerce.
14 Document of the IMF, *Lesotho - Recent Economic Developments*,
  SM/75/123, p. 1.
15 See note 12, p. 24.
16 Ibid. p. 76.
17 Ibid. p. 24 and 76.
18 *Interview* with Arne Lexander, surveyor at the Ministry of Agriculture,
  November 1975. See also his surveys of the Leribe and Thaba Bosiu areas.
19 *Interviews* with villagers in the Leribe-Khomokhoana area, November
  1975; *speech by* the acting head of the Leribe project, *M. Salae* also
  in November 1975.
20 Complaints presented to the Court and to the *Special Investigation
  committee to the Leribe project*. Ministry of Agriculture 1975.
21 *Project Progress Report* 1.2.75. to 31.7.75. Lesotho Rural Development
  of the *Khomokhoana* and adjacent areas, by M. Salae.
22 See note 11.
23 Ibid.
24 Ibid., see also *Second Five Year Plan*, pp. 22-25.
25 *Business and Development in Lesotho. A Newsletter of the LNDC*, no. 1,
  Maseru March 1976, p. 3.
26 Ibid.
27 *Speech by Joel Moitse*, Minister of Industry, Labour and Commerce, to
  traders 29 November 1974.
28 Traders invited to Foreign Minister C.D. Molapo, December 1975; *press
  release by LNDC* (interview by Joe Molife with Ilmar Rosthal) at the
  opening of a new "Cash and Carry Wholesale Market", Maseru November
  1975.
29 See note 25, pp. 8 and 14.
30 *Interviews* with the chief manager of Standard Bank Lesotho, (confirmed
  by the Registrar of Financial Institutions) and the head of the Lesotho Bank, Maseru November and December 1975. More money than before
  was also invested in Lesotho in the sectors of diamond mining, construction and tourism.
31 *The Sky is the Limit in Lesotho*, prospect published by the LNDC,
  Maseru 1970.
32 Officers of the CPDO participating in discussion on the customs union
  revenue distribution in November 1975. Selwyn P.
33 *Customs and Excise Union Agreement* between the Government of Lesotho,
  Botswana, South Africa and Swaziland 1969, Lesotho Government Gazette
  no. 58, 1969.

34 *Monetary Agreement* between the Government of Lesotho, South Africa and Swaziland, 1974, Lesotho Government Gazette no. 1974.

35 Mentioned in article 12 of the Customs Union Agreement, see note 33.

36 Leistner, G.M.E., *Cooperation for Development in Southern Africa*, Africa Institute of South Africa, Pretoria 1972.

37 *Economic Development Programme for the Republic of South Africa* 1972-1977. Pretoria 1972.

38 *Interview* with the acting head of LNDC, Ilmar Rosthal, Maseru November 1975. Pamphlets of LNDC.

39 See note 37.

40 Clarke, D.G., *Some Determinants of Demand for Foreign African Labour in South Africa*, (mimeo) Geneva 1977.

41 A common monthly income in 1970 among gold mine workers was R 25. The same job was paid R 100 in 1975. In 1980, the average gold miners wage per month was R 170 and in 1984 it had increased to R 350. In real terms this was annual increase of 10 - 20 per cent. Miners remittances increased during the late 1970 and early 1980s and became the dominant and expanding part of National Income.

42 Leeuvenburg, Jeff, *Transkei. A Study in Economic Regression*, The Africa Bureau, London January 1977, p. 7.

43 Speeches by Leabua Jonathan at pitsos in different districts in 1971, 1973 and 1975.

44 The South African Government decided in 1974 to allocate new funds for the encouragement of less labour intensive techniques in the mining industry. (See also Five Year Plan 1975, Pretoria.)

45 The Lesotho Labour Department collects statistics from the South African Recruitment organizations.

46 See for example Leys, R., *Labour Migration, Lesotho*, IDR Project Papers, D 75.1., Progress Report for the Period April to November 1974, Institute for Development Research, Copenhagen 1975.

47 Top Companies in South Africa. Supplement to the *Financial Mail*, (Johannesburg) April 1973 and April 1974.

48 Ibid.

49 Ibid.

50 *Pioneer Industries Encouragement Act 1969.*

51 Rupert, Anton "International Business Partnership - the Multinational Concept", *South African International*, vol. 1, no. 2.

52 See note 4.

53 First, R., Steele, J., Gurney, C., *The South African Connection - Western Investment in Apartheid*, Harmondsworth 1973.

54 *Interviews* with Thahane, head of CPDO, and Sekhunyana, Minister of Finance, in Stockholm July 1973.

55 Leabua Jonathan at press conference, Maseru February 1970.

56 Cervenka, Zdenek, ed. *Landlocked countries in Africa*, The Scandinavian Institute of African Studies, Uppsala 1973, p. 239, T. Thahane, "Lesotho - The Realities of Landlockedness".

57 *Interviews* with Officers at the Lesotho Desk of ODA, London October 1972.

58 Legum, C., ed. *African Contemporary Records*, London 1972 and 1973.

59 Ibid. Examples given in interview with K. Rakhetla, Minister and former Permanent Secretary at the Ministry of Industry, Stockholm March 1976.

60 *Interviews* with personnel at LNDC, CPDO (Nov. 1975) and see note 59.

61 Annual Report 1973 and 1974, *EDESA Finanz*, Zürich.

62 These visits are ususally recorded in the *Radio Lesotho News*.
63 Walton J., *Father of Kindness and Horses. History of Frasers Ltd*, Wepener 1958.
64 Facts given by one of the managers of Frasers Lesotho Ltd, Maseru December 1975.
65 *Trade Registry*, at Ministry of Industry and Commerce for 1974 and 1975.
66 See note 64.
67 First et al., see note 53.
68 *Lesotho Telephone Directory*, yearly advertisements.
69 *Interview* with Dr. B. Wacher, Wool and Mohair Division of the Lesotho Marketing Corporation.
70 Percentage figure of profit was given by J.T. Surti for his own trade. Surti is one of the few traders who compete with Fraser and is active in the Butha Buthe district.
71 Rakhetla see note 59.
72 *Barclay's International* 1973 and 1974, confirmed by Department of statistics, Maseru 1975.
73 Ibid.
74 *Barclay's International*, February 1973.
75 *Rennies' Company News*, October 1975.
76 *Lesotho National Development Corporation Annual Report* 1972. *Lesotho Telephone Directory*, see also LNDC list of companies 1975.
77 Savosnic, Kurt, et al. *Development Plan for Tourism in Lesotho*, 3.4.20, *Annual Statistical Bulletin* 1975, table 20.
78 *Interview* with the former Minister of Industry, Commerce and Labour, Joel Moitse, November 1975.
79 See note 59.
80 See note 38.
81 Document of the IBRD, *The Economy of Lesotho*, Report no. 331a-LSO, Washington June 25, 1974; *Interview* with Arne Lexander surveyor at the Ministry of Agriculture, Maseru December 1975.
82 *The Economy...*, see note 81, p. 70.
83 *Budget Speech by the Minister of Finance*, Department of Information, Maseru 1971.
84 *Basutoland 1958*, H.M.S.O., London 1959.
85 Ibid.
86 See note 41.
87 Information given by Theresa Ntsane, Permanent Secretary responsible of personnel questions in the Cabinet Office, Maseru November 1975.
88 Information by Dr. B. Wacher, adviser in the Wool and Mohair Division of the Livestock Marketing Corporation, Maseru December 1975.
89 *Estimated and Actual Revenue and Expenditure* of the Kingdom of Lesotho, 1973/74. (Both revenue and expenditure are, in Lesotho, divided between a "Current budget" and a "Capital budget").
90 *Lesotho 1968*, see note 12.
91 Figures from *The Economy of Lesotho*. See note 81 and Current and Capital Accounts of the Government of Lesotho 1974/75 and 1975/76.
92 *Owen Horwood's report* has not been made public, but is quoted for example in Coutts, W., Cabinet Circular Notice, no. 20, Maseru 1966.
93 Press articles republished in clippings, weekly from the Department of Information, Maseru 1970 and 1974 and information by the secretary to the Prime Minister Desmond Sixlise.
94 *Interview* with K. Rakhetla, Minister of Industry, Stockholm March 1976.
95 *Report on the Structure and Administration of the Lesotho Government*, Coutts, W., Cabinet Circular Notice no. 20, Maseru 1966.
96 The *Basutoland Federation of Labour*, (BFL), estimates the Government revenue from recruitment offices to 1.5 million rand during the first year of the agreement 1974/75. This revenue from the recruitment offices in Lesotho was not recorded separately and is not stated officially.

97 See note 33.
98 *Estimated and Actual Revenue and Expenditure of the Kingdom of Lesotho*, 1972/73.
99 *Estimated and Actual Revenue and Expenditure of the Kingdom of Lesotho*, for the years 1973/74, 1974/75 and 1975/76 and estimates by officers at the Central Planning and Development Office.
100 According to representatives of the Lesotho and Botswana Governments participating in bargaining in November 1975, both the liberation of Mozambique and Angola and the labour strikes in the Republic had favourable effects on the bargaining results. General conclusions about the actual causes of the favourable results for the Customs Union partners to South Africa are, however, not possible to draw at this stage.
101 Ibid.
102 See note 99, *Capital and Current Accounts for 1973/74*.
103 Ibid. for 1974/75 and 1975/76.
104 The South African and British radio and press reported after the events of January–February 1974, that 200 to 1,000 people were killed by the Lesotho Para-Military Unit and by the armed youth league, known as "The Peace Corps".
105 Letter on visit to Lesotho, by the *Swedish Ambassador* to Lesotho, stationed in Pretoria, to the Swedish Foreign Office, 22 April 1974. Archive of the Swedish International Development Agency, (SIDA) in Stockholm.
106 See notes 6 and 14.
107 *Annual Statistical Bulletin 1975*, table 58 and *interview* with the Registrar of Financial Institutions, Maseru November 1975.
108 *Financial Institutions Act 1974*.
109 *Interview* with the Registrar, see note 107.
110 See note 34.
111 (IMF), *Surveys of African Economies*, Vol. 5, Washington 1973; confirmed in *interviews* with the chief manager of the Standard Bank, Maseru November 1975, and (IMF) Lesotho-Recent Economic Developments, Nov 1985.
112 Ibid p. 147, Maseru November 1975; *interview* with the head of Lesotho Bank.
113 *Interview* with the former Minister of Industry etc., Joel Moitse, Maseru November 1975; Barclay's International 1974; according to the chief manager of the Standard Bank competition has increased on the supply side of the credit market. This had in 1976 not yet had effects on statistical records.
114 *Deferred Pay Fund Act*, January 1975; *interviews* with the BFL leaders Maseru November 1975.
115 Information from documents published by the LNDC.
116 Ibid. and *interview* with the acting head of the LNDC, see note 38, *Assets and Liabilities of the LNDC 1975*; *interview* see note 107.
117 Information given by officers of the CPDO, see note 41.
118 *Petition*, see note 114.
119 *Interview* with the head of the Lesotho Bank, November 1975.
120 Ibid., *interview* with the Registrar, see note 107; Surveys, see note 111.
121 Reference in *interview* with the head of Lesotho Bank to estimates by Lesotho Chamber of Commerce (P.B. Jandrell) see note 30.
122 Standard Bank Statistics quoted in *interview* with the chief manager of Standard Bank, see note 34.
123 See note 119.
124 The most important insurance companies operating in Lesotho are Sanlam, Homes Trust (both South African parastatal companies) and Protea partly owned by Frasers.
125 See note 111.

126 Muzorewas, Basil C., *Money, Financial Institutions and Economic Development in Lesotho* (M.A. Thesis), Department of Economics, University of Botswana, Lesotho and Swaziland (UBLS), Gaborone 1972, p. 20.
127 *Interview*, see note 107.
128 See note 126.
129 See note 61.
130 *Interview* with the local representatives of EDESA, N.N. Raditapoli.
131 See note 61.
132 See note 130.
133 See note 61.
134 See note 130.
135 *Press release by the LNDC* on a new joint venture on Mohair Processing, Maseru 7 July 1975.
136 *South African Mohair Board, Annual Statistics*, 1970 and 1975, Pretoria; *South African Wool Board, Annual Statistics*, 1970 and 1975, Pretoria.
137 *United Nations Statistical Yearbook*, New York 1975.
138 Ibid. 1970.
139 *Annual Statistical Report* 1976, table 25.
140 See note 3, p. 289, BNP Manifesto 1970.
141 *International Diamond Annual*, ed. Wilson, A.N., Vol 1, Johannesburg 1971, p. 65.
142 Kresten, P., *Report on assignment to the UNDP*, Maseru 1973 and *interview* with Peter Kresten.
143 *Annual Report of the Department of Mines and Geology*, Maseru 1974.
144 Ibid., and *interview* with Peter Kresten.
145 See note 142 and note 6.
146 Kolisang, G.M., *The Export of Apartheid to Lesotho, report to the United Nations' Anti-Apartheid Commission*, New York 1969.
147 See note 141.
148 *Annual Report by the Commissioner of Police*, Maseru 1968.
149 See note 12, p. 134.
150 *The Friend*, 10.4.1970, "Diggers blamed for clashes in Lesotho", *The Friend*, 14.4.1970, "BCP leaders appeal may end violence", *Economist* (first week in April) "Rule by Hand Grenade", *The Friend*, 9.4.1970, "Top Lesotho men agreed to talk", *Rand Daily Mail*, 8.4.1970 "150 people killed", *The Star* 8.4.1970 "Air dash by police" and "Rhodesian sees Lesotho police attack on gang".
151 *Interview* april 1970 with Timothy Thahane, officer at the CPDO at the time and special representative of the government in bargaining with the diamond diggers.
152 See note 150.
153 See note 151.
154 Gregory, T., *Ernest Oppenheimer and the Economic Growth of South Africa*, Cape Town 1962.
155 Kresten, P., *Special Report, The Kimberlites of the Kao-Lemphane Area*, Maseru January 1973.
156 See note 141.
157 Ibid., p. 22.
158 Ibid.
159 Ibid., p. 24.
160 Ibid.
161 Ibid., p. 14.
162 Ibid.
163 See note 12, p. 134.
164 Ibid.
165 *Interviews* with employees at the Department of Mines and Geology, Maseru 1970.
166 *Lesotho Weekly Bulletin*, Department of Information, 4.8.1973, 22.9.1973 and 8.9.1973.

Ibid., March 1974.
See note 166.
Speech by Harry Oppenheimer at the occasion of the signing of the agreement with the Lesotho Government on diamond mining and trade, 24 March 1975, Maseru.
See note 6, p. 145.
See note 41.
See note 170.
Ibid., p. 144.

References

Literature

Africa Institute, *South Africa's Development Aid to African States*, After a manuscript by Leistner, G.M.E., Pretoria 1970.

Amin, S., *Accumulation on a World Scale*, New York 1974.

Amin, S., *Le Développement Inégal. Essai sur les Formations Sociales du Capitalisme Périphérique*, Paris 1973.

Ashley, M.J., *Education and Social Change. Report from Social Commission*, No. 44, The Study Project on Christianity in Apartheid Society, Johannesburg 1973.

Barrat, J. et al., *Accelerated Development in Southern Africa*, South African Institute of International Affairs, Johannesburg 1974.

Bibliography on Basutoland/Lesotho by Centre for International Studies, Ohio University, Athens 1966.

Bodenheimer, S., "Dependence and Imperialism, The Roots of Latin American Underdevelopment", *NACLA Newsletter*, (New York), Vol. IV No. 3., May–June 1970, pp. 18–27.

Breytenbach, W.J., *Crocodiles and Commoners in Lesotho*, Africa Institute of South Africa, Pretoria 1975.

Carter, C.M., Karis, Y., Stults, N.M., *South Africa's Transkei. The Politics of Domestic Colonialism*, London 1967.

Campbell, J., *Travels in South Africa 1820*, London 1822.

Casalis, E., *The Basuto: Twenty-three Years in South Africa*, Africana Collectanea Series, Cape Town 1965 (Reprint from 1855, Paris).

Cervenka, Z., ed., *Land-locked Countries in Africa*, The Scandinavian Institute of African Studies, Uppsala 1973.

Collection of Articles in Swedish Newspapers (in Swedish) on *Southern Africa*, by journalists travelling to Botswana, Lesotho, Swaziland and Zambia financed by SIDA, Stockholm 1975.

Dye, T., *Understanding Public Policy*, Englewood Cliffs 1972.

Ewers, T., and Wogau, P.v., "Dependencia: lateinamerikanische Beiträge zur Theorie der Unterentwicklung", *das Argument*, no. 3 1973.

First, R., Steele, J., Gurney, C., *The South African Connection—Western Investment in Apartheid*, Harmondsworth 1973.

Frank, A.G., *Capitalism and Underdevelopment in Latinamerica. Historical Studies of Chile and Brazil*, New York 1967.

Frank, L., *The Basotho National Party—from Traditionalism to Neo-colonialism*, Denver 1970.

Germond, R.C., *Chronicles of Basutoland*, Morija 1967.

Gregory, T., *Ernest Oppenheimer and the Economic Growth of South Africa*, Cape Town 1962.

Halpern, J., *South African Hostages*, London 1965.

Hettne, B., *Utvecklingsstrategier i Kina och Indien* (Development Strategies in China and India) Göteborg 1971.

Hobson, J.A., *Imperialism. A Study*, London 1905.

Hobson, J.A., *The South African War*, London 1903.

Jacotett, E., *Growth of the Church in the Mission Field*, Morija 1959.

Jingoes, S.J., *A Chief is a Chief by the Peoples* (Autobiography recorded and compiled by J. and C. Perry), Cape Town 1975.

Khaketla, B.M., Lesotho 1970. *An African Coup under the Microscope*, London 1971.

Keen, K., *Two Decades of Development in Basutoland, 1830-1850*, Bulletin of Department of History, University of Gothenburg 1975.

Laclau, E., "Feudalism and Capitalism in Latin America", *New Left Review*, No. 67 1971.

Leeuvenburg, Jeff, *Transkei. A Study in Economic Repression*, The Africa Bureau, London Jan. 1977.

Legassick, M., "Race, Industrialization and Social Change in Southern Africa". *African Affairs*, Vol. 75, No. 299.

Leistner, G.M.E., *Cooperation for Development in Southern Africa*, Africa Institute of South Africa, Pretoria 1972.

Leys, C., "Underdevelopment and Dependency: Critical Notes", *Journal of Contemporary Asia*, Vol. 7, no. 1, 1977, p. 92.

Livingstone, D., *Missionary Travels and Research in South Africa*, London 1857.

Livingstone, D., *Missionary Correspondence 1841-1856*, ed. Shapera, I., London 1861.

Macartney, W.J.A., "The General Election in Lesotho 1970", *Government and Opposition*, Oct. no. 4 1973, pp. 473-495.

Marquard, L., *Peoples and Policies in South Africa*, London 1968.

Mason, R.J., and van der Merwe, N.J., "Radio-carbonic Dating of Iron Age Sites in the Southern Transvaal", *South Africa Journal of Science*, 60 V 1964.

Mikkelsen, Vagn, Imperialism og Avhängighed. En dröftelse av periferiens udvikling og studiet av avhängighet (Imperialism and Dependence). *Politica* 2-3, 1976 (Århus).

Palmer, V., and Poulter, S., *The Legal System of Lesotho*, Charlottenville 1972.

Potholm, C.P. and Dale, R., ed., *Southern Africa in Perspective*, New York 1972.

Rupert, A., "International Business Partnership—The Multinational Concept", *South African International*, Vol. 1, No. 2.

Selwyn, P., *Industries in the Southern African Periphery*, London 1975.

Senghaas, D., ed., *Imperialismus und Strukturelle Gewalt. Analysen über abhängige Reproduktion*, Frankfurt a.M. 1972.

Spence, J., *The Politics of Dependence in Lesotho*, London 1968.

Wallensteen, P., "*Dealing with the Devil: Relations between South Africa and its Neighbours*", Department of Peace and Conflict Research, Uppsala University 1971.

Wallman, S., "The Modernization of Dependence—a Further Note on Lesotho", *Journal of Southern African Studies*, March 1977.

Wallman, S., *Take Out Hunger: Two Case Studies of Rural Development in Basutoland*, London 1969.

Walton, J., *Father of Kindness and Horses. History of the Frasers' Family*, Wepener 1958.

Warren, B., "Imperialism and Capitalist Industrialization". *New Left Review* 81, 1973.

Weisfelder, R., *Defining National Purpose in Lesotho*, International Studies Series No. 3, Athens 1969.

Weisfelder, R., "Power Struggle in Lesotho", *Africa Report*, Vol. 12, no. 1, African American Inst. Washington, Jan. 1967.

Wellmer, G., Mission and Migrant Labour, *Ministry*, vol. 10, no. 1, 1970.

Wikar's Journal 1778–1779, ed. Mossop, E.E., Cape Town 1935.

Wilson, M. and Thompson, L., ed., *Oxford History of South Africa*, London 1969, Parts I and II.

Wilson, F., *Labour in South African Gold Mines 1899–1969*, Cambridge 1972.

Wolpe, H., "Capitalism and Cheap Labour Power in South Africa from Segregation to Apartheid", *Economy and Society*, 1, 74.

Mimeographed Papers

Amin, S., *The Future of Southern Africa*, introduction to a forthcoming book based on papers for the Conference on Socio-economic Change in Southern Africa, (organized by IDEP and OAU). Dar-es-Salaam University 6–10 Dec. 1975.

Cardoso, F.H., *Current Thesis on Latin American Development and Dependency: A critique.* and *The Consumption of Dependency Theory in the U.S.*, papers for the Conference on Latin America, Bergen 17–19 June 1976.

Chakela, K.Q., *Review and Bibilography, Water and Soil Resources in Lesotho, 1935–1970*, Department of Physical Geography, Uppsala University of Uppsala Febr. 1973.

Clarke, D.G., *Some Determinants of Demands for Foreign African Labour in South Africa*, Geneva 1977.

Damane, M., *The Statecraft of Moshoeshoe the Great*, Maseru 12 March 1975.

Devitt, P., *A Micro-Study of Power Politics at a Village in the Roma Valley*, *M.A. Thesis*, Department of Social Anthropology, Witwatersrand University, Johannesburg 1969.

Good. D., and Williams, M., *South Africa: The Crisis in Britain and the Apartheid Economy*, Anti-Apartheid Movement, London 1976.

Haliburton, R., *Politics and Religion*, paper for the Conference on History of Southern Africa, Gaborone 1973.

Kaplan, D., *Capitalist Development in South Africa. Class Conflict and State*, IDS, Sussex.

Kowet, D., *Botswana, Lesotho and Swaziland, Department of Political Science, Uppsala University 1974.*

Leys, R., *Labour Migration Lesotho, Progress report* for the period April to Nov. 1974, IDR project Papers D 75.1., Institute for Development Research, Copenhagen 1975.

Musorewa, B., *Money, Financial Institutions and Economic Development in Lesotho,* (M.A. Thesis), Department of Economics, UBLS, Gaborone 1972.

Opinions of Ruling and Exiled Leaders of Lesotho, Report no. 15, Department of Peace and Conflict Research, Uppsala University 1976.

Russet, P.N., *An Emprical Assessment of Global Inequalities and Dependence,* paper for Conference on Głobal Dominance and Dependence, Peace Research Institute (PRIO), Oslo Sept. 1974.

Shaw, T., *Southern Africa: Dependence, Interdependence and Independence in a Regional Subsystem,* Dalhouse 1973.

Simson, H., "The Causes of Apartheid Revisited", *Studies on South African Imperialism,* Report no. 17, Department of Peace and Conflict Research, Uppsala University 1977.

Simson, H., *Historical Notes on South Africa,* Department of Economic History, Uppsala University 1975.

Spray, P., *The Economic History of Basutoland,* IDS, Sussex 1975.

Weisfelder, R.F., *Lesotho: An Unstable Irritant within South Africa,* paper for Meeting of African Studies Association, Boston 1970.

Weisfelder, R.F., *Early Voices of Basutoland,* paper for Conference on History of Southern Africa, Gaborone 1973.

Weisfelder, R., *The Basotho Monarchy. A Spent Force or a Dynamic Political Factor,* paper for Meeting of African Studies Association, Denver 1971.

Wuyts, M., *On the Nature of Underdevelopment: An Analysis of Two Views on Underdevelopment,* Economic Research Bureau, University of Dar-es-Salaam, March 1976.

Väyrinen, R., *Some Theoretical Aspects of Subimperialism,* Tampere Peace and Conflict Research Institute (TAPRI), Tampere 1974.

Periodicals

Newspapers and Magazines

Barclay's International Review (monthly), London.
Barclay's (Bank) Review (quarterly), London.
Drum (weekly), Johannesburg.
Labour News (monthly), Gaborone.
Leselinyana, (Protestant weekly), Morija.
Lesotho Weekly Bulletin, Department of Information, Maseru.
Makatolle (BCP weekly), Maseru.
Mareng a Meso, Johannesburg.

Moeletsi (Catholic weekly), Mazenod.
Nketu (BNP weekly), Maseru.
Rand Daily Mail (daily), Johannesburg.
Rennies Company News, (monthly), Hong Kong.
Sunday Times (weekly), Johannesburg.
The Friend (daily), Bloemfontein.
The Star (daily), Johannesburg.

Annual Reports

Annual Report of EDESA (Economic Development of East and Southern Africa), Zürich.
Annual Report of the Commissioner of Police, Maseru.
Annual Report of the Department of Mines and Geology, Maseru.
Annual Report of the South African Mohair Exports, (incl. Lesotho), South African Mohair Board, Pretoria.
Annual Report of the South African Wool Exports, (incl. Lesotho), South African Wool Board, Pretoria.
Annual Statistical Bulletin, Bureau of Statistics, Maseru.
Annual Survey of the South African Institute of Race Relations, Johannesburg.
Business and Development in Lesotho. A Newsletter of the LNDC, Maseru.
Catalogue of the University of Botswana, Lesotho and Swaziland, Roma.
Catholic Directory of Southern Africa, Cape Town.
Estimated and Actual Revenue and Expenditure of the Kingdom of Lesotho, Current and Capital Budgets, Department of Finance, Maseru.
Legum, C., ed., *Africa Contemporary Records*, London.
Lesotho National Development Corporation. *Annual Report*, Maseru.
Lesotho Telephone Directory, Maseru.
Top Companies in South Africa, Supplement to the Financial Mail, (April), Johannesburg.
United Nations Statistical Yearbook, New York.
Wilson, A.N., *International Diamond Annual*, Johannesburg.

Government Documents, Published and Unpublished.

Lesotho:

Speeches and Statements to the Press

Address by the Prime Minister, at the Reception for the Yugoslav Economic Mission, Maseru 10 Sept. 1970.

Budget Speech by the Minister of Finance, Maseru March 1967.
Budget Speech by the Minister of Finance, Maseru March 1971.
Message from his Excellency Dr. Leabua Jonathan, to 8 General Conference of the World Anto-communist League, Rio de Janeiro 24 April 1975.
Ministry of Foreign Affairs' Note, No. 5, 21.1.1975.
Press conference with Leabua Jonathan, 16 February 1970.
Press Release by the LNDC, at the opening of the "Cash and Carry Market" in Maseru, Nov. 1975 (Joe Molife interviewing I. Rosthal).
Press release by the LNDC, on a new joint venture in mohair processing, Maseru 7 July 1975.
Radio Statement by the Prime Minister, in connection with the announcement of a "National Government", 14 Nov. 1975.
Speech by H. Oppenheimer, at the occasion of the signing of the agreement with the Lesotho government on diamond mining and trade, Maseru 24 March 1975.
Speech by Joel Moitse, Minister of Industry, Labour and Commerce to Traders, 29 Nov. 1974.
Speech by M. Salae (my notes), acting head of the Khoomokhoana project, 15 Nov. 1975.
Speech by the Prime Minister, moving the 1968/69 Develeopment Fund Expenditure in the House of Assembly, Maseru March 1968.
Statement by the Prime Minister Leabua Jonathan *Towards Self-reliance,* early in 1973.

Prospects

A Small Country, but What a Market, Prospect by the LNDC, Maseru 1973.
Leabua Jonathan, A Tribute to the Prime Minister of the Kingdom of Lesotho, Information Department, Maseru Oct. 1972.
The Honourable Chief Leabua Jonathan, Information Dep., Maseru Aug. 1970.
The Sky is the Limit in Lesotho, LNDC, Maseru 1970.

Plans and Reports

Agricultural Census Report 1970, Bureau of Statistics, Maseru 1973.
Agricultural Statistics 1950, 1960 and 1965–70, Bureau of Statistics, Maseru 1973. *Assets and Liabilities of the LNDC,* 1970 and 1975.
Basutoland 1958, H.M.S.O., London 1959.
Basutoland 1962, H.M.S.O., London 1963.
Complaints to the Special Investigation Committee to the Leribe Project, Ministry of Agriculture, Maseru 1975.
Donor Conference Minutes, CPDO, Maseru June 1975.
Elkan, W., *Report to the Government of Basutoland on the Manpower Situation,* ILO/TAO/Basutoland R.1.

Debates of the Legislative Council, 1947, kept at UBLS Library, Roma.

Hansards, Official Reports from the Parliamentary Debates of the National Assembly, (April 1966–May 1966, printed, October 1966–October 1969 mimeo).

Hansards, Official Reports from the Debates of the Interim National Assembly (April 1973–November 1975 mimeo).

Kresten, P., (UNDP mineralogist, Dep. of Mines and Geology), *Special Report, The Kimberlites of the Kao-Lemphane Area,* Maseru Jan. 1973.

Lesotho 1966, H.M.S.O., London 1967.

Lesotho 1967, Department of Information, Maseru 1968.

Lesotho 1971, Department of Information, Maseru 1972.

Lesotho. First Five-Year Development Plan 1970/71–1974/75, Maseru 1970.

Lesotho. Second Five-Year Development Plan 1975/76–1979/80.

Leribe Pilot Agricultural Scheme—Economic Surveys of a Random Sample of Farmers 1970/71–1972/73, Hellman, C., Ministry of Agriculture, Maseru Aug. 1974.

Lexander, A., (FAO Rural Sociologist, Ministry of Agriculture), *People, Land and Livestock in the Thaba Bosiu Rural Development Project Area,* Thaba Tseka Project Area and Leribe Agricultural Scheme (based on information collected during 1969/70 Agricultural Survey).

Project Progress Report 1.2.75 to 31.7.75. Lesotho Rural Development of the Khomokhoana and adjacent areas, Salae, M., Maseru 1975.

Report of the Basutoland Independence Conference 1966, suppl. to Government Gazette no. 35 38, London June 1966.

Report on Constitutional Reforms and Chieftainship Affairs, Maseru 1958.

Report on the Structure and Administration of Lesotho Government, Coutts, W., Cabinet Circular Notice No. 20, Maseru 1966.

Savosnic, K. et al., *Development Plan for Tourism for the Kingdom of Lesotho,* Associated Research Consultants Ltd, Nairobi 1974.

Summary and objectives of the Second Five-Year Plan, CPDO, Maseru 1975.

Thaba Bosiu Rural Development Projects, Evaluation Study no. 1, Maseru April 1975.

Trade Registry, at Ministry of Industry and Commerce for 1974 and 1975.

Urban and Rural Consumption Surveys, figures from 1968, Bureau of Statistics, Maseru 1973.

Laws

Customs and Excise Union Agreement between the Governments of Lesotho, Botswana, South Africa and Swaziland 1969, Lesotho Government Gazette no. 58, 1969.

Deferred Pay Fund Act, Jan. 1975.

The Emergency Regulations 1970, Extraordinary Gazettes. No. 6, 13 and 16.

Financial Institutions Act, 1974.

Judgement of Mr Justice Landsowne in Mantsebo v. Bereng 1943.

Land Administration Act 1973 and Government Proposition to the Interim Parliament in 1974.

Laws of Lerotholi, Theal, G.M. Basutoland Records, Cape Town 1883.

Monetary Agreement between the Government of Lesotho, South Africa and Swaziland 1974.

Native Court Proclamation No. 62, 1938 (enforced in 1946).

Pioneer Industries Encouragement Act 1969.

The Order of the Office of the King, Dec. 1970.

Great Britain:

Beattie, A., Public and Private Sector Manpower Surveys in Lesotho, ODA, London 1971.

Native Administration Proclamation (Basutoland) No. 61, 1938.

Selwyn, P., Report on Assignment to Lesotho, IDS, Sussex 1971.

Report of Economic Commission appointed by the Secretary of State for Dominion Affairs, Financial and Economic Position of Basutoland (Pim Report) London 1935.

Republic of South Africa:

Economic Development Programme for the Republic of South Africa 1972–1977, Pretoria 1972.

Government decisions on the Recommendations of the Commission for the Socio-Economic Development of the Bantu Areas within the Union of South Africa, White Paper F/1956.

Setting the Record Straight, The Republic of South Africa in defence of the Bantu Education System to the United Nations, Pretoria 1969.

Summary of the Report of the Commission for the Socio-economic Development of the Bantu Araas (Tomlinson), UG 61/1955.

Verwoerd, Dr. H.F., on I. Crisis in World Conscience and II. The Road to Freedom for Basutoland, Bechuanaland and Swaziland, Department of Information, Fact Paper 107, Pretoria Sept. 1963.

International Organizations:

All-African People's Conference, 5–12 Dec. 1958.

Document of IMF, Lesotho. Recent Economic Developments, SM/75/123, Washington 28 May 1975.

Document of IBRD and IDA, The Economy of Lesotho, Report No. 331a LSO, Washington June 1974.

IMF Surveys of African Economies, Vol. 5, Washington 1973.

International Development Strategy for the Second UN Development Decade, A/8124 and Add. 1, Item 42, 24 Oct. 1970, 1883 plenary meeting, General Assembly, 24 session, Resolution No. 2626 (XXV), New York 1970.

Kresten, P., *Report on Assignment to the UNDP*, Maseru 1973.

Mafeje, A., *Land Tenure and Development of Agriculture in South Africa*, FAO 1975.

Measurement of Changes in National Levels of Living, Social Affairs Division of OECD, MS/5967.126, Paris 1967.

Repressive Legislation of the Republic of South Africa, UN on Apartheid, New York 1969.

Report of the Fact-finding and Consiliation Mission on Freedom of Association concerning Lesotho, ILO, Geneva 1975.

UNDP Reports in 1970 and 1975, *UN and other aid personnel assistance to Lesotho*, Maseru 1970 and 1975.

Verbatim Records of the 49 session of the Committee of the Twenty-Four, AC/AC T09/PO, Accra 14 May 1962.

Other Documents

Basutoland, Bechuanaland Protectorat and Swaziland, History of Discussions with Union of South Africa 1909–1939, London Dec. 1952 (kept at UBLS Library).

Letter by the Swedish Ambassador to Lesotho, to the Foreign Office in Stockholm, Pretoria 22 April 1974.

Ministry of Foreign Affairs' Note No. 5, 21.1.1975.

Readings in BoLeswa Government, Select Documents, ed. Macartney, W.J.A., UBLS, Roma 1971.

Preamble and Resolution agreed on by the Annual Conference of the BFL, Maseru 2 July 1973.

Staff Lists and Establishment Lists of the Government of Lesotho, Maseru 1972.

Statement by the General Secretary of the BCP, K. Chakela to the Press, Stockholm June 1973.

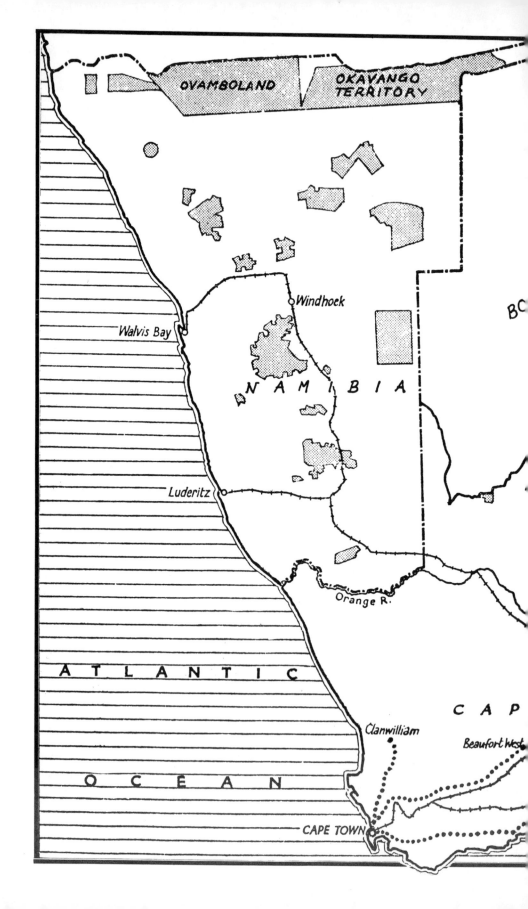

SOUTH AFRICA

— ·· — ·· — Political boundaries
African areas, including land scheduled for purchase

—+—+—+— Principal railways
············ National Roads

0 60 120 180 240 300 360 420 km

Bulawayo

Beitbridge

MOZAMBIQUE

Limpopo R.

Crocodile

Mafeking

TRANSVAAL
Pretoria
JOHANNESBURG

Mbabane
SWAZI-
LAND

Maputo

Vaal R.

ORANGE FREE

Kimberley

STATE

Bloemfontein Maseru

LESOTHO

Tugela R.

Pietermaritzburg

Durban

Orange R.

O VINCE

INDIAN

Great Kei R.

OCEAN

East London

Great Fish R.

Port Elizabeth